THE TRINITY FORU

THE JOURNEY
Our Quest for Faith and Meaning

OS GUINNESS

Edited by Ginger Koloszyc
Reader's Guide by Karen Lee-Thorp

NAVPRESS

Bringing Truth to Life
P.O. Box 35001, Colorado Springs, Colorado 80935

OUR GUARANTEE TO YOU

We believe so strongly in the message of our books that we are making this quality guarantee to you. If for any reason you are disappointed with the content of this book, return the title page to us with your name and address and we will refund to you the list price of the book. To help us serve you better, please briefly describe why you were disappointed. Mail your refund request to: NavPress, P.O. Box 35002, Colorado Springs, CO 80935.

Library of Congress Catalog Card Number: 2001030755

ISBN 1-57683-160-4

Cover design by Dan Jamison
Cover illustration of map by Digital Vision / Nanette Hoogslag
Cover photo of lake by Masterfile / Greg Stott
Creative Team: Steve Webb, Karen Lee-Thorp, Darla Hightower, Pat Miller

Unless otherwise identified, all Scripture quotations in this publication are taken from the HOLY BIBLE: NEW INTERNATIONAL VERSION® (NIV®). Copyright © 1973, 1978, 1984 by International Bible Society. Used by permission of Zondervan Publishing House. All rights reserved.

Library of Congress Cataloging-in-Publication Data
Guinness, Os.
    The journey : our quest for faith and meaning / by Os Guinness ; edited by Ginger Koloszyc ; reader's guide by Karen Lee-Thorp.
        p. cm.
Includes bibliographical references.
ISBN 1-57683-160-4
    1. Apologetics. 2. Meaning (Philosophy)—Religious aspects—Christianity. I. Koloszyc, Ginger. II. Lee-Thorp, Karen. III. Title.

BT51103 .G85 2001
239—dc21   2001030755

Printed in the United States of America

1 2 3 4 5 6 7 8 9 10 / 05 04 03 02 01

FOR A FREE CATALOG OF
NAVPRESS BOOKS & BIBLE STUDIES,
CALL 1-800-366-7788 (USA)
OR 1-416-499-4615 (CANADA)

THE TRINITY FORUM

Contents

THE TRINITY FORUM

"Contributing to the transformation and renewal of society through the transformation and renewal of leaders."

The Trinity Forum would like to recognize the following people for their work on this project:

Project Director: Os Guinness

Selections and Introductions: Os Guinness, with Mark Filiatreau

Academic Consultants: William Edgar, Richard B. Keyes, Peter Kreeft, James W. Sire, Ravi Zacharias

Researchers: Mark Filiatreau, Margaret Gardner

Editor: Ginger Koloszyc

Copy Editors: Amy Boucher, Peter Edman

NOT SO MUCH A BOOK
AS A WAY OF THINKING

The 'Why' and 'How' of the Trinity Forum Study Series

THINKERS FROM THE TIME OF SOCRATES TO OUR OWN DAY HAVE BELIEVED THAT THE unexamined life is not worth living. Today's unique challenge is to lead an examined life in an unexamining age. The sheer pace and pressure of our modern lives can easily crowd out time for reflection. To make matters worse, we live in a war zone against independent thinking. Television jingles, advertising hype, political soundbites, and "dumbed-down" discourse of all kinds assault an individual's ability to think for himself or herself. Carefully considered conclusions about life and the best way to live it are too often the casualties.

Into this challenging landscape The Trinity Forum launches its *Study Series*, inviting individuals to think through today's issues carefully and deliberately — in the context of faith — to reach deeper and more firmly established convictions.

About The Trinity Forum

The Trinity Forum was founded in 1991. Its aim: to contribute to the transformation and renewal of society through the transformation and renewal of leaders. Christian in commitment, but open to all who are interested in its vision, it has organized dozens of forums for leaders of all sectors of modern life — from business to education, from fashion to government and the media.

Hundreds of leaders from many faiths across the United States, Canada, and Europe have taken part in these forums.

A distinctive feature of The Trinity Forum is its format. There are no lectures, addresses, or talks of any kind. A curriculum of readings on a given topic is sent in advance and then explored at the forum in a Socratic-style open discussion led by moderators. This give-and-take challenges the participants to wrestle with the issues themselves and—importantly—to reach their own thought-out conclusions.

By popular demand, The Trinity Forum now offers these curricula to a wider audience, enhanced as the *Trinity Forum Study Series* and designed for individual readers or study groups in homes, churches, and colleges. Each Study is intended to help thoughtful people examine the foundational issues through which faith acts upon the public good of modern society. A reader's guide at the back of each book will aid those who want to discuss the material with a group. Those reading the book on their own may also find that the reader's guide will help them focus on the Study's big ideas. The reader's guide contains basic principles of small group leadership, an overview of the Study's main ideas, and suggested selections for groups that don't have time to discuss every reading in the Study.

Adult in seriousness and tone, yet popular rather than scholarly in style, the *Trinity Forum Study Series* probes each topic through the milestone writings that have shaped its development. This approach will be fresh and exciting to many and, we trust, stimulating to all. It is worth laying out some of the assumptions and convictions that guide this approach, for what is presented here is not so much a book as it is a way of thinking.

Defining Features of the Trinity Forum Study Series

First, the Trinity Forum Study Series *explores the issues of our day in the context of faith.* As stated earlier, The Trinity Forum is Christ-centered in its commitment, but opens its programs to all who share its aims—whether believers, seekers, or skeptics. The same committed but open spirit marks this series of books.

For people of faith, it should be natural to take into account the place of faith when discussing the issues of life, both historically and presently. But it should also be natural for all citizens of Western society, of whatever faith. For no one can understand Western civilization without understanding the Christian faith which, for better or worse, has been its primary shaping force. Yet a striking feature of many of today's thought-leaders and opinion-shapers is their "tone deafness" toward faith of any kind—which means that, unwittingly or otherwise, they do not hear the music by which most people orchestrate their lives.

For example, a national media executive recently admitted his and his colleagues' befuddlement about Americans' deep reliance upon faith. Citing the outpouring of public prayer in response to a tragic school shooting in Kentucky, he confessed, "We simply don't get it." These readings aim to remedy that neglected dimension of understanding, and thereby reintroduce to the modern discussion the perspective of faith that is vital both for making sense of the past and dealing with the present.

Second, the Trinity Forum Study Series *presents the perspective of faith in the context of the sweep of Western civilization, recognizing the vital place of the past in the lives of nations as well as individuals.* A distinctive feature of the modern world is its passion for the present and fascination with the future at the expense of the past. Progress, choice, change, novelty, and the myth of newer-the-truer and latest-is-greatest reign unchallenged, while ideas and convictions from earlier times are boxed up in the cobwebbed attic of nostalgia and irrelevance. By contrast, Winston Churchill said, "The further backward you can look, the farther forward you can see." For him, as well as the American framers in the eighteenth century and the writers of the Bible before them, remembering is not foremost a matter of nostalgia or historical reverie, and it is far more than mental recall. For all of them, it is a vital key to identity, faith, wisdom, renewal, and the dynamism of a living tradition, for both nations and individuals.

By reintroducing important writings from the past, the *Trinity Forum Study Series* invites readers to a living conversation of ideas and imagination with the great minds of our heritage. Only when we know where we have come from do we know who we are and where we are going.

Third, the Trinity Forum Study Series *presents the perspective of faith in the context of the challenge of other faiths.* If the first feature of this series is likely to offend some unthinking secularists, this one may do the same to unthinking believers. But the truth is, some believers don't appear to know their own faith because they know *only* their own faith. Familiarity breeds inattention. It is true, as essayist Ronald Knox quipped, that comparative religion can make us "comparatively religious." But it is also true that contrast is the mother of clarity.

One important benefit of understanding one's own faith in distinction to others is the ability to communicate ideas and positions persuasively in the public square. Believers properly hold their beliefs on the basis of divine authority. Such beliefs, however, must be conveyed compellingly in a society that does not accept the same authority. An important part of meeting that challenge effectively is the ability to grasp and highlight the differences between faiths.

This series of books, therefore, sets out the perspectives of the Christian faith in the context of the challenge of other faiths. If "all truth is God's truth," and if differences truly make a difference, then such contrasts between one faith and another are not only challenging, but illuminating and important for both individuals and society.

Fourth, the Trinity Forum Study Series *is unashamed about the necessity for tough-minded thinking.* Much has been made recently of Christian anti-intellectualism and the scandal of the lack of a Christian mind. As Bertrand Russell put it, "Most Christians would rather die than think—in fact, they do." But failure to think is not confined to any one community or group. Former Secretary of State Henry Kissinger is quoted as saying, "In Washington D.C. there is so little time to think that most people live forever off the intellectual capital from the day they arrive."

In contrast, Abraham Lincoln's greatness was fired in times of thoughtful reflection during the Civil War. Today's profound crises call for similar thoughtful reflection and courage by men and women prepared to break rank with a largely unthinking and conformist age. Just as an earlier generation broke with accepted practices of little exercise and bad eating, restoring a vogue for fitness, so our generation must shake off the lethargy of "dumbed down" discourse and recover the capacity to think tough-mindedly as the issues and our times require.

Fifth, the Trinity Forum Study Series *recognizes that many of the urgent public issues of our day are cultural rather than political.* Much recent discussion of public affairs oscillates uneasily between heavily moral issues (such as abortion) and more strongly political issues (such as campaign finance reform). Yet increasingly, many of the urgent concerns of our day lie in-between. They are neither purely moral nor purely political, but integrate elements of both. In other words, many key issues are morally grounded "pre-political" issues, such as the role of "trust" in capitalism, "character" in leadership, "truth" in public discourse, "stewardship" in philanthropy and environmentalism, and "voluntarism" in civil society.

To be sure, it is a symptom of our present crisis that such foundational issues have to be debated at all. But the *Trinity Forum Study Series* addresses these often neglected issues, always presenting them in the context of faith and always addressing them in a nonpartisan manner that befits such cultural discussion.

Finally, the Trinity Forum Study Series *assumes the special need for, and the possibility of, a social and cultural renaissance in our time.* As we consider our present crises with clear-eyed realism, one of the great challenges is to be hopeful with a real basis for hope while always being critical of what is wrong without collapsing into alarmism or despair. To be sure, no freedom, prosperity, or success lasts forever in this life, in either spiritual or secular affairs. But, equally, the grand cycle of birth, growth, and decline is never deterministic, and no source of renewal is more sure and powerful than spiritual revival. The *Study Series* is born of this conviction.

Giving up hope in the worthwhileness of the worthwhile—in God, the good, the true, the just, and the beautiful—is another name for the deadly sin of sloth. Venturing out, under God, to be entrepreneurs of life is another name for faith. Thus, while always uncertain of the outcome of our times, always modest about our own contribution, and always confident in God rather than ourselves, those who present the *Trinity Forum Study Series* desire to encourage people to move out into society with constructive answers and a sense of a confidence born of faith and seasoned by history. In so doing we seek to sow the seeds for a much-needed renaissance in our own time.

INTRODUCTION—
THE JOURNEY

"I AM AT A POINT IN MY LIFE WHERE I REALIZE THERE HAS TO BE SOMETHING MORE." The elegantly dressed speaker had come up after a Trinity Forum dinner near San Francisco. He cut straight to the point and there was an intensity in his voice that immediately set him apart from the surrounding small talk. There had been some remarks on the search for meaning in the modern world. Many of the guests were eminent names in the world of high finance in the city and high technology in Silicon Valley farther south. And the conversation was flushed with the success of the last two decades of the twentieth century, which had witnessed the greatest legal creation of wealth in history, much of it in that part of the world.

The words "something more" hadn't been used, but in personal conversations afterward no fewer than four people separately used the same two words. With very different stories they each said they knew they needed "something more" in their lives. As so often in life, the very things people strive to achieve turn out to be less than they desired once they have achieved them. They are not enough in themselves, and their incompleteness points beyond them to the need for something more.

"Like many of my friends around here," the man continued, "I've learned a lesson I wish I'd known when I started out: 'Having it all' just isn't enough. There's a limit to the successes worth counting and the toys worth accumulating. Business school never gave me a calculus for assessing the deeper things of life."

For all the aura of wealth and success on this occasion, it would be as wrong to limit the search for meaning to the wealthy and the successful as it would be to the intelligent. As G. K. Chesterton wrote, "We all feel the riddle of the earth without anyone to point it out. The mystery of life is the plainest part of it."

Similar conversations take place every day in living rooms, classrooms, cafés, pubs, on beaches, airplanes, and trains across the world. Nothing is more human for people of all backgrounds—for all of us—than a desire to unriddle the mystery of life. One of the bedrock realities of our existence is that none of us will be here for long. C. S. Lewis stated the obvious that we all try to avoid: "One hundred percent of us die." How then do we make the most of this brief and marvelous time lived in the face of death? It is often said that there are three requirements for a fulfilling life: a clear sense of personal identity, a deep sense of life's meaning, and a strong sense of purpose and mission. But even the first and the last are rooted in the middle one, the faith that represents one's convictions about the meaning of life.

True, many people today have been spurred to search for meaning because they are haunted by having too much to live with and too little to live for. But there are countless other spurs to the search, and the search itself is human and universal. Indeed, for each of us the outcome of the search—discovery of faith and meaning—is the single most important secret of a life rich with significance.

This study is for all who long for "something more," for all who desire to unriddle life, for all who are pursuing a life rich with significance, for all who wish there were a seeker's road map to the quest for meaning. Does that describe you? Let's begin by considering the idea of the journey of life.

OUR HUMAN ODYSSEY

"Midway on our life's journey I found myself in a dark wood." So begins Dante's metaphysical adventure story *The Divine Comedy,* his three-part pilgrimage to discover the fate of souls after death. Life as a journey . . . from the Hebrew *Exodus* to Homer's *Odyssey* to Virgil's *Aeneid* to Dante's *Divine Comedy* to John Bunyan's *Pilgrim's Progress* to Mark Twain's *Huckleberry Finn* to Herman Hesse's *Siddhartha,* no picture of human life is more universal than to see it as a journey, a voyage, a quest, a pilgrimage, a personal odyssey. We are all midway on life's journey—or at least we are all at some point unknown to us between the beginning and the end of this odyssey of our human existence.

Webster defines the word *odyssey* as "a long wandering or voyage usually marked by many changes of fortune." The word, of course, comes to us from the epic age of Greece. More importantly, it aptly describes the progress and setbacks, the twists and turns and ups and downs of our human experience of living. Rooted in an older oral tradition, Homer's *Odyssey* (written around 725 B.C.) represents his storyteller's genius for addressing our fundamental questions as wanderer-seekers: What does life mean? And how should we live it?

Questions arise if our human lot is to journey for "three score years and ten"—give or take a few years. Who are we? Where have we come from? Why are we here? Where are we going? What does it all add up to? What dangers and diversions can make us lose our way and even our very selves?

We usually raise such questions with idealism in our youth, only to have them shouldered aside by the busy importance of midlife, which itself is often cowed into silence by the faint tolling bell of our own mortality—in deepening wrinkles, graying hair, shortening breath, thickening waistlines, and more of our sentences beginning "In my day . . ."

WHAT'S IT ALL ABOUT?

"Here I am in the twilight years of my life, still wondering what it's all about. . . . I can tell you this, fame and fortune is for the birds."

—Lee Iacocca, *Straight Talk*

"In the greatest confusion there is still an open channel to the soul. It may be difficult to find because by mid-life it is overgrown, and some of the wildest thickets that surround it grow out of what we describe as our education. But the channel is always there, and it is our business to keep it open, to have access to the deepest part of ourselves—to that part of us which is conscious of a higher consciousness, by means of which we make final judgments and put everything together. The independence of this consciousness . . . is what the life struggle is all about."

—Saul Bellow

As Friedrich Nietzsche said well, he who knows *why* can bear any *how*. Odysseus could bear the buffeting of storms and escape the oblivion of enchantments because he was a man on his way home to Ithaca and his wife and son. But for life's journey to be a homecoming we have to know our bearings and, more importantly, there has to be a home.

A WORLD ON THE MOVE

The idea of life-as-journey is not esoteric today. Few people, however, realize how much journeying and movement are major themes of the past century. Less obvious perhaps than such grand triumphs as the moon landing or such dark tragedies as Auschwitz, travel is so typical of our times that ours is literally a world on the move. Consider some of its dimensions.

One is the reality of migration in the daily lives of millions. From Mexicans crawling through Southern Californian ravines to Vietnamese boat people bobbing on the South China Sea to terrified Tutsis fleeing the murderous wrath of the Hutus in Rwanda, millions of our fellow human beings have experienced the twentieth and twenty-first centuries as life on the move in an age of displacement and migration. Driven by war, disease, hunger, persecution, and genocide, the number of people driven out of countries rivals the number of those shut up inside.

As critic George Steiner observes, the border is one of the most powerful ideas to shape modern experience—from the Berlin Wall to international air space to the "glass ceiling" of the corporate world. But we also have the impact of shifting borders and borderlessness. The net effect is that more and more people have been uprooted and made to feel at home nowhere. Thus ours is a day of exiles, émigrés, expatriates, immigrants, refugees, deportees, illegal aliens, undesirable aliens, resident aliens, migrant workers, drifters, vagabonds, and bums. The journeying of the pilgrims, explorers, conquerors, and colonizers of the past have been overshadowed by the restlessness of the modern nomads and the wandering of today's stateless.

LIGHT IN THE WINDOW

"Give me your tired, your poor
Your huddled masses yearning to breathe free,
The wretched refuse of your teeming shore.
Send these, the homeless, tempest-tost to me,
I lift my lamp beside the golden door!"

—Emma Lazarus,
"The New Colossus"

There is of course a very positive side of modern migration, as represented by the history of the United States as a "nation of immigrants" and epitomized by Ellis Island and Emma Lazarus's poem on the Statue of Liberty. It is true, too, that much of our awareness of journeying has been heightened by the creative insights of exiles and expatriates themselves. Dante and Petrarch wrote as exiles from Florence, John Calvin as an expatriate from France, Jean-Jacques Rousseau from Switzerland, and John Keats from England. But the volume of exiles and expatriates in the twentieth century has risen to a flood, led by American writers and artists in Paris, Henry James and T. S. Eliot in England, Albert Einstein in Princeton, W. H. Auden in New York, Aleksandr

Solzhenitsyn in Vermont, and countless refugees from Nazism and Communism in the United States at large.

Enormous differences divide these twentieth-century travelers—differences of geography, culture, and psychology. But all experience some sense of a loss of home, of history, and of a sense of "the fatherland," the "mother tongue," the "language of childhood." The "homesickness" of nostalgia is the experience of our time. Too many of us, in W. H. Auden's words, feel that we are "altogether elsewhere."

Another dimension of modern journeying is shaped by national experience. Americans, for example, have always demonstrated an intense "nomadism" even within the United States, born not only of the forces of immigration but of mobility and westward expansion. Gertrude Stein said that when American migration had reached the Pacific, there was nowhere else to go but "west in the head." And into the head Americans went. De Tocqueville called it the Americans' "strange unrest" and H. G. Wells their "headlong hurry."

Sadly, there is no need to underscore the dark record that has created the poignant myth of "the wandering Jew."

NOWHERE AT HOME

Walking one drizzly day in Oxford, philosopher Isaiah Berlin suddenly waved his umbrella in the air and asked: "What do you think is common to all Jews? I mean, to the Jew from San'a, from Marrakech, from Riga, from Glasgow? A sense of social unease. Nowhere do almost all Jews feel entirely at home."

—*The New Republic,* March 1995

Yet another dimension of modern journeying concerns the leadership class in the modern world. Mobility is now essential to success. Nothing represents this better than the sight of busy executives crisscrossing the airports of five continents with crowded calendars and cellular telephones in hand and luggage-on-wheels in tow like well-trained pets.

But behind this common sight is a major shift. Whereas old money and the so-called "aristocracy of birth" traveled little and had a strong sense of rootedness and local loyalties, the new "aristocracy of brains" is more cosmopolitan and migratory. Success in the modern world is closely tied to mobility. Advancement in business and the professions requires a willingness to follow the "siren call of opportunity" wherever it leads. As one observer says, "The new elites are at home only in transit." Theirs is essentially "a tourist's view of the world." Even privilege provides no exemption from movement.

LIFE TOWARD HOME

But the greatest dimension of our sense of journey is deeper still. It is created by the nearly universal intuition that journeying is the most apt metaphor for human life itself—or at least that the human odyssey at its highest is that life with a quest for purpose, meaning, destination, and home.

In his typically imperious manner, Pablo Picasso used to say, "I do not seek, I find." But for the rest of us a humbler attitude is appropriate. Life is a quest; to find is a blessing. As poet Joseph Brodsky wrote, the "truth of the matter is that exile is a metaphysical condition." To ignore it or dodge it is to cheat ourselves out of the meaning of what is happening to us. Human life is not only life on the road, but life in search of home.

This sense of life-as-journey can be seen in the world's quest stories. Today the quest theme is captured in such popular films as *2001: A Space Odyssey* and *Raiders of the Lost Ark,* but it began around 1500 B.C. with the Sumerian tale of Gilgamesh. The king of Uruk, Gilgamesh, is seized by a fear of death on losing his only friend. He therefore sets out to cross the world—fruitlessly but heroically—to find the secret of immortality.

In some quest stories the search is hopeless from the start. In Herman Melville's *Moby Dick*, for example, the search is mad and the quest meaningless— except to Captain Ahab himself, who dies with all his crew apart from Ishmael, who alone survives to tell the tale. In other quest stories, such as the varied legends of the Holy Grail, the search is symbolic. The quest is for someone or something that will make the searcher a whole person—some truth or revelation that will unlock the secret of the meaning of life. Whether the searcher takes the high road or the low, whether the search is successful, like that of the Arthurian knight Parsifal, or unsuccessful, like that of Cervantes' Don Quixote, it always invests the traveler with an aura of dignity and heroism. Philosophy itself, it could be argued, rose as part of that quest, a passionate pursuit of wisdom to decode the meaning of human existence.

Today such quests are rarer at the serious level. Many thinkers have openly given up the idea that life has meaning or that there is such a thing as truth. Others talk about "searching" but condemn themselves to fruitless seeking without end because they are open-minded about everything except finding and concluding. Eric Hobsbawn, the eminent historian, wrote recently, "The old maps and charts which guided human beings singly and collectively through life, no longer represent the landscape through which we move, the sea on which we sail. . . . We do not know where our journey is taking us, or even ought to take us."

DON'T KNOW, DON'T CARE

"The tragedy of modern man is not that he knows less and less about the meaning of his own life, but that it bothers him less and less."

—Václav Havel, *Letters to Olga*

Alienation, some modern philosophers have said, is the exile of the emotions in a world that can never fulfill us. By the same token, loneliness at the everyday level is not so much aloneness as longing—anxiety about whom we are not with but would like to be. And restlessness is a yearning beyond words for the home to which we can no longer return.

HUMANS AS HOMELESS

"But it is truest to say that the soul is an exile and a wanderer, driven forth by the divine decrees and laws, and then, on an island buffeted by the seas, imprisoned within the body 'like an oyster in its shell,' as Plato says, because it does not remember or recall 'what home and what high felicity' it has left, not leaving Sardis for Athens or Corinth or Lemnos or Scyros, but Heaven and the Moon for earth and life on earth."

—Plutarch

"The human race is constantly rushing to and fro."

—Seneca

"Has anyone ever considered the philosophy of travel? It might be worthwhile. What is life but a form of motion and a journey through a foreign world?"

—George Santayana

"To be rooted is perhaps the most important and least recognized need of the human soul."

—philosopher Simone Weil

"Exile accepted as a destiny, in the way we accept an incurable illness, should help us see through our self-delusions."

—poet Czeslaw Milosz

"Life is itself exile, and its inevitability does not lessen our grief or alter the fact."

—novelist William H. Gass

"The first thing I remember about the world—and I pray it may be the last—is that I was a stranger in it. This feeling, which everyone has in some degree, and which is at once the glory and desolation of *homo sapiens,* provides the only thread of consistency that I can detect in my life."

—journalist Malcolm Muggeridge

"We're threatened with eviction, for this is a point of entry and departure, there are no permanent guests! And where else have we to go when we leave here? . . . We're lonely. We're frightened."

—Tennessee Williams

"After all, all of life is moving. First you have an assigned home in your mother's body, then you get in a crib, and finally you get in a coffin. When I heard he was dead I thought: That's a stop. No more moving."

—A friend on hearing of the suicide of
psychoanalyst Bruno Bettelheim, 1990

"The main thing that I sensed back in my childhood was this inescapable *yearning* that I could never satisfy. Even now at times I experience a terrible loneliness and isolation. . . . Oh, God, how I remember that feeling, though. Sitting on the front steps on a summer night and hearing a lawnmower in the distance and a screen door slamming somewhere. It would actually make my heart *ache*."

—actress Jessica Lange

THE ROAD LESS TRAVELED

"The unexamined life is not worth living." Socrates' famous statement during his trial is probably the most-quoted but least-followed statement of all antiquity. For although all human beings are serious about the meaning of life at some point on their journeys, most people are unconcerned most of the time. We live life like a headlong rush down the road. But considering our lack of purpose and direction, we might as well be ambling along with barely a thought about why we are here or where we are going. If we want to do better, however, our challenge as modern people is to pursue an examined life in an unexamining age.

Oddly enough, this unconcern is a characteristic of the leadership of Western countries to a surprising degree and in striking ways—especially in the United States. Professor Peter L. Berger, the eminent social scientist, has observed that the United States is a "nation of Indians ruled by Swedes"—in other words, that the United States has a populace as religious as India's, the most religious country in the world, but is ruled by leadership that is as secular as Sweden's, the most secular country in the world. Not surprisingly, this situation raises questions at the personal level as well as the political level.

Needless to say, the problem created is not one of hostility but "tone deafness." Too often it means that American leaders are "unmusical." They simply cannot hear or follow the musical score by which most of their fellow citizens orchestrate their lives.

THE NEW YORK VIEW OF AMERICA

"Millions of people out there believe what nobody believes any more."

—New York attorney

A history professor in New York accompanied a class on a tour of French cathedrals and art museums. After a week of this, one of the brightest students in the class observed that they had been viewing all these paintings and statues of a mother with a child, and in every case the child was a boy. "How can anyone deny that that's not evidence of sexism?" she wanted to know.

—*First Things*, March 1995

"Ignorant people in preppy clothes are more dangerous to America than oil embargoes."

—author V. S. Naipaul, after a year of college teaching

People in Manhattan "are constantly creating these real unnecessary neurotic problems for themselves 'cause it keeps them from dealing with the more unsolvable, terrifying problems about the universe."

—Woody Allen, *Manhattan*

This "tone deafness" of many American leaders is all the more odd if viewed from the perspective of history. Quite simply, in America faith has been the leading hope of the founding pioneers, the early home of intellectual life, a vital harbinger of such pivotal national events as revolution and abolition, and the hub of a myriad of reforms and concerns, including the women's movement. In short, understanding the United States without seeing the importance of faith is like describing Switzerland without mentioning the Alps. Yet many American leaders have the equivalent of an Alpless map of Switzerland when they come to understanding their own country.

Consider the fact that the Christian faith is the single strongest animating feature in Western civilization. Many of the greatest thinkers, writers, artists, musicians, scientists, and reformers in the history of the West and the United States have been people of deep faith—Augustine, Gutenberg, Blaise Pascal, Rembrandt van Rijn, Isaac Newton, Johann Sebastian Bach, Jonathan Edwards, William Wilberforce, and Fyodor Dostoyevsky, to name a few. Yet somehow faith today is considered to be appropriate only for the uneducated and uncultured.

Or consider that most Americans throughout the generations have understood themselves and their lives, public as well as private, from the perspective of their Christian faith—and more than 85 percent of Americans say they still do. Yet serious mention of this faith in many segments of public life is considered intrusive and undemocratic.

Or again consider that most of the greatest and most successful movements of reform in American history, including the abolition of slavery and the rise of the women's movement, have been inspired by the Christian faith and led by people of faith. Yet faith itself is commonly regarded as reactionary.

In sum, we are at an odd moment in the life of our civilization, a time when someone examining the animating faith must choose Robert Frost's road "less traveled by."

INVITATION TO TRAVEL

This book, *The Journey*, offers a series of readings that chart a thinking person's quest for meaning—including the special questions and considerations that influence this journey. More particularly the readings highlight four general stages of the journey that countless people have passed through.

The Journey has been prepared for two kinds of people. One are those who do not view themselves as committed believers, but who are serious about the big questions on the journey of life and are open to the possibility of those questions being answered. The other are those who are already followers of Christ at some stage on the journey of faith who wish to reflect seriously on *why* they believe what they believe.

Needless to say, these roadmaps are not a required route for travelers. Nothing is more fully human, and therefore more fully free, than the road to faith. There is no one way to faith and no sure-fire, twelve-step recipe to achieve it. When all is said and done, there are as many ways to faith as people who come to believe. But there is a special encouragement and precedent in the routes that some of the greatest minds and hearts have followed before.

The thinking person's road to faith is not for everyone. But if Christian truth is simple enough for a child to paddle in yet deep enough for an elephant to swim in, as early Christians expressed it, it is certainly for thoughtful people too. There are, after all, issues that reflective people cannot afford to miss, just as there are possibilities they will not wish to experience.

We are all distinct individuals who are at different stages on the journey. For some the road is simple; for others it is tortuous. When Peter Drucker was asked by fellow business consultant Ken Blanchard why he had become a Christian, he answered simply, "Because there's no better deal." For some the outer journey is hard enough, for others the inner journey may prove even more strenuous and long. But for all of us the invitation stands: to set out on the most important journey of our lives—from the understanding to the will and from the will to action—bringing us to that place of faith in God that is the first step toward home.

To avoid misunderstanding and be more specific: These readings are not so much a single *proof* for God's existence as a series of *pointers* to help indicate the way to that conclusion. They are not *exhaustive*—for most of us that would be tiresome as well as excessive—but they are *sufficient*, at least to prompt the beginning of deeper reflection. And they are not a *demonstration* for spectators but an *invitation* for participants—to "taste and see" in the celebrated mixed metaphor of the Psalms or to "come and see" in the words of the Gospels.

The reason for this insistence is simple. If God is who he says he is, he is the source, guide, and goal of life—no greater, more perfect, and more loving being exists. It therefore would be absurd to have his existence turn for us on a ten-step proof that depends solely on a logic beyond the capacity of all but a few clever minds. Far better to indicate a path whose exploration requires whole people in a wholly passionate and honest search, including our active and inquiring minds.

Yet the very strength of those words should carry its own warning. Most modern people have grown unaccustomed to big-picture or first-principle thinking. So as soon as we discuss the human journey and go beyond the shallows of convention and cliché, the issues can quickly become deep, or controversial, or personal. After all, when all is said and done "the human journey" is an abstraction. For truly our individual lives are the topic, our births and deaths frame the picture, our goals and standards are under scrutiny, our successes and failures are in the balance. Thus, the answer that benefits each of us most is not the one that tells us something we did not know before and do not need now. It is the answer that gives expression to the truth that we have been mutely struggling inside ourselves to grasp.

Significantly—at a time when the name "Christian" was still an insult and the unfortunately abstract term "Christianity" was centuries off—the very earliest name for followers of Christ was "the Way." Jesus announced simply that he was "the way and the truth and the life." A narrow way rather than a broad way, he added, so the road "less traveled by" is nothing new. Yet it always was and is that faith in Jesus Christ appeals to us all on the human journey of life. As novelist Walker Percy put it:

You can get all *A*'s and still flunk life.

Or as G. K. Chesterton put it a little earlier:

> Man has always lost his way. He has been a tramp ever since Eden; but he always knew, or thought he knew, what he was looking for. . . . For the first time in history he begins really to doubt the object of his wanderings on earth. He has always lost his way; but now he has lost his address.

Or again, as Augustine wrote much earlier still in what might be the epigraph for all these readings:

> For you have formed us for yourself, and our hearts are restless until they find their rest in you.

ONE
A TIME FOR QUESTIONS

THE FOUR PARTS OF THIS STUDY FOLLOW THE FOUR STAGES THAT ARE INTEGRAL TO THE quest for meaning—and therefore to a thinking person's journey toward faith. The first stage of the journey is when we become aware of a sense of questioning or need that forces us to consider where we are in life. In spurring our quest for meaning, beyond the meaning we know, it spurs us to become seekers.

The term "seeker" is in vogue today, but used far too casually. Often it is only a synonym for the spiritually unattached. Seekers, in this loose sense, are those who do not identify themselves as Christian, Jew, Muslim, Buddhist, atheist, and so forth, and who do not attend or belong to any church, synagogue, mosque, or meeting place.

Such seekers are rarely looking for anything in particular. Often they are drifters, not seekers, little different from the "hoppers and shoppers" who surf the media and cruise the malls of the postmodern world. Cool, noncommittal, ever-open, and concerned only to cover all bases, they have been well-described as "conversion prone" and therefore eternally ready to be converted and reconverted ad nauseam. They are like a character Anita Brookner describes in her novel Altered States: "Her life was an improvisation, without roots, without commitments, without guarantees."

True seekers are quite different. On meeting them you feel their seriousness, their restlessness, and their desire to close on an answer. Something in life has awakened questions—perhaps something positive, like a sense of awe in the face of beauty; perhaps something negative, like a crisis or a collapsed confidence. But those questions have forced them to consider where they are in life. They have become seekers. Something has spurred them to a quest for meaning, and they have to find an answer.

True seekers are looking for something. They are people for whom life, or a part of life, has suddenly become a point of wonder, a question, a problem, or an irritation. This happens so intensely or so persistently that they are stirred to look for an answer beyond their present answers and to clarify their position in life. However the need arises, and whatever it calls for, the sense of need consumes searchers and launches them on their quest.

Mention of a "sense of need" raises an important caution. The point is not that people believe in God because of need—that would be irrational and make the believer vulnerable to the accusation that faith is a crutch. Rather they disbelieve in what they believed in before because of new needs their previous beliefs could not answer. The question of what and why they then come to believe comes at a later stage.

The point is not that people believe in God because of need—that would be irrational and make the believer vulnerable to the accusation that faith is a crutch. Rather they disbelieve in what they believed in before because of new needs their previous beliefs could not answer.

SPUR TO THE SEARCH

"I carried about me a cut and bleeding soul, that could not bear to be carried by me, and where I could put it, I could not discover. Not in pleasant groves, not in games and singing, nor in the fragrant corners of a garden. Not in the company of a dinner table, not in the delights of the bed: not even in my books and poetry. It floundered in a void and fell back on me. I remained in a haunted spot, which gave me no rest, from which I could not escape. For where could my heart flee from my heart? Where could I escape myself? Where would I not dog my own footsteps?"

—Augustine of Hippo, *Confessions*

"He knew what he disbelieved long before he knew what he believed."

—Malcolm Muggeridge's biographer, describing his conversion

At stake in this first stage of the journey is the urgency that spurs the quest away from complacency about life and from false sources of sufficiency (ourselves, our possessions, our successes, or our present sense of answers) and toward the deeper sort of answer required by the search.

POINT TO PONDER:

A World Within the World that Makes a World of Difference

To understand why a sense of questioning or need arises in our lives, we need to explore some of the features of how we human beings live and think and see the world.

A key part of human living is that we all have a philosophy of life. Sometimes called a vision of life, a worldview, or a world-and-life view, this philosophy of life is the framework or road map within which we interpret all our experience of life—how we see reality, how we view our own identity, how we decide issues of morality, and so on.

LIKE LIGHT

"I believe in Christianity as I believe in the sun—not only because I see it, but because by it I see everything else."

—C. S. Lewis

"He used to say that he had three educations: one from school, one at the pool hall, and one from the Bible. Without the latter, he said, you can't understand what you learned from the other two places."

—Jana Tull Steed, *Duke Ellington*

"The truly powerful ideas are the ones that do not have to justify themselves."

—Dallas Willard

With most of us, most of the time our worldviews are unconscious, but that is not to say they are unimportant. Even when we do not see them, we see by them. We derive them from a variety of sources—our parents, our education, our cultural background, our friends, as well as our own experiences and discoveries. Some people, such as humanists, are quite candid that these beliefs are their own inventions. Others, such as Jews and Christians, claim a different status because their worldviews have been revealed from that which is outside of human experience.

But for all the differences, our ways of viewing life are fundamental and necessary because they provide us with a sense of meaning and belonging; they help us make sense of our lives and find security in our worlds. And this, of course, is why we feel it so keenly when life throws at us questions our worldviews cannot answer or problems they cannot resolve—especially if

Our ways of viewing life are fundamental and necessary because they provide us with a sense of meaning and belonging; they help us make sense of our lives and find security in our worlds.

"An unexamined life is
not worth living."
—SOCRATES

Calvin and Hobbes © 1992 Watterson.
Reprinted with permission of Universal
Press Syndicate. All rights reserved.

we must face that our worldview is inadequate and therefore we must look for another.

Naturally, most people regard their own worldviews as true, even if they dismiss those of others as inadequate or incomplete. Some people, however, regard all worldviews as false—their own included—though this position becomes a difficult one for a person to live with. But anyone who appreciates how necessary and universal our human worldviews are understands the force of Socrates' saying, "An unexamined life is not worth living." The readings in this section give a flavor of different viewpoints on the universal human need to find meaning in life.

VIEWS OF WORLDVIEWS

"One must take the best and most irrefragable of human theories, and let this be the raft on which he sails through life—not without risk, as I admit, if he cannot find some word of God which will surely and safely carry him."

—Plato

"Fear made the gods."

—Lucretius

"Religion is the opium of the people."

—Karl Marx

"Take away the life-lie from the average man and you take away his happiness."

—Henrik Ibsen

"This is the true joy in life—that being used for a purpose recognized by yourself as a mighty one. That being a force of nature, instead of a feverish, selfish little clod of ailments and grievances complaining that the world will not devote itself to making you happy."

—George Bernard Shaw

"No man can live without any basis of philosophy, however primitive, naïve, childish, or unconscious."

—philosopher Nikolai Berdyaev

The human task is "to sustain alone a weary but unyielding Atlas, the world that his own ideals have fashioned."

—Bertrand Russell

"It is as undignified to think another man's philosophy as to wear another man's cast-off clothes."

—psychologist Havelock Ellis

"Man inhabits, for his own convenience, a homemade universe within the greater alien world of external matter and his own irrationality. Out of the illimitable blackness of that world the light of his customary thinking scoops, as it were, a little illuminated cave—a tunnel of brightness, in which, from the birth of consciousness to its death, he lives, moves and has his being. . . . We ignore the outer darkness; or if we cannot ignore it, if it presses too insistently upon us, we disapprove of being afraid."

—**Aldous Huxley**

"There is, in fact, a religious sense deeply rooted in each and every man's unconscious depths."

—**Viktor Frankl,** *Man's Search for Ultimate Meaning*

"I think we are all healthier if we think there is some importance to what we are doing. I can only speak from personal experience, but when it seems like my life is meaningless, I feel closest to despair. I like life to have meaning. That is not to say you have to jump into meaning and find it where there is none. Or come up with answers too quickly, which is what we tend to do in North America."

—**Norman Mailer**

Plato

Plato (about 427–347 B.C.), along with his mentor Socrates and his disciple Aristotle, was a giant of the mind and a leading shaper of Western civilization and its intellectual tradition. Born a year after the death of Pericles, Plato came from a family that was prominent in Athenian politics. He, however, refused to enter politics after he became disgusted by the corruption and violence of Athenian democracy—which culminated in the execution of his friend and teacher Socrates in 399 B.C. Living in troubled times, he sought his cure from the ills of society in philosophy, not politics. He became convinced that justice would not arrive "until either real philosophers gain political power or politicians become by some miracle true philosophers."

Ironically, the defeat of Athens by Sparta in 404 B.C. and the collapse of the Periclean Golden Age led to a new Athenian dominance of the world—through education, culture, and the Greek ideal of Paidea, the formation of a people's character through living up to their highest ideals. Plato is the greatest of the fourth-century geniuses of education; his celebrated parable of the cave is one of the most beautiful, imaginative, and influential sections of his classic work, The Republic.

The following reading is an excerpt from Plato's parable of the cave. In the allegory, Socrates explains to Glaucon that we human beings are in an underground cave that has a wide entrance through which sunlight streams. We have been chained there since childhood with our backs to the entrance, unable to move our legs or heads. Above and behind us, some distance off, a fire is burning. Its rays fall on the back wall of the cave that we face.

A road with a wall behind it runs between us and the fire. Behind the wall people are carrying all sorts of figures and objects. Some are talking, some silent, but the effect is to cast shadows on the back wall of the cave at which we look. Because our shackles do not allow us to turn around, we cannot see anything but the shadow-pictures on the wall. Naturally we take the shadows to be reality and the echoing voices to be the speech of the shadow-figures.

If this is our human situation, what does it say of the nature of humanness and our claim to knowledge and reality? Of our path to liberation? And, if we achieve freedom, of our responsibility to those still caught in the world of shadows?

THROUGH A GLASS DARKLY

"People say that a good seat in the backyard affords as accurate and inspiring a vantage point on the planet earth as any observation tower on Alpha Centauri. They are wrong. We see through a glass darkly. We find ourselves in the middle of a movie, or, God help us, a take for a movie, and we don't know what's on the rest of the film."

—Annie Dillard

"If, when I am asleep, I am a man dreaming I am a butterfly, how do I know, when I am awake, I am not a butterfly dreaming I am a man?"

—Chuang Chou

"No one can be sure, apart from faith, whether he is sleeping or waking, because when we are asleep, we are just as firmly convinced that we are awake as we are now."

—Blaise Pascal

The Parable of the Cave ⮚

And now, I said, let me show in a figure how far our nature is enlightened or unenlightened: Behold! human beings living in a underground den, which has a mouth open towards the light and reaching all along the den; here they have been from their childhood, and have their legs and necks chained so that they cannot move, and can only see before them, being prevented by the chains from turning round their heads. Above and behind them a fire is blazing at a distance, and between the fire and the prisoners there is a raised way; and you will see, if you look, a low wall built along the way, like the screen which marionette players have in front of them, over which they show the puppets.

I see.

And do you see, I said, men passing along the wall carrying all sorts of vessels, and statues and figures of animals made of wood and stone and various materials, which appear over the wall? Some of them are talking, others silent.

You have shown me a strange image, and they are strange prisoners.

Like ourselves, I replied; and they see only their own shadows, or the shadows of one another, which the fire throws on the opposite wall of the cave?

True, he said; how could they see anything but the shadows if they were never allowed to move their heads?

And of the objects which are being carried in like manner they would only

Behold! human beings living in a underground den, which has a mouth open towards the light and reaching all along the den; here they have been from their childhood, and have their legs and necks chained so that they cannot move, and can only see before them.

see the shadows? . . . To them, I said, the truth would be literally nothing but the shadows of the images.

That is certain.

And now look again, and see what will naturally follow if the prisoners are released and disabused of their error. At first, when any of them is liberated and compelled suddenly to stand up and turn his neck round and walk and look towards the light, he will suffer sharp pains; the glare will distress him, and he will be unable to see the realities of which in his former state he had seen the shadows. . . .

And if he is compelled to look straight at the light, will he not have a pain in his eyes which will make him turn away to take in the objects of vision which he can see, and which he will conceive to be in reality clearer than the things which are now being shown to him? . . . When he approaches the light his eyes will be dazzled, and he will not be able to see anything at all of what are now called realities.

Not all in a moment, he said.

He will require to grow accustomed to the sight of the upper world. And first he will see the shadows best, next the reflections of men and other objects in the water, and then the objects themselves; then he will gaze upon the light of the moon and the stars and the spangled heaven; and he will see the sky and the stars by night better than the sun or the light of the sun by day?

Certainly.

Last of all he will be able to see the sun, and not mere reflections of him in the water, but he will see him in his own proper place, and not in another; and he will contemplate him as he is.

Certainly.

He will then proceed to argue that this is he who gives the season and the years, and is the guardian of all that is in the visible world, and in a certain way the cause of all things which he and his fellows have been accustomed to behold?

Clearly, he said, he would first see the sun and then reason about him.

And when he remembered his old habitation, and the wisdom of the den and his fellow-prisoners, do you not suppose that he would felicitate himself on the change, and pity them? . . .

Yes, he said, I think that he would rather suffer anything than entertain these false notions and live in this miserable manner.

Imagine once more, I said, such a one coming suddenly out of the sun to be replaced in his old situation; would he not be certain to have his eyes full of darkness? . . .While his sight was still weak, and before his eyes had

At first, when any of them is liberated and compelled suddenly to stand up and turn his neck round and walk and look towards the light, he will suffer sharp pains; the glare will distress him, and he will be unable to see the realities of which in his former state he had seen the shadows.

become steady (and the time which would be needed to acquire this new habit of sight might be very considerable) would he not be ridiculous? Men would say of him that up he went and down he came without his eyes; and that it was better not even to think of ascending; and if any one tried to loose another and lead him up to the light, let them only catch the offender, and they would put him to death.

No question, he said.

This entire allegory, I said, you may now append, dear Glaucon, to the previous argument; the prison-house is the world of sight, the light of the fire is the sun, and you will not misapprehend me if you interpret the journey upwards to be the ascent of the soul into the intellectual world according to my poor belief, which, at your desire, I have expressed whether rightly or wrongly God knows. But, whether true or false, my opinion is that in the world of knowledge the idea of good appears last of all, and is seen only with an effort; and, when seen, is also inferred to be the universal author of all things beautiful and right, parent of light and of the lord of light in this visible world, and the immediate source of reason and truth in the intellectual; and that this is the power upon which he who would act rationally, either in public or private life must have his eye fixed.

My opinion is that in the world of knowledge the idea of good appears last of all, and is seen only with an effort.

I agree, he said, as far as I am able to understand you.

Moreover, I said, you must not wonder that those who attain to this beatific vision are unwilling to descend to human affairs; for their souls are ever hastening into the upper world where they desire to dwell; which desire of theirs is very natural, if our allegory may be trusted.

Yes, very natural.

And is there anything surprising in one who passes from divine contemplations to the evil state of man, misbehaving himself in a ridiculous manner; if, while his eyes are blinking and before he has become accustomed to the surrounding darkness, he is compelled to fight in courts of law, or in other places, about the images or the shadows of images of justice, and is endeavouring to meet the conceptions of those who have never yet seen absolute justice?

Anything but surprising, he replied.

Any one who has common sense will remember that the bewilderments of the eyes are of two kinds, and arise from two causes, either from coming out of the light or from going into the light, which is true of the mind's eye, quite as much as of the bodily eye; and he who remembers this when he sees any one whose vision is perplexed and weak, will not be too ready to laugh; he will first ask whether that soul of man has come out of the brighter light, and is unable to see because unaccustomed to the dark, or having turned from darkness to the day is dazzled by excess of light. And he will count the one happy in his condition and state of being, and he will pity the other; or, if he have a mind to laugh at the soul which comes from below into the light, there will be more reason in this than in the laugh which greets him who returns from above out of the light into the den.

That, he said, is a very just distinction.

. . . Our argument shows that the power and capacity of learning exists in the soul already; and that just as the eye was unable to turn from darkness to light without the whole body, so too the instrument of knowledge can only by the movement of the whole soul be turned from the world of becoming into that of being, and learn by degrees to endure the sight of being, and of the brightest and best of being, or in other words, of the good.

Very true.

And must there not be some art which will effect conversion in the easiest and quickest manner; not implanting the faculty of sight, for that exists already, but has been turned in the wrong direction, and is looking away from the truth?

Yes, he said, such an art may be presumed.

And whereas the other so-called virtues of the soul seem to be akin to bodily qualities, for even when they are not originally innate they can be implanted later by habit and exercise, the virtue of wisdom more than anything else contains a divine element which always remains, and by this conversion is rendered useful and profitable; or, on the other hand, hurtful and useless. Did you never observe the narrow intelligence flashing from the keen eye of a clever rogue—how eager he is, how clearly his paltry soul sees the way to his end; he is the reverse of blind, but his keen eyesight is forced into the service of evil, and he is mischievous in proportion to his cleverness? . . . What if there had been a circumcision of such natures in the days of their youth . . .—if, I say, they had been released from these impediments and turned in the opposite direction, the very same faculty in them would have seen the truth as keenly as they see what their eyes are turned to now.

Very likely.

Yes, I said; and there is another thing which is likely, or rather a necessary inference from what has preceded, that neither the uneducated and uninformed of the truth, nor yet those who never make an end of their education,

Neither the uneducated and uninformed of the truth, nor yet those who never make an end of their education, will be able ministers of State.

will be able ministers of State; not the former, because they have no single aim of duty which is the rule of all their actions, private as well as public; nor the latter, because they will not act at all except upon compulsion, fancying that they are already dwelling apart in the islands of the blest.

Very true, he replied.

Then, I said, the business of us who are the founders of the State will be to compel the best minds to attain that knowledge which we have already shown to be the greatest of all—they must continue to ascend until they arrive at the good; but when they have ascended and seen enough we must not allow them to do as they do now.

What do you mean?

I mean that they remain in the upper world: but this must not be allowed; they must be made to descend again among the prisoners in the den, and partake of their labours and honours, whether they are worth having or not. . . . The intention of the legislator, who did not aim at making any one class in the State happy above the rest; the happiness was to be in the whole State, and he held the citizens together by persuasion and necessity, making them bene-factors of the State, and therefore benefactors of one another; to this end he created them, not to please themselves, but to be his instruments in binding up the State.

I mean that they remain in the upper world: but this must not be allowed; they must be made to descend again among the prisoners in the den, and partake of their labours and honours, whether they are worth having or not.

From Plato, *The Republic,* translated by Benjamin Jowett (1892).

OTHERWISE NOT WORTH LIVING?

"If on the other hand I tell you that to let no day pass without discussing goodness and all the other subjects about which you hear me talking and examining both myself and others is really the very best thing that a man can do, and that life without this sort of examination is not worth living, you will be even less inclined to believe me."

—Socrates, *Apology*

QUESTIONS FOR THOUGHT AND DISCUSSION

1. What is Plato illustrating "in a figure" in his description of the cave? Who are "the strange prisoners"? The "shadows"? What is the status of our human knowledge and perceptions, as Plato sees it?

2. In the paragraph "And now look again . . .," what does the prisoners' liberation symbolize? Before experiencing this freedom, what has been their "error"?

3. What is the meaning of the "light"? Why would looking at the light be painful initially? What process must the former prisoner go through before he can "see him [the sun] in his own proper place"? What does contemplating "him as he is" entail?

4. Once fully in the sun, what would the former prisoner's attitude be toward those in the cave and their notions?

5. What would the prisoners think of the freed man, should he choose to come back into the cave? What does Plato mean by "it was better not even to think of ascending"? Who are "the offenders"? How does he say they would be treated? What kind of prejudice is Plato really describing?

6. How does Plato interpret his allegory?

7. In the paragraph that begins "This entire allegory . . .," read from "But, whether true or false" to the end of the paragraph. What do you make of his assessment? Do you agree or not?

8. Why does Plato say that one who has "attain[ed] this beatific vision" would be unwilling to go back to the cave of human affairs? But what reasons does he give for doing so?

9. According to his way of thinking, who is qualified for leadership? Why? What are their responsibilities?

10. How would an atheist understand Plato's parable of the cave? A Hindu? A Jew or a Christian? How does the allegory challenge you to think about your beliefs and worldview? Why is it so unsettling to think that the way you've always seen the world may not be the only way, or even the true way?

Viktor Frankl

Viktor Emil Frankl (1905–1997) is an internationally renowned psychiatrist, author, founder of "logotherapy," a school of psychiatric analysis and counseling, and a celebrated survivor of the Nazi concentration camps. Born in Vienna, he earned his M.D. and his Ph.D. from the University of Vienna. He was the founder and head of the Youth Counseling Centers in Vienna from 1928–1938 and head of the neurology department at Rothschild Hospital from 1940 until his arrest by the Nazis in 1942.

After the war he served as a professor of neurology and psychiatry at the University of Vienna and head of the Neurological Poliklinik Hospital of Vienna from 1946–1970. His many books have been published in more than nineteen languages, and he has been awarded many honors, including the Albert Schweitzer Award and Germany's Cross of Merit. The following reading from Man's Search for Meaning, *of which millions of copies have been sold, describes the death-camp inmates' absolute need for meaning and hope.*

WHY LIVE?

"When all hope is gone, death becomes a duty."

—Voltaire

"When all hope is gone, Jews invent new hopes."

—Elie Wiesel, *A Jew Today*

"There is but one truly serious philosophical problem, and that is suicide. Judging whether life is worth living amounts to answering the fundamental question of philosophy. . . . I see many people die because they judge that life is not worth living. I see others paradoxically getting killed for the ideas or illusions that give them a reason for living (what is called a reason for living is an excellent reason for dying). I therefore conclude that the meaning of life is the most urgent of questions."

—Albert Camus, *The Myth of Sisyphus*

"The truth is that among those who actually went through the experience of Auschwitz—the number of those whose religious life was deepened—in spite of, not because of, this experience—by far exceeds the number of those who gave up their belief. To paraphrase what La Rochefoucauld once remarked with regard to love, one might say that just as the small fire is extinguished by the storm while a large fire is enhanced by it—likewise a weak faith is weakened by predicaments and catastrophes, whereas a strong faith is strengthened by them."

—Viktor Frankl, *Man's Search for Ultimate Meaning*

Experiences in a Concentration Camp 🐦

The prisoner who had lost faith in the future—his future—was doomed. With his loss of belief in the future, he also lost his spiritual hold; he let himself decline and become subject to mental and physical decay.

The prisoner who had lost faith in the future—his future—was doomed. With his loss of belief in the future, he also lost his spiritual hold; he let himself decline and become subject to mental and physical decay. Usually this happened quite suddenly, in the form of a crisis, the symptoms of which were familiar to the experienced camp inmate. We all feared this moment—not for ourselves, which would have been pointless, but for our friends. Usually it began with the prisoner refusing one morning to get dressed and wash or to go out on the parade grounds. No entreaties, no blows, no threats had any effect. He just lay there, hardly moving. If this crisis was brought about by an illness, he refused to be taken to the sick-bay or to do anything to help himself. He simply gave up. There he remained, lying in his own excreta, and nothing bothered him any more. . . .

"He who has a why to live for can bear with almost any how."
—FRIEDRICH NIETZSCHE

As we said before, any attempt to restore a man's inner strength in the camp had first to succeed in showing him some future goal. Nietzsche's words, "He who has a *why* to live for can bear with almost any *how*," could be the guiding motto for all psychotherapeutic and psychohygienic efforts regarding prisoners. Whenever there was an opportunity for it, one had to give them a *why*—an aim—for their lives, in order to strengthen them to bear the terrible *how* of their existence. Woe to him who saw no more sense in his life, no aim, no purpose, and therefore no point in carrying on. He was soon lost. The typical reply with which such a man rejected all encouraging arguments was, "I have nothing to expect from life any more." What sort of answer can one give to that?

We had to learn ourselves and, furthermore, we had to teach the despairing men, that it did not really matter what we expected from life, but rather what life expected from us.

What was really needed was a fundamental change in our attitude toward life. We had to learn ourselves and, furthermore, we had to teach the despairing men, that *it did not really matter what we expected from life, but rather what life expected from us.* . . .

THE WILL TO MEANING

"According to logotherapy [Frankl's school of psychology], the striving to find a meaning in one's life is the primary motivational force in man. That is why I speak of a *will to meaning* in contrast to the pleasure principle (or, as we could also term it, the *will to pleasure*) on which Freudian psychoanalysis is centered, as well as in contrast to the *will to power* stressed by Adlerian psychology.

"Man's search for meaning is a primary force in his life and not a 'secondary rationalization' of instinctual drives. This meaning is unique and specific in that it must and can be fulfilled by him alone; only then does it achieve a significance that will satisfy his own will to meaning. There are some authors who contend that meanings and values are 'nothing but defense mechanisms, reaction formations and sublimations.' But as for myself, I would not be willing to live merely for the sake of my 'defense mechanisms,' nor would I be ready to die merely for the sake of my 'reaction formations.' Man, however, is able to live and even to die for the sake of his ideals and values!

"A poll of public opinion was conducted a few years ago in France. The results showed that 89 percent of the people polled admitted that man needs 'something' for the sake of which to live. Moreover, 61 percent conceded that there was something, or someone, in their own lives for whose sake they were even ready to die. I repeated this poll at my clinic in Vienna among both the patients and the personnel, and the outcome was practically the same as among the thousands of people screened in France; the difference was only 2 percent. In other words, the will to meaning is in most people *fact*, not *faith*."

   —Victor Frankl, *Man's Search for Meaning*

"It is not enough for me to be able to say 'I am'; I want to know *who I am* and in relation to whom I live. It is not enough for me to ask questions; I want to know how to answer the one question that seems to encompass everything I face: What am I here for?"

   —Abraham Heschel

Human life "essentially involves *meaning*. Meaning is not a luxury for us. It is a kind of spiritual oxygen, we might say, that enables our souls to live."

   —Dallas Willard, *The Divine Conspiracy*

I remember an incident when there was occasion for psychotherapeutic work on the inmates of a whole hut, due to an intensification of their receptiveness because of a certain external situation.

It had been a bad day. On parade, an announcement had been made about the many actions that would, from then on, be regarded as sabotage and therefore punishable by immediate death by hanging. Among these were crimes such as cutting small strips from our old blankets (in order to improvise ankle supports) and very minor "thefts." A few days previously a semi-starved prisoner had broken into the potato store to steal a few pounds of potatoes. The theft had been discovered and some prisoners had recognized the "burglar." When the camp authorities heard about it they ordered that the guilty man be given up to them or the whole camp would starve for a day. Naturally the 2,500 men preferred to fast.

On the evening of this day of fasting we lay in our earthen huts—in a very low mood. Very little was said and every word sounded irritable. Then, to make matters even worse, the light went out. Tempers reached their lowest ebb. But our senior block warden was a wise man. He improvised a little talk about all that was on our minds at that moment. He talked about the many comrades who had died in the last few days, either of sickness or of suicide. But he also mentioned what may have been the real reason for their deaths: giving up hope. He maintained that there should be some way of preventing possible future victims from reaching this extreme state. And it was to me that the warden pointed to give this advice.

He talked about the many comrades who had died in the last few days, either of sickness or of suicide. But he also mentioned what may have been the real reason for their deaths: giving up hope.

God knows, I was not in the mood to give psychological explanations or to preach any sermons — to offer my comrades a kind of medical care of their souls. I was cold and hungry, irritable and tired, but I had to make the effort and use this unique opportunity. Encouragement was now more necessary than ever.

So I began by mentioning the most trivial of comforts first. I said that even in this Europe in the sixth winter of the Second World War, our situation was not the most terrible we could think of. I said that each of us had to ask himself what irreplaceable losses he had suffered up to then. I speculated that for most of them these losses had really been few. Whoever was still alive had reason for hope. Health, family, happiness, professional abilities, fortune, position in society — all these were things that could be achieved again or restored. After all, we still had all our bones intact. Whatever we had gone through could still be an asset to us in the future. And I quoted from Nietzsche: *"Was mich nicht umbringt, macht mich stärker."* (That which does not kill me, makes me stronger.)

"That which does not kill me, makes me stronger."
—FRIEDRICH NIETZSCHE

Then I spoke about the future. I said that to the impartial the future must seem hopeless. I agreed that each of us could guess for himself how small were his chances of survival. I told them that although there was still no typhus epidemic in the camp, I estimated my own chances at about one in twenty. But I also told them that, in spite of this, I had no intention of losing hope and giving up. For no man knew what the future would bring, much less the next hour. Even if we could not expect any sensational military events in the next few days, who knew better than we, with our experience of camps, how great chances sometimes opened up, quite suddenly, at least for the individual. For instance, one might be attached unexpectedly to a special group with exceptionally good working conditions — for this was the kind of thing which constituted the "luck" of the prisoner.

But I did not only talk of the future and the veil which was drawn over it. I also mentioned the past; all its joys, and how its light shone even in the present darkness. Again I quoted a poet—to avoid sounding like a preacher myself—who had written, *"Was Du erlebt, kann keine Macht der Welt Dir rauben."* (What you have experienced, no power on earth can take from you.) Not only our experiences, but all we have done, whatever great thoughts we may have had, and all we have suffered, all this is not lost, though it is past; we have brought it into being. Having been is also a kind of being, and perhaps the surest kind.

What you have experienced, no power on earth can take from you.

Then I spoke of the many opportunities of giving life a meaning. I told my comrades (who lay motionless, although occasionally a sigh could be heard) that human life, under any circumstances, never ceases to have a meaning, and that this infinite meaning of life includes suffering and dying, privation, and death. I asked the poor creatures who listened to me attentively in the darkness of the hut to face up to the seriousness of our position. They must not lose hope but should keep their courage in the certainty that the hopelessness of our struggle did not detract from its dignity and its meaning. I said that someone looks down on each of us in difficult hours—a friend, a wife, somebody alive or dead, or a God—and he would not expect us to disappoint him. He would hope to find us suffering proudly—not miserably—knowing how to die.

And finally I spoke of our sacrifice, which had meaning in every case. It was in the nature of this sacrifice that it should appear to be pointless in the normal world, the world of material success. But in reality our sacrifice did have a meaning. Those of us who had any religious faith, I said frankly, could understand without difficulty. I told them of a comrade who on his arrival in camp had tried to make a pact with Heaven that his suffering and death should save the human being he loved from a painful end. For this man, suffering and death were meaningful; his was a sacrifice of the deepest significance. He did not want to die for nothing. None of us wanted that.

The purpose of my words was to find a full meaning in our life, then and there, in that hut and in that practically hopeless situation. I saw that my efforts had been successful. When the electric bulb flared up again, I saw the miserable figures of my friends limping toward me to thank me with tears in their eyes. But I have to confess here that only too rarely had I the inner strength to make contact with my companions in suffering and that I must have missed many opportunities for doing so.

MEANING ON DEATH ROW

"Let me just restate what happened when I spoke to the prisoners of San Quentin in 1966, at the request of the prison's director. After I had addressed these prisoners, who were the toughest criminals in California, one stood up and said, 'Dr. Frankl, would you be kind enough to say a few words through the mike to Aaron Mitchell, who is expecting to die in the gas chamber in a couple of days? The people on death row are not allowed to come down to the Chapel, but perhaps you will say a few words particularly to him' (an embarrassing position, but I had to accept this challenge and say a few words). I improvisingly said, 'Mr. Mitchell, believe me, I understand your situation. I myself had to live for some time in the shadow of the gas chamber. But also believe me that even then I did not give up my conviction of the unconditional meaningfulness of life, because either life has meaning—and then it retains this meaning even if the life is short lived—or life has no meaning—and then adding evermore years just perpetuates this meaninglessness. And believe me, even a life that has been meaningless all along, that is, a life that has been wasted, may—even in the last moment—still be bestowed with meaning by the very way in which we tackle this situation.'"

—Viktor Frankl, *Man's Search for Ultimate Meaning*

QUESTIONS FOR THOUGHT AND DISCUSSION

1. Frankl observed in the concentration camp that prisoners who lost hope in their future were doomed. Why does he say that such a person had "lost his spiritual hold"? How did the doom manifest itself?

2. Read the paragraph starting "What was really needed . . ." What sort of transition is he speaking of? What is he saying about hope?

3. Read the box, "The Will to Meaning." What does Frankl mean in the last paragraph when he says "the will to meaning is in most people *fact*, not *faith*"?

4. What do you think of Frankl's impromptu talk to boost morale? Which of his points do you find convincing and which not?

5. What does he mean by "Having been is also a kind of being, and perhaps the surest kind"? Why is remembering past joys and achievements an effective generator of hope?

6. Read the paragraph starting "Then I spoke of the many opportunities . . ." What do you think of his reasoning? What is the relationship of hope to suffering? Is it only stimulated by crises? What is the difference between "knowing how to die" and "giving up"?

7. Frankl's description of the "will to meaning" comes out of an extreme situation. How would it apply in more ordinary life?

8. What gives the prisoners strength in the concentration camp? Are they hoping to get out of prison?

9. Think back over crises that you or your friends have faced. What did they reveal of what you believe and what you rely on in life?

HE WHO HAS A WHY

"What can we know? What must we do? What can we hope for? What is man?"

—Immanuel Kant

"Where do we come from? What are we? Where are we going?"

—Paul Gauguin

"I can't believe it's all accidental. We're still trying to find out, like plumbers trying to mend Swiss watches, what makes it tick, aren't we?"

—film director David Lean

POINT TO PONDER:

The Real Divide
Is Between the Serious and the Indifferent

An obvious thought arises. If it is so important to have beliefs, or a worldview and a philosophy of life, why aren't people more conscious of it? Why don't they care more about the issue? Why do most seem not to mind the "unexamined life" that Socrates thought was not worth living?

One obvious answer is that having a worldview is similar to enjoying health. Good health is usually enjoyed most when it is talked about least. In the same way a philosophy of life that is working well is one of which we are barely aware. Like a good pair of glasses or contact lenses, it is something we see with *rather than* see.

Another obvious answer is that many people are only too happy to leave such questions to others, especially designated experts—whether priests in traditional society or pundits and psychiatrists today.

But there is a deeper answer still. Many thinkers over the centuries have observed that we human beings need a source of meaning and belonging, yet we also mount characteristic defenses against thinking and caring too deeply about the meaning of life. We appear to be driven, in fact, not to think and care too deeply about the human condition, especially about the fact that we will all die.

The following readings address the two most common forms of defense. One is what Blaise Pascal called "diversion," John Bunyan "Vanity Fair," and Søren Kierkegaard the Philistinism that "tranquilizes itself in the trivial"—the human drive toward an entertaining, distracting busyness that shields us from looking too closely at our situations or pursuing our journey. The other is the theme that recurs widely in life and literature: "bargaining," the idea that in order to gain what we most want in life we can either try to delay time— Augustine's notorious prayer, "Lord, give me chastity, but not yet"—or else try to strike a bargain with God (or fate or the Devil)—by selling our souls.

> *Human beings have characteristic defenses against thinking and caring too deeply about the meaning of life. We appear to be driven, in fact, not to think and care too deeply about the human condition, especially about the fact that we will all die.*

THE UNMENTIONABLE

"Death and the sun are not to be looked at steadily."

—Rochefoucauld

"All but Death, can be Adjusted."

—Emily Dickinson

"We all fear truth."

—Friedrich Nietzsche, *Ecce Homo*

"Humankind cannot bear very much reality."

—T. S. Eliot

"Any man who says he is not afraid of death is a liar."

—Winston Churchill

Such defenses are, of course, inadequate. And no one who seriously ponders the human condition can be complacent. Thus thinking and caring deeply are marks of the genuine seeker. And thus the real divide is not between believers and unbelievers but between those who are prepared to think seriously about life and those who are indifferent.

The real divide is not between believers and unbelievers but between those who are prepared to think seriously about life and those who are indifferent.

TRANQUILIZED BY THE TRIVIAL
"Almost five thousand years agone, there were Pilgrims walking to the Cœlestial City, as these two honest persons are; and Beelzebub, Apollyon, and Legion, with their companions, perceiving by the path that the Pilgrims made, that their Way to the City lay through this Town of *Vanity*, they contrived here to set up a Fair; a Fair, wherein should be sold *all Sorts of Vanity*, and that it should last all the year long."

—John Bunyan, *The Pilgrim's Progress*

"Think no more, lad; laugh, be jolly.
Why should men make haste to die?
Empty heads and tongues a-talking
Make the rough road easy walking,
And the feather pate of folly
Bears the falling sky."

—A. E. Housman, "A Shropshire Lad"

"Modern man is drinking and drugging himself out of awareness, or he spends his time shopping, which is the same thing."

—psychologist Ernest Becker, *The Denial of Death*

"The search is what anyone would undertake if he were not sunk in the everydayness of his own life."

—Walker Percy, *The Moviegoer*

Blaise Pascal

Blaise Pascal (1623–1662) is among the greatest Christian and Western thinkers, and was a scientist, mathematician, and Christian apologist. Born in Clermont-Ferrand, France, he was brought up by his father after his mother died when he was four years old. Pascal showed great precocity from the earliest age, taking part in mathematical experiments, including those that led to the invention of the barometer and the hydraulic press. He is sometimes also called "the grandfather of the computer" because of his invention of the first calculating machine.

Pascal's greatest work is Pensées (thoughts). Never finished, or even started as a normal book, it is his collected thoughts for a grand vindication of the Christian faith against the influence of the libertines of his day. His style is brilliant, but Pascal's force comes from the wealth of his personal experience and his philosophical and psychological insights. Incomplete though it is, Pensées has become a Western classic. The following reading covers some of his pithy and original thoughts on "diversion," our drive toward an entertaining, distracting busyness that protects us from thinking too deeply about our human condition.

THE SKULL AT THE BANQUET

"I drink not from more joy in wine nor to scoff at faith—no, only to forget myself for a moment, that only do I want of intoxication, that alone."

—The Rubaiyat of Omar Khayyam

"Let sanguine healthy-mindedness do its best with its strange power of living in the moment and ignoring and forgetting, still the evil background is really there to be thought of, and the skull will grin in at the banquet."

—William James, *Varieties of Religious Experience*

Diversion

If our condition were truly happy we should not need to divert ourselves from it.

Being unable to cure death, wretchedness, and ignorance, men have decided, in order to be happy, not to think about such things.

I have often said that the sole cause of man's unhappiness is that he does not know how to stay quietly in his room.

I have often said that the sole cause of man's unhappiness is that he does not know how to stay quietly in his room.

The only good thing for men therefore is to be diverted from thinking of what they are, either by some occupation which takes their mind off it, or by some novel and agreeable passion which keeps them busy, like gambling, hunting, some absorbing show, in short by what is called diversion.

That is why gaming and feminine society, war and high office are so popular. It is not that they really bring happiness nor that anyone imagines that true bliss comes from possessing the money to be won at gaming or the hare that is hunted: no one would take it as a gift. What people want is not the easy peaceful life that allows us to think of our unhappy condition, nor the dangers of war, nor the burdens of office, but the agitation that takes our mind off it and diverts us. That is why we prefer the hunt to the capture. . . .

What people want is not the easy peaceful life that allows us to think of our unhappy condition, nor the dangers of war, nor the burdens of office, but the agitation that takes our mind off it and diverts us. That is why we prefer the hunt to the capture.

That is all that men have been able to devise for attaining happiness; those who philosophize about it, holding that people are quite unreasonable to spend all day chasing a hare that they would not have wanted to buy, have little knowledge of our nature. The hare itself would not save us from thinking about death and the miseries distracting us, but hunting it does so. Thus when Pyrrhus was advised to take the rest towards which he was so strenuously striving, he found it very hard to do so.

Telling a man to rest is the same as telling him to live happily. It means advising him to enjoy a completely happy state which he can contemplate at leisure without cause for distress. It means not understanding nature.

Thus men who are naturally conscious of what they are shun nothing so much as rest; they would do anything to be disturbed.

Men who are naturally conscious of what they are shun nothing so much as rest; they would do anything to be disturbed.

It is wrong then to blame them; they are not wrong to want excitement— if they only wanted it for the sake of diversion. The trouble is that they want it as though, once they had the things they seek, they could not fail to be truly happy. That is what justifies calling their search a vain one. All this shows that neither the critics nor the criticized understand man's real nature.

"But," you will say, "what is his object in all this?" Just so that he can boast tomorrow to his friends that he played better than someone else. Likewise others sweat away in their studies to prove to scholars that they have solved some hitherto insoluble problem in algebra. Many others again, just as foolishly in my view, risk the greatest dangers so that they can boast afterwards of having captured some stronghold. Then there are others who exhaust themselves observing all these things, not in order to become wiser, but just to show they know them, and these are the biggest fools of the lot, because they know what

"Look, I'm dying. Gotta go."

they are doing, while it is conceivable that the rest would stop being foolish if they knew too. . . .

That is why men cannot be too much occupied and distracted, and that is why, when they have been given so many things to do, if they have some time off they are advised to spend it on diversion and sport, and always to keep themselves fully occupied.

From *Pensées* by Blaise Pascal, translated by A. J. Krailsheimer (Penguin Classics, 1966). Copyright © 1966 by A. J. Krailsheimer. Reproduced by permission of Penguin Books Ltd.

PHILOSOPHERS TOO

"Most fortunately it happens, that since reason is incapable of dispelling these clouds, Nature herself suffices to that purpose, and cures me of this philosophical melancholy and delirium, either by relaxing this bend of mind, or by some avocation and lively impression of my senses, which obliterates all these chimeras. I drive, I play a game of backgammon, I converse, and am merry with my friends; and when, after three or four hours' amusement, I would return to these speculations, they appear so cold, and strained and ridiculous, that I cannot find it in my heart to enter into them further."

—David Hume, *Treatise of Human Nature*

"I have to read at least one detective book a day to drug myself against the nuclear threat."

—Bertrand Russell, in an interview

A SPRINTING, SQUINTING AGE

"Our own age is not likely to be distinguished in history for the large numbers of people interested in finding the time to think. Plainly, this is not the Age of Meditative Man. It is a sprinting, squinting, shoving age. Substitutes for repose are a billion dollar business. Almost daily, new antidotes for contemplation spring into being and leap out from store counters. Silence, already the world's most critical shortage, is in danger of becoming a nasty word. Modern man may or may not be obsolete, but he is certainly wired for sound and he twitches as naturally as he breathes."

—Norman Cousins, *Human Options*

QUESTIONS FOR THOUGHT AND DISCUSSION

1. How would you describe Pascal's "diversion" in your own words?

2. What does Pascal say is behind our desire for diversion? What is it that people are trying to avoid?

3. Why does Pascal say, "we prefer the hunt to the capture"? What evidence could you give to support his point?

4. Pascal says that those seeking diversion and their critics don't understand human nature. How so? Do you agree?

5. At one level we need entertainment and escape, but when does it become a danger? When is it a drug from dealing with deeper issues?

6. What are the modern variations of Pascal's examples of "diversions"? What kind of person is susceptible to diversion?

7. How do you use diversion in your life?

#

Johann Wolfgang von Goethe (1749–1832) fits the description of a "Renaissance man" as well as anyone. Born in Frankfurt-am-Main, he was a poet, dramatist, scientist, lawyer, and court official. He was educated privately and began to study law, but as happened at several points of his life, a love affair inspired him to begin writing verse dramas. Upon receiving his degree he came under the influence of the movement known as Romanticism, which began in Germany; he was soon a determining voice within it.

In 1771 Goethe became an influential newspaper critic. A few years later he began his verse drama Faust, which he worked on for most of his life. Part I of Faust was published in 1808 and is a classic of world literature. Using earlier versions of the story of a man who sells his soul to the Devil for worldly gain, it is now an archetypal theme of Western culture that resonates powerfully with the modern theme of human striving for mastery and control over life.

Dr. Faust is the grandfather of all bargaining-with-the-Devil stories. Sometimes traced to Simon Magnus in the New Testament, the Faust figure is based on a shadowy German necromancer in the sixteenth century. But from Christopher Marlowe to Goethe to Berlioz to Honoré Balzac to Oscar Wilde to Thomas Mann, whether in poetry, drama, novels, or opera, the picture is of the restless, insatiable striver — not just curious but lusting to know, to experience, and to possess. Here Faust is an old scholar who yearns to comprehend all experience rather than all knowledge. The pact is that he will be given a knowledge with godlike power that will last until he is so satisfied that he begs that the present moment never ends. If that happens, he will have to surrender his soul to the Devil.

The story raises the same issues of the calculus of success that Jesus raised two thousand years ago: "What good is it for a man to gain the whole world, yet forfeit his soul?" One point is clear in all the stories of devil's bargains: The Devil is a reliable businessman who keeps his side of the deal and insists that we keep ours too.

Intriguingly, Faust was Sigmund Freud's most quoted book, and the last book he chose to read on the day of his death by euthanasia was Balzac's The Wild Ass's Skin. Readers of Freud's books become very aware that bargaining with the Devil was very much on his mind.

In the following passages, Professor Faust and the Devil Mephistopheles are in Faust's study.

ALWAYS READ THE SMALL PRINT

"Fools that must laugh on earth will weep in hell."

—Christopher Marlowe, *Dr. Faustus*

"Possess me and thou shalt possess all things. But thy life is forfeit to me. So hath God willed it. Express a desire and thy desire shall be fulfilled. But let thy wishes be measured against thy life. Here it lies. Every wish will diminish me and diminish thy days. Dost thou desire me? Take and God will grant thy wish. Amen."

—Honoré Balzac, *The Wild Ass's Skin*

Faust

FAUST.

> The pain of life, that haunts our narrow way,
> I cannot shed with this or that attire.
> Too old am I to be content with play,
> Too young to live untroubled by desire.
> What comfort can the shallow world bestow?
> Renunciation!—Learn, man, to forgo!
> This is the lasting theme of themes,
> That soon or late will show its power,
> The tune that lurks in all our dreams,
> And the hoarse whisper of each hour.
> Yet, each new day I shudder when I wake
> With bitter tears to look upon the sun,
> Knowing that in the journey he will make
> None of my longings will come true, not one;
> To see the tendrils of my joys that start,
> Cankered with doubts, the mind's self-conscious tares,
> To feel creation stir a generous heart,
> Only to fail before life's mocking cares.
> And when soft night has shrouded all the west,
> My anxious soul will beg her peace supreme;
> But still I lie forsaken, for my rest
> Is shattered by the wildness that I dream.
> The god who dwells enthroned within my breast
> Can stir my inner vision's deepest springs,

> But he who binds my strength to his behest
> Brings no command to sway external things.
> Thus life has taught me, with its weary weight,
> To long for death, and the dear light to hate. . . .

MEPHISTOPHELES.
> Leave off this traffic with your groping grief,
> That like a vulture feeds upon your mind;
> No company so vile but brings relief,
> And marks you for a man among mankind.
> By this I don't suggest
> We thrust you in among the common herd.
> I'm not the grandest person or the best,
> But if you care to take me at my word
> And join with me, and make a common quest,
> I'm very much at your disposal,
> That's my proposal:
> I'll make a pact with you,
> Without ado,
> Find out what you crave,
> And see you through,
> Your comrade and your slave.

I'm very much at your disposal, / That's my proposal: / I'll make a pact with you, / Without ado, / Find out what you crave, / And see you through, / Your comrade and your slave.

FAUST.
> And what return am I required to make?

MEPHISTOPHELES.
> A question time can settle—why insist?

FAUST.
> Nay, nay, the devil is an egoist.
> The help he gives is not for Heaven's sake.
> State your conditions clearly, thus and thus:
> Such servants in the house are dangerous.

MEPHISTOPHELES.
> Then here below in service I'll abide,
> Fulfilling tirelessly your least decree,

If when we meet upon the other side
You undertake to do the same for me.

FAUST.

The other side weighs little on my mind;
Lay first this world in ruins, shattered, blind;
That done, the new may rise its place to fill. . . .
If I be quieted with a bed of ease
Then let that moment be the end of me!
If ever flattering lies of yours can please
And soothe my soul to self-sufficiency,
And make me one of pleasure's devotees,
Then take my soul, for I desire to die:
And that's a wager!

If ever flattering lies of yours can please / And soothe my soul to self-sufficiency, / And make me one of pleasure's devotees, / Then take my soul, for I desire to die: / And that's a wager!

MEPHISTOPHELES.

Done!

FAUST.

. . . And rightly is my offer thus construed!
What I propose, I do not lightly dare:
While I abide, I live in servitude,
And whether yours or whose, why should I care? . . .
Now let your muffled mysteries emerge,
Breed magic wonders naked to our glance,
Now plunge we headlong in time's racing surge,
Swung on the sliding wave of circumstance.
Bring now the fruits of pain or pleasure forth,
Sweet triumph's lure, or disappointment's wrath,
A man's dynamic needs this restless urge.

What I propose, I do not lightly dare: / While I abide, I live in servitude, / And whether yours or whose, why should I care?

MEPHISTOPHELES.

Wealth shall be yours, beyond all fear or favor,
Be pleased to take your pleasures on the wing,
Voluptuous beauty taste in everything,
And may you flourish on the joys you savor.
Fall to, I say; but plunge, and don't be coy. . . .

(Exit Faust.)

He'll find the bargain over which he haggled / Shall leave him dumb-struck, writhing, sticking fast.

MEPHISTOPHELES (*IN THE LONG ROBES OF FAUST*).
  He'll find the bargain over which he haggled
  Shall leave him dumb-struck, writhing, sticking fast;
  Before his lips shall float a rich repast,
  To mock insatiable appetite;
  In vain he'll cry for comfort in his plight;
  Whether or not he owns the devil's might,
  His doom of ruin is secured at last.

From *Faust, Part I*, by Johann Wolfgang von Goethe, translated by Philip Wayne (Penguin Classics, 1949). Copyright © 1949 by the Estate of Philip Wayne. Reproduced by permission of Penguin Books Ltd.

SEX IS WORTH DYING FOR

Michel Foucault, the French social theorist, was sometimes described as the most famous intellectual in the world before his death in 1984. He was also a homosexual and—despite his knowledge of the danger of wantonly spreading AIDS—was preoccupied by death and fascinated by the death-defying freedom of sex in the San Francisco bath houses.

Many homosexuals at the time were like young people caught up in an underclass culture of violence. Expecting to die young, they grew totally careless of moral sanctions and physical safeguards. Their way of life was admittedly risky. But in the bargainer's calculations, risk becomes its own reward and flirting with death becomes the preferred alternative to the boredom of straight ways of living.

Foucault's biographer comments:

Foucault's work was drawing to an end; and his life, like [his friend] Roussel's, was ending in an ambiguous gesture, as if he had finally grasped the full significance, too late, of the fatal temptation he had first identified nearly ten years earlier, long before AIDS had become a tangible threat: "The Faustian pact, whose temptation has been instilled in us by the deployment of sexuality, is now as follows: to exchange life in its entirety for sex itself, for the truth and the sovereignty of sex. Sex is worth dying for."

From James Miller, *The Passion of Michel Foucault* (New York: Simon & Schuster, 1993). Copyright © 1993 by James E. Miller.

QUESTIONS FOR THOUGHT AND DISCUSSION

1. Read Faust's opening monologue. What are his musings all about? What is frustrating him? What do you see as areas that would make him susceptible to a soul bargain? What sort of man does Faust appear to be?

2. Read Mephistopheles' response. What is his appeal to Faust? How does he tempt him?

3. What do you think of Faust's deal with the Devil? Is Faust a shrewd negotiator or a fool? Why does he think he can outwit Mephistopheles?

4. What sort of person is most vulnerable to the temptation of "Faustian bargaining"? And at what stage of life?

5. Do you think people take more easily to diversion or bargaining as a means of blocking out the questions of life? Which are you drawn to more?

6. In what other ways do we try to make a kind of bargain with life, or fate, or God?

POINT TO PONDER:

Jolted by Life

Most people most of the time may not give much thought to where they are in life or what they believe. But everyone does at some time. It is therefore worth reflecting on the experiences and events in life that jolt us out of complacency, unmask our most successful diversions, and expose the folly of our most determined attempts at bargaining.

Sometimes the shaking loose comes simply from the passages of life, which remind us that life is moving whether we like it or not. Sometimes the disillusionment of old beliefs comes from a long, drawn-out experience of insurmountable contradictions. Arthur Koestler and his former comrades, for instance, described their disenchantment with communism as "the god that failed." But often, and more interestingly, the jolt comes in the flash of a moment—C. S. Lewis's experience of being "surprised by joy" or Peter Berger's "signals of transcendence"—as the following series of readings show.

But often, and more interestingly, the jolt comes in the flash of a moment—C. S. Lewis's experience of being "surprised by joy" or Peter Berger's "signals of transcendence."

As Berger defines it in A Rumor of Angels, a signal of transcendence is an experience found in our everyday world of reality that appears to point beyond that world to a higher reality. Put differently, the logic of these experiences bleeps like a signal that, if followed, carries a message that impels us to transcend our present experience. In each case the message is a double one. Partly, the experience contradicts what we once believed, by raising issues that puncture the adequacy of that belief. Partly, too, it rouses in us a desire for something that, if discovered to be true, would provide a surer, richer answer to the issue raised.

Whatever the occasion, life is never the same again. Old views no longer satisfy. Problems crave solutions. New answers are imperative. We need to start traveling in the right direction before it is too late. The quest is underway. In the sculptor Alberto Giacometti's words, such experiences are like a "hole torn in life."

INTIMATIONS OF MORTALITY

When asked why there were people "without religion": "Sir, you need not wonder at this, when you consider how large a proportion of almost every man's life is passed without thinking of it. I myself was for some years totally regardless of religion. It had dropped out of my mind. It was at an early part of my life. Sickness brought it back and I hope I have never lost it since."

—Dr. Samuel Johnson, *The Life of Johnson*

"It is unusual to find yourself in the middle of a shooting war, but many of life's accidents can have a similar effect. You play tennis twice a week with a dynamic 38-year-old businessman. In the locker room a silent clot throttles an artery and before he can call for help, a large part of his heart muscle has been strangled. His attack touches his wife, his business associates, and all his friends of a similar age, including you. Or a distant phone call notifies you that your father or mother has been hospitalized. You carry with you to the bedside a picture of the dynamo you last saw, clearing land or dashing off to the League of Women Voters. In the hospital you see that this dynamo has passed, all at once and incontrovertibly, into the twilight of ill health and helplessness.

"As we reach midlife in the middle thirties or early forties, we become susceptible to the idea of our own perishability. If an accident that interrupts our life occurs at this time, our fears of mortality are heightened. We are not prepared for the idea that time can run out on us, or for the startling truth that if we don't hurry to pursue our own definition of a meaningful existence, life can become a repetition of trivial maintenance duties. Nor are we anticipating a major upheaval of the roles and rules that may have comfortably defined us in the first half of life, but that must be reordered around a core of strongly felt personal values in the second."

—Gail Sheehy, *Passages*
(From *Passages*, by Gail Sheehy. Copyright © 1974, 1976 by Gail Sheehy.
Used by permission of Dutton,
a division of Penguin Putnam, Inc.)

"It is very dangerous to go into eternity with possibilities which one has oneself prevented from becoming realities. A possibility is a hint from God."

—Søren Kierkegaard

"Whatever opinion we may hold of the subject of death, we may be sure that it is meaningless and valueless. Death has not required us to keep a day free."

—Samuel Beckett

"As he attempts to reappraise his life, a man discovers how much it has been based on illusions, and he is faced with the task of *de-illusionment*. By this expression I mean a reduction of illusions, a recognition that long-held assumptions and beliefs about self and world are not true. This process merits special attention because illusion plays so vital a role in our lives throughout the life cycle."

—Daniel Levinson, *The Seasons of a Man's Life*

MIDLIFE CRISIS AS MIDLIFE OPPORTUNITY

"But five years ago something very strange began to happen to me. At first I began having moments of bewilderment, when my life would come to a halt, as if I did not know how to live or what to do; I would lose my presence of mind and fall into a state of depression. But this passed, and I continued to live as

Kudzu by Doug Marlette. © 2000, dist. by Los Angeles Times Syndicate. Reprinted by permission.

before. Then the moments of bewilderment recurred more frequently, and they always took the same form. Whenever my life would come to a halt, the questions would arise: Why? and what next?

"At first I thought these were pointless and irrelevant questions. I thought that the answers to them were well known and that if I should ever want to resolve them, it would not be too hard for me; it was just that I could not be bothered with it now, but if I should take it upon myself, then I would find the answers. But the questions began to come up more and more frequently, and their demands to be answered became more and more urgent. And like points concentrated into one spot, these questions without answers came together to form a single black stain."

—Leo Tolstoy, *Confessions*
(After Tolstoy had written his great classics *War and Peace* and *Anna Karenina* he became rich, famous, and celebrated—and then began to face his deeper questions.)

THE SEVEN AGES OF MAN

"All the world's a stage,
And all the men and women merely players:
They have their exits and their entrances;
And one man in his time plays many parts,
His acts being seven ages. At first the infant,
Mewling and puking in the nurse's arms.
And then the whining school-boy, with his satchel
And shining morning face, creeping like snail
Unwillingly to school. And then the lover,
Sighing like furnace, with a woeful ballad
Made to his mistress' eyebrow. Then a soldier,
Full of strange oaths and bearded like the pard,
Jealous in honour, sudden and quick in quarrel,
Seeking the bubble reputation
Even in the cannon's mouth. And then the justice,
In fair round belly with good capon lined,
With eyes severe and beard of formal cut,
Full of wise saws and modern instances;
And so he plays his part. The sixth age shifts
Into the lean and slipper'd pantaloon,
With spectacles on nose and pouch on side,
His youthful hose, well saved, a world too wide
For his shrunk shank; and his big manly voice,
Turning again toward childish treble, pipes

And whistles in his sound. Last scene of all,
That ends this strange eventful history,
Is second childishness and mere oblivion,
Sans teeth, sans eyes, sans taste, sans everything."

—William Shakespeare, *As You Like It*, Act II

❧ C. S. Lewis ❧

Clive Staples Lewis (1898–1963) was a scholar and writer, and is probably the most respected and widely read religious author of the twentieth century. Born in Belfast, Northern Ireland, he was educated at University College, Oxford. After brief service in World War I, he resumed his studies at Oxford and was elected Fellow and Tutor in English Language and Literature at Magdalen College. From 1954 he held the chair of Professor of Medieval and Renaissance Literature at Cambridge.

Lewis's works of literary scholarship were all acclaimed, but his enormous reputation rests on his writings for the common person. Three dozen of his titles are still available, with over sixty million in print—making Lewis the best-selling Christian author of all time. He became popular through the best-selling Screwtape Letters and through his broadcast talks on the BBC radio during World War II. His children's stories, The Chronicles of Narnia, and his science-fiction trilogy are likewise considered classics.

Lewis, known to friends as Jack, was the leading light in the Inklings, an informal discussion group that met in his rooms or in an Oxford pub, the Eagle and Child. He was a close friend of J. R. R. Tolkien and Charles Williams, who were members of this group, as well as many other important writers, such as Dorothy Sayers. The following reading, from a 1941 essay, outlines his experiences of being "surprised by joy" that jolted him to begin his quest of faith.

Such experiences of joy pierce us like a rapier with their unnamable longings. But when we pursue these longings, we find that they do not contain the joy that broke our hearts with longing. In short, such joys point beyond themselves to an eternal joy—God.

LISTEN TO THE SIGNALS

"Everlasting!—for the end would be despair. No—no end! No end!"

—Goethe, *Faust*

"Joy wills eternity—wills deep, deep eternity."

—Friedrich Nietzsche

"The blazing evidence of immortality is our dissatisfaction with any other solution."

—Ralph Waldo Emerson

"In every real man the will for life is also the will for joy."

—Karl Barth

The Weight of Glory ‽

In speaking of this desire for our own far-off country, which we find in our-selves even now, I feel a certain shyness. I am almost committing an indecency. I am trying to rip open the inconsolable secret in each one of you—the secret which hurts so much that you take your revenge on it by calling it names like Nostalgia and Romanticism and Adolescence; the secret also which pierces with such sweetness that when, in very intimate conversation, the mention of it becomes imminent, we grow awkward and affect to laugh at ourselves; the secret we cannot hide and cannot tell, though we desire to do both. We cannot tell it because it is a desire for something that has never actu-ally appeared in our experience. We cannot hide it because our experience is constantly suggesting it, and we betray ourselves like lovers at the mention of a name. Our commonest expedient is to call it beauty and behave as if that had settled the matter. Wordsworth's expedient was to identify it with certain moments in his own past.

But all this is a cheat. If Wordsworth had gone back to those moments in the past, he would not have found the thing itself, but only the reminder of it; what he remembered would turn out to be itself a remembering. The books or the music in which we thought the beauty was located will betray us if we trust to them; it was not *in* them, it only came *through* them, and what came through them was longing.

These things—the beauty, the memory of our own past—are good images of what we really desire; but if they are mistaken for the thing itself they turn into dumb idols, breaking the hearts of their worshippers. For they are not the thing itself; they are only the scent of a flower we have not found, the echo of a tune we have not heard, news from a country we have never yet visited. Do you think I am trying to weave a spell? Perhaps I am; but remember your fairy tales. Spells are used for breaking enchantments as well as for inducing them. And you and I have need of the strongest spell that can be found to wake us from the evil enchantment of worldliness which has been laid upon us for nearly a hundred years.

In speaking of this desire for our own far-off country, which we find in ourselves even now, I feel a certain shyness. I am almost committing an indecency.

Almost our whole education has been directed to silencing this shy, persistent, inner voice; almost all our modern philosophies have been devised to convince us that the good of man is to be found on this earth. And yet it is a remarkable thing that such philosophies of Progress or Creative Evolution themselves bear reluctant witness to the truth that our real goal is elsewhere. When they want to convince you that earth is your home, notice how they set about it. They begin by trying to persuade you that earth can be made into heaven, thus giving a sop to your sense of exile in earth as it is. Next, they tell you that this fortunate event is still a good way off in the future, thus giving a sop to your knowledge that the fatherland is not here and now. Finally, lest your longing for the transtemporal should awake and spoil the whole affair, they use any rhetoric that comes to hand to keep out of your mind the recollection that even if all the happiness they promised could come to man on earth, yet still each generation would lose it by death, including the last generation of all, and the whole story would be nothing, not even a story, for ever and ever. . . .

A LONGING FOR THE LONGING

"As I stood beside a flowering currant bush on a summer day there suddenly arose in me without warning, and as if from a depth not of years but of centuries, the memory of that earlier morning at the Old House when my brother had brought his toy garden into the nursery. It is difficult to find words strong enough for the sensation which came over me; Milton's 'enormous bliss' of Eden (giving the full, ancient meaning to 'enormous') comes somewhere near it. It was a sensation, of course, of desire; but desire for what? Not, certainly, for a biscuit tin filled with moss, nor even (though that came into it) for my own past—and before I knew what I desired, the desire itself was gone, the whole glimpse withdrawn, the world turned commonplace again, or only stirred by a longing for the longing that had just ceased. It had taken only a moment of time; and in a certain sense everything else that had ever happened to me was insignificant in comparison."

—from *Surprised by Joy,* C. S. Lewis's autobiography

Do what they will, then, we remain conscious of a desire which no natural happiness will satisfy.

Do what they will, then, we remain conscious of a desire which no natural happiness will satisfy. But is there any reason to suppose that reality offers any satisfaction to it? "Nor does the being hungry prove that we have bread." But I think it may be urged that this misses the point. A man's physical hunger does not prove that that man will get any bread; he may die of starvation on a raft in the Atlantic. But surely a man's hunger does prove that he comes of a race which repairs its body by eating and inhabits a world where eatable substances exist. In the same way, though I do not believe (I wish I did) that my desire for Paradise proves that I shall enjoy it, I think it a pretty good indication that such a thing exists and that some men will. A man may love a woman and not win her; but it would be very odd if the phenomenon called "falling in love" occurred in a sexless world.

FAR, FAR MORE THAN HAPPINESS

"In a sense the central story of my life is about nothing else . . . it is that of an unsatisfied desire which is itself more desirable than any other satisfaction. I call it Joy, which is here a technical term and must be sharply distinguished both from Happiness and from Pleasure. Joy (in my sense) has indeed one characteristic, and one only, in common with them; the fact that anyone who has experienced it will want it again. Apart from that, and considered only in its quality, it might almost equally well be called a particular kind of unhappiness or grief. But then it is a kind we want. I doubt whether anyone who has tasted it would ever, if both were in his power, exchange it for all the pleasures in the world. But then Joy is never in our power and pleasure often is."

—from *Surprised by Joy*

QUESTIONS FOR THOUGHT AND DISCUSSION

1. What does C. S. Lewis mean by "this desire for our own far-off country"? Do you think it is a common experience among people for a memory or moment of beauty to trigger this longing?

2. Why does Lewis disagree with Wordsworth's explanation for such sensations? What do you think of his reasoning? What is he saying that "we really desire"?

3. Read the first box, "A Longing for the Longing." What words strike you in his description of the experience?

4. Read the second box, "Far, Far More than Happiness." What is he saying in the first sentence? Is this only word play? What would you say is the difference between happiness and joy? What is the essence of pleasure as compared to joy? Do you agree or disagree that "Joy is never in our power and pleasure often is"? What does he mean?

5. What seems to you the one end, which when reached would justify your desire and satisfy it completely?

6. Have you ever experienced "a desire which no natural happiness will satisfy"? What was its focus?

7. Lewis's experience is somewhat artistic. Do you relate to it or not? Why?

Peter L. Berger

Peter Ludwig Berger (born 1929) is University Professor and Director of the Institute for the Study of Economic Culture at Boston University. Born in Austria, he came to the United States after World War II and completed graduate studies at the New School for Social Research in New York. One of the world's leading sociologists, he has had a distinguished academic career. As well as his scholarly books, he has written several popular, best-selling books—supremely A Rumor of Angels, an exploration of the status of religion in modern, secular society.

The reading below, taken from A Rumor of Angels, opens up his notion of "signals of transcendence"—human experiences that are instinctive yet assume and require answers that point beyond themselves if they are as meaningful as we assume they must be. Among the other arguments he discusses as signals of transcendence that imply the necessity of faith are his argument from humor and his argument from damnation. This passage is his argument from "order."

IT'S ALL RIGHT

"Then she turns toward me, reaches for me. 'I'm scared. I'm scared.'

"I put my arms around her and hold her. I hold her as I held my children when they were small and afraid in the night; as, this summer, I hold my grandchildren. I hold her as she, once upon a time and long ago, held me. And I say the same words, the classic, maternal, instinctive words of reassurance. 'Don't be afraid. I'm here. It's all right.'

"'Something's wrong. I'm scared. I'm scared.'

"I cradle her and repeat, 'It's all right.'

"What's all right? What am I promising her? I'm scared too. I don't know what will happen when Hugh [her husband] goes to the neurologist. I don't know what's going to happen to my mother this summer. I don't know what the message may be the next time the phone rings. What's all right? How can I say it?

"But I do. I hold her close and kiss her, and murmur, 'It's all right, Mother. It's all right.'

"I mean these words. I do not understand them, but I mean them. Perhaps one day I will find out what I mean. They are implicit in everything I write. I caught a hint of them during that lecture, even as I was cautioning against false promises. They are behind everything, the cooking of meals, walking the dogs, talking with the girls. I may never find out with my intellectual self what I mean, but if I am given enough glimpses perhaps these will add up to enough so that my heart will understand. It does not; not yet."

—Madeleine L'Engle, *The Summer of the Great-Grandmother*
(Copyright © 1974 by Madeleine L'Engle. Reprinted by permission of Farrar,
Straus & Giroux, Inc.)

OR IS IT?

"Behold, we know not anything:
I can but trust that good shall fall
At last—far off—at last, to all
And every winter change to spring.
So runs my dream; but what am I?
An infant crying in the night;
An infant crying for the light;
And with no language but a cry."

—Alfred, Lord Tennyson, 1850, after the death of a close friend

"For life is at the start a chaos in which one is lost. The individual suspects this, but he is frightened at finding himself face to face with this terrible reality, and tries to cover it over with a curtain of fantasy, where everything is clear. It does not worry him that his 'ideas' are not true, he uses them as trenches for the defense of his existence, as scarecrows to frighten away reality."

—Jose Ortega y Gasset, *The Revolt of the Masses*

"I think that taking life seriously means something such as this: that whatever man does on this planet has to be done in the lived truth of the terror of creation, of the grotesque, of the rumble of panic underneath everything. Otherwise it is false."

—Ernest Becker, *The Denial of Death*

Signals of Transcendence ✍

By *signals of transcendence* I mean phenomena that are to be found within the domain of our "natural" reality but that appear to point beyond that reality. In other words, I am not using transcendence here in a technical philosophical sense but literally, as the transcending of the normal, everyday world that I earlier identified with the notion of the "supernatural." By prototypical human gestures I mean certain reiterated acts and experiences that appear to express essential aspects of man's being, of the human animal as such. . . .

Consider the most ordinary, and probably most fundamental, of all—the ordering gesture by which a mother reassures her anxious child.

A child wakes up in the night, perhaps from a bad dream, and finds himself surrounded by darkness, alone, beset by nameless threats. At such a moment the contours of trusted reality are blurred or invisible, and in the

By signals of transcendence I mean phenomena that are to be found within the domain of our "natural" reality but that appear to point beyond that reality.

terror of incipient chaos the child cries out for his mother. It is hardly an exaggeration to say that, at this moment, the mother is being invoked as a high priestess of protective order. It is she (and, in many cases, she alone) who has the power to banish the chaos and to restore the benign shape of the world. And, of course, any good mother will do just that. She will take the child and cradle him in the timeless gesture of the Magna Mater who became our Madonna. She will turn on a lamp, perhaps, which will encircle the scene with a warm glow of reassuring light. She will speak or sing to the child, and the content of this communication will invariably be the same—"Don't be afraid—everything is in order, everything is all right." If all goes well, the child will be reassured, his trust in reality recovered, and in this trust he will return to sleep.

Yet this common scene raises a far from ordinary question, which immediately introduces a religious dimension: Is the mother lying to the child? The answer, in the most profound sense, can be "no" only if there is some truth in the religious interpretation of human existence.

All this, of course, belongs to the most routine experiences of life and does not depend upon any religious preconceptions. Yet this common scene raises a far from ordinary question, which immediately introduces a religious dimension: *Is the mother lying to the child?* The answer, in the most profound sense, can be "no" only if there is some truth in the religious interpretation of human existence. Conversely, if the "natural" is the only reality there is, the mother is lying to the child—lying out of love, to be sure, and obviously *not* lying to the extent that her reassurance is grounded in the fact of this love—but, in the final analysis, lying all the same. Why? *Because the reassurance, transcending the immediately present two individuals and their situation, implies a statement about reality as such.*

To become a parent is to take on the role of world-builder and world-protector. This is so, of course, in the obvious sense that parents provide the environment in which a child's socialization takes place and serve as mediators to the child of the entire world of the particular society in question. But it is also so in a less obvious, more profound sense, which is brought out in the scene just described. The role that a parent takes on represents not only the order of this or that society, but order as such, the underlying order of the universe that it makes sense to trust. It is this role that may be called the role of high priestess. It is a role that the mother in this scene plays willy-nilly, regardless of her own awareness or (more likely) lack of awareness of just what it is she is representing. "*Everything* is in order, *everything* is all right"—this is the basic formula of maternal and parental reassurance. Not just this particular anxiety, not just this particular pain—but *everything* is all right. The formula can, without in any way violating it, be translated into a statement of cosmic scope—"Have trust in being." This is precisely what the formula intrinsically implies. And if we are to believe the child psychologists (which we have good reason to do in this instance), this is an experience that is absolutely essential to the process of becoming a human person. Put differently, at the very center of the process of becoming fully human, at the core of *humanitas,* we find an experience of trust in the order of reality. Is this experience an illusion? Is the individual who represents it a liar?

If reality is coextensive with the "natural" reality that our empirical reason can grasp, then the experience is an illusion and the role that embodies it is a lie. For then it is perfectly obvious that everything is *not* in order, is *not* all right. The world that the child is being told to trust is the same world in which he will eventually die. If there is no other world, then the ultimate truth about this one is that eventually it will kill the child as it will kill his mother. This would not, to be sure, detract from the real presence of love and its very real comforts; it would even give this love a quality of tragic heroism. Nevertheless, the final truth would be not love but terror, not light but darkness. The nightmare of chaos, not the transitory safety of order, would be the final reality of the human situation. For, in the end, we must all find ourselves in darkness, alone with the night that will swallow us up. The face of reassuring love, bending over our terror, will then be nothing except an image of merciful illusion. In that case the last word about religion is Freud's. Religion is the childish fantasy that our parents run the universe for our benefit, a fantasy from which the mature individual must free himself in order to attain whatever measure of stoic resignation he is capable of.

It goes without saying that the preceding argument is not a moral one. It does not condemn the mother for this charade of world-building, if it be a charade. It does not dispute the right of atheists to be parents (though it is not without interest that there have been atheists who have rejected parenthood for exactly these reasons). The argument from ordering is metaphysical rather than ethical. To restate it: In the observable human propensity to order reality there is an intrinsic impulse to give cosmic scope to this order, an impulse that implies not only that human order in some way corresponds to an order that transcends it, but that this transcendent order is of such a character that man can trust himself and his destiny to it. There is a variety of human roles that represent this conception of order, but the most fundamental is the parental role. Every parent (or, at any rate, every parent who loves his child) takes upon himself the representation of a universe that is ultimately in order and ultimately trustworthy. This representation can be justified only within a religious (strictly speaking a supernatural) frame of reference. In this frame of reference the natural world within which we are born, love, and die is not the

Put differently, at the very center of the process of becoming fully human, at the core of humanitas, *we find an experience of trust in the order of reality. Is this experience an illusion? Is the individual who represents it a liar?*

only world, but only the foreground of another world in which love is not anni-hilated in death, and in which, therefore, the trust in the power of love to banish chaos is justified.

Man's ordering propensity implies a transcendent order, and each ordering gesture is a signal of this transcendence.

Thus man's ordering propensity implies a transcendent order, and each ordering gesture is a signal of this transcendence. The parental role is not based on a loving lie. On the contrary, it is a witness to the ultimate truth of man's situation in reality. In that case, it is perfectly possible (even, if one is so inclined, in Freudian terms) to analyze religion as a cosmic projection of the child's experience of the protective order of parental love. What is projected is, however, itself a reflection, an imitation, of ultimate reality. Religion, then, is not only (from the point of view of empirical reason) a projection of human order, but (from the point of view of what might be called *inductive faith*) the ultimately true vindication of human order.

QUESTIONS FOR THOUGHT AND DISCUSSION

1. Read the box, "It's All Right." What is going through Madeleine L'Engle's mind and heart as she mothers her own mother? How do you understand her statement, "How can I say it? But I do"? What is compelling her? What does she really mean in saying, "It's all right"?

2. How does Peter Berger define "signals of transcendence"? How does the act of a mother reassuring her child fit this definition?

3. Read the paragraph, "A child wakes up in the night . . ." Is this a fair description? What was your experience as a child? As a parent?

4. What do you think of Berger's reasoning in his answers to the question, "Is the mother lying to the child?" Which of his answers (no, she's not lying; or yes, she is) resonates with you more? Why?

5. How does Berger describe the role of the parent as "high priestess" of protective order?

6. Do you believe a mother's reassurance is ultimately a lie or somehow a justifiable act of faith in the meaning of the universe? Is the mother only speaking of the circumstance or is she speaking of something deeper?

7. How would an atheist or a Hindu respond to Berger? What sort of ultimate reality and meaning is assumed and required if the instinctive assurance "everything is going to be all right" is to be justified?

G. K. Chesterton

Gilbert Keith Chesterton (1874–1936) is one of the twentieth century's best-known journalists, essayists, humorists, authors, debaters, and social observers. Born in London, he studied at the Slade School of Art before embarking on the writing career that brought him acclaim and popularity until his death. He began with art and book reviews, but editors soon saw his exuberant talents for wit and insight and gave him the latitude to write whatever he wanted. His essays included every subject under the sky — one early anthology is aptly titled All Things Considered *— the rocky government politics of his day, ideas, art, popular culture, religion, his neighborhood in Battersea, and "What I Found in My Pocket."*

For much of his life Chesterton wrote two or three articles a week for English newspapers. His huge frame, black cape, hat, and swordstick made him a legendary presence on Fleet Street. He lectured around England, toured the United States twice (lecturing at the University of Notre Dame for one semester), visited and wrote about Poland and the Mideast, and was awarded several honorary degrees. His enormous output includes dozens of books of fiction, social criticism (such as What's Wrong with the World), *literary criticism, history, poetry, and religious subjects, as well as his collected newspaper columns. The appeal of his detective-priest in his Father Brown series led to his election as the first president of the Mystery Writers Club of England.*

Chesterton championed the common person and considered his calling to be one of challenging and confuting the politically correct modernists of his day through wit, paradox, and insight. In the following passage from his autobiography, he describes how it was gratitude and wonder that jolted him onto the journey toward faith.

WHOM TO THANK?

"We thank people for birthday presents of cigars and slippers. Can I thank no one for the birthday present of birth?"

—G. K. Chesterton, *Orthodoxy*

"If my children wake up on Christmas morning and have somebody to thank for putting candy in their stocking, have I no one to thank for putting two feet in mine?"

—G. K. Chesterton, *Orthodoxy*

"I would maintain that thanks are the highest form of thought; and that gratitude is happiness doubled by wonder."

—G. K. Chesterton, *Orthodoxy*

"The best definition of man is the ungrateful biped."

—Fyodor Dostoyevsky

"Man's first faculty is forgetting."

—Albert Camus

"The worst moment for an atheist is when he is genuinely thankful, but has nobody to thank."

—Dante Gabriel Rossetti

The Autobiography of G. K. Chesterton

In truth, the story of what was called my Optimism was rather odd. When I had been for some time in these, the darkest depths of the contemporary pessimism, I had a strong inward impulse to revolt; to dislodge this incubus or throw off this nightmare. But as I was still thinking the thing out by myself, with little help from philosophy and no real help from religion, I invented a rudimentary and makeshift mystical theory of my own. It was substantially this; that even mere existence, reduced to its most primary limits, was extraordinary enough to be exciting. Anything was magnificent as compared with nothing.

Even if the very daylight were a dream, it was a day-dream; it was not a nightmare. The mere fact that one could wave one's arms and legs about (or those dubious external objects in the landscape which were called one's arms and legs) showed that it had not the mere paralysis of a nightmare. Or if it was a nightmare, it was an enjoyable nightmare.

In fact, I had wandered to a position not very far from the phrase of my Puritan grandfather, when he said that he would thank God for his creation if he were a lost soul. I hung on to the remains of religion by one thin thread of thanks. I thanked whatever gods might be, not like Swinburne, because no life lived for ever, but because any life lived at all; not, like Henley for my unconquerable soul (for I have never been so optimistic about my own soul as all that) but for my own soul and my own body, even if they could be conquered.

I invented a rudimentary and makeshift mystical theory of my own. It was substantially this; that even mere existence, reduced to its most primary limits, was extraordinary enough to be exciting. Anything was magnificent as compared with nothing.

I hung on to the remains of religion by one thin thread of thanks.

This way of looking at things, with a sort of mystical minimum of gratitude, was of course, to some extent assisted by those few of the fashionable writers who were not pessimists; especially by Walt Whitman, by Browning and by Stevenson; Browning's "God must be glad one loves his world so much," or Stevenson's "belief in the ultimate decency of things." But I do not think it is too much to say that I took it in a way of my own; even if it was a way I could not see clearly or make very clear.

What I meant, whether or not I managed to say it, was this; that no man knows how much he is an optimist, even when he calls himself a pessimist, because he has not really measured the depths of his debt to whatever created him and enabled him to call himself anything. At the back of our brains, so to speak, there was a forgotten blaze or burst of astonishment at our own existence. The object of the artistic and spiritual life was to dig for this submerged sunrise of wonder; so that a man sitting in a chair might suddenly understand that he was actually alive, and be happy. . . .

And I am, by the nature of the task, especially concerned with the fact that these doctrines seem to me to link up my whole life from the beginning, as no other doctrines could do; and especially to settle simultaneously the two problems of my childish happiness and my boyish brooding. And they specially affected one idea; which I hope it is not pompous to call the chief idea of my life; I will not say the doctrine I have always taught, but the doctrine I should always have liked to teach. That is the idea of taking things with gratitude, and not taking things for granted. . . .

One idea; which I hope it is not pompous to call the chief idea of my life; I will not say the doctrine I have always taught, but the doctrine I should always have liked to teach. That is the idea of taking things with gratitude, and not taking things for granted.

The real difficulty of man is not to enjoy lamp-posts or landscapes, not to enjoy dandelions or chops; but to enjoy enjoyment. To keep the capacity of really liking what he likes; that is the practical problem which the philosopher has to solve. And it seemed to me at the beginning, as it seems to me now in the end, that the pessimists and optimists of the modern world have alike missed and muddled this matter; through leaving out the ancient conception of humility and the thanks of the unworthy. . . .

The pessimist was proud of pessimism, because he thought nothing good enough for him; the optimist was proud of optimism, because he thought nothing was bad enough to prevent him from getting good out of it. There were valuable men of both these types; there were men with many virtues; but they not only did not possess the virtue I was thinking of, but they never thought of it. They would decide that life was no good, or that it had a great deal of good; but they were not in touch with this particular notion, of having a great deal of gratitude even for a very little good. And as

I began to believe more and more that the clue was to be found in such a principle, even if it was a paradox, I was more and more disposed to seek out those who specialized in humility, though for them it was the door of heaven and for me the door of earth.

For nobody else *specializes* in that mystical mood in which the yellow star of the dandelion is startling, being something unexpected and undeserved. . . . Since the time of which I speak, the world has in this respect grown even worse. A whole generation has been taught to talk nonsense at the top of its voice about having "a right to life" and "a right to experience" and "a right to happiness." The lucid thinkers who talk like this generally wind up their assertion of all these extraordinary rights, by saying that there is no such thing as right and wrong. It is a little difficult, in that case, to speculate on where their rights came from; but I, at least, leaned more and more to the old philosophy which said that their real rights came from where the dandelion came from; and that they will never value either without recognizing its source. And in that ultimate sense uncreated man, man merely in the position of the babe unborn, has no right even to see a dandelion; for he could not himself have invented either the dandelion or the eyesight.

I have here fallen back on one idle figure of speech from a fortunately forgotten book of verses; merely because such a thing is light and trivial, and the children puff it away like thistledown; and this will be most fitting to a place in which formal argument would be quite a misfit. But lest anyone should suppose that the notion has no relation to the argument, but is only a sentimental fancy about weeds or wild flowers, I will lightly and briefly suggest how even the figure fits in with all the aspects of the argument. For the first thing the casual critic will say is "What nonsense all this is; do you mean that a poet cannot be thankful for grass and wild flowers without connecting it with theology; let alone your theology?" To which I answer, "Yes; I mean he cannot do it without connecting it with theology, unless he can do it without connecting it with thought. If he can manage to be thankful when there is nobody to be thankful to, and no good intentions to be thankful for, then he is simply taking refuge in being thoughtless in order to avoid being thankless."

If he can manage to be thankful when there is nobody to be thankful to, and no good intentions to be thankful for, then he is simply taking refuge in being thoughtless in order to avoid being thankless.

THE WONDER OF WONDERING—FOR MOST PEOPLE ANYWAY

"Men go to admire the heights of mountains, the great floods of the seas, the courses of rivers, the shores of the ocean, and the orbits of the stars, and neglect themselves."

—Augustine, *Confessions*

"When I look back at my past and think how much time I wasted on nothing, how much time has been lost in futilities, errors, laziness, incapacity to live; how little I appreciated it, how many times I sinned against my heart and soul—then my heart bleeds. Life is happiness, every minute can be an eternity of happiness! *Si la jeunesse savait* [If youth only knew]!"

—Fyodor Dostoyevsky to his brother Mikhail
after his last-minute reprieve from execution in 1849

"It is said by men who know about these things that the smallest living cell probably contains over a quarter of a million protein molecules engaged in the multitudinous coordinated activities which make up the phenomenon of life. At the instant of death, whether of man or microbe, that ordered, incredible spinning passes away in an almost furious haste of those same particles to get themselves back into the chaotic, unplanned earth.

"I do not think, if someone finally twists the key successfully in the tiniest and most humble house of life, that many of these questions will be answered, or that the dark forces which create lights in the deep sea and living batteries in the waters of tropical swamps, or the dread cycles of parasites, or the most noble workings of the human brain, will be much if at all revealed. Rather, I would say that if 'dead' matter has reared up this curious landscape of fiddling crickets, song sparrows, and wondering men, it must be plain even to the most devoted materialist that the matter of which he speaks contains amazing, if not dreadful powers, and may not impossibly be, as Hardy has suggested, 'but one mask of many worn by the Great Face behind.'"

—Loren Eiseley, *The Secret of Life*

One summer Samuel Beckett was visiting London, where he took the opportunity of going to Lord's cricket ground to see England play Australia. Drinking beer and watching cricket with friends were favorite pastimes of his. It was a beautiful, sky-blue day and as they say there, someone remarked that it was "The sort of day that makes one glad to be alive."

To which the author of *Waiting for Godot* immediately replied, "Oh, I don't think I would go quite so far as to say that."

QUESTIONS FOR THOUGHT AND DISCUSSION

1. What was the "rudimentary and makeshift mystical theory" that G. K. Chesterton developed as his philosophy of life? Why did he develop

this way of thinking as an antidote to contemporary pessimism? Where do you see pessimism in our culture?

2. What are some of the things for which Chesterton was thankful? Do you think it is reasonable to be thankful for such things? What makes you say that?

3. Refer to the paragraph starting "In fact, I had wandered . . ." What does he mean in saying he "hung on to the remains of religion by one thin thread of thanks"? What helped him hold on to that thread?

4. Do you think his experience is typical? What jolts him into gratitude? What does he say is the "object of the artistic and spiritual life"?

5. How does Chesterton say the pessimist leaves out "humility and the thanks of the unworthy"? How does the optimist do it? How does it affect the way they each see good in the world?

6. What is the connection between Chesterton's analysis of pessimism and optimism and his own jolt of gratitude in being alive? Does he feel closer to optimism or pessimism?

7. What does Chesterton mean by a "mystical minimum of gratitude" that requires someone to be grateful? Why does he argue that thankfulness requires faith or thoughtlessness?

8. Do you ever feel this gratitude for the sheer pleasure of being alive? If so, what does it make you think about life and the meaning of life? If not, to what do you attribute this difference between you and Chesterton?

W. H. Auden

Wystan Hugh Auden (1907–1973), English poet and dramatist, is one of the major poets of the twentieth century. Born in York, he was educated at Christ Church, Oxford, after which he lived in Berlin and served in the Spanish Civil War. Such experiences deeply influenced his work. In the 1930s he became the best known of a circle of left-wing poets that included Stephen Spender and Christopher Isherwood.

Auden's early poetry was marked by a naïve optimism in human nature and activist causes; the passage that follows describes how he was massively disillusioned of these beliefs when he confronted the realities of Nazism. This was a critical moment in his quest, the experience that made him a seeker. Auden immigrated to the United States in 1939, but returned to Oxford near the end of his life. The experience described here is from Humphrey Carpenter's biography.

GOOD, BAD, OR BOTH?

"I have found little that is 'good' about human beings on the whole. In my experience most of them are trash, no matter whether they subscribe to this or that ethical doctrine or none at all."

—Sigmund Freud, *Psychoanalysis and Faith*

"The plight of modern man: a sinner with no word for it or, worse, who looks for the word for it in a dictionary of psychology and thus only aggravates the problem."

—Ernest Becker, *The Denial of Death*

"The overall intention may be stated simply enough. Before the second world war I believed in the perfectibility of social man . . . but after the war I did not because I was unable to. I had discovered what one man could do to another. . . . I must say that anyone who moved through those years without understanding that man produces evil as a bee produces honey, must have been blind or wrong in the head. . . . My own conviction grew that what had happened was that men were putting the cart before the horse. They were looking at the system rather than the people. It seemed to me that man's capacity for greed, his innate cruelty and selfishness, was being hidden behind a kind of pair of political pants. I believed then, that man was sick—not exceptional man, but average man. I believed that the condition of man was to be a morally diseased creation and that the best job I could do at the time was to trace the connection between his diseased nature and the international mess he gets himself into."

—William Golding, on why he wrote *Lord of the Flies*

The Fatal Flaw of Liberalism ☙

Two months after the outbreak of war, in November 1939, he went to a cinema in Yorkville, the district of Manhattan where he and Isherwood had lived for a few weeks in the spring. It was largely a German-speaking area, and the film he saw was *Sieg im Poland,* an account by the Nazis of their conquest of Poland. When Poles appeared on the screen he was startled to hear a number of people in the audience scream "Kill them!" He later said of this: "I wondered then, why I reacted as I did against this denial of every humanistic value. The answer brought me back to the church."

"I wondered then, why I reacted as I did against this denial of every humanistic value. The answer brought me back to the church."
— W. H. AUDEN

He had been through many changes of heart since reaching adulthood, but all the dogmas he had adopted or played with—post-Freudian psychology, Marxism, and the liberal-socialist-democratic outlook that had been his final political stance before leaving England—had one thing in common: they were all based on a belief in the natural goodness of man. They all claimed that if one specific evil were removed, be it sexual repression, the domination of the proletariat by the bourgeoisie, or Fascism, then humanity would be happy and unrest would cease. Even the viewpoint which Auden had reached in the summer of 1939 during his "honeymoon," a viewpoint (expressed in "The Prolific and the Devourer") which might be called liberal humanism with religious and pacifist overtones, was still based on a belief in man's natural goodness. Its message was, in the words of the poem which summed it up, "We must love one another or die": that is, only the exercise of love between human beings would save humanity from self-destruction. The implication was that if humanity followed this precept and so obeyed a "divine law" it *could* save itself, being fundamentally good. Auden's experience in the Yorkville cinema in November 1939 radically shook this belief. He now became convinced that human nature was not and never could be good. The behaviour of those members of the audience who shouted "Kill them!" was indeed, as he said, "a denial of every humanistic value."

In the weeks that followed this experience he considered its implications. It was not just a question of shattered optimism: the whole ground of his outlook had shifted beneath his feet. If humanity were not innately good, then on what basis could he legitimately object to the murderous shouts of the Germans in that cinema audience, or indeed to the behaviour of Hitler himself? Were not the Nazis merely being true to their own nature, to all our natures? What reason could he give for his strong, instinctive, ineradicable

If humanity were not innately good, then on what basis could he legitimately object to the murderous shouts of the Germans in that cinema audience, or indeed to the behaviour of Hitler himself?

hatred of the Nazis and all that they stood for? He had to find some new objective ground from which to argue against Hitler. "There had," as he put it, "to be some reason why [Hitler] was utterly wrong."

Auden began to remark to his friends on this desperate need for objective criteria from which to oppose Hitler: "The English intellectuals who now cry to Heaven against the evil incarnated in Hitler have no heaven to cry to," he told Erika Mann's brother Golo; "they have nothing to offer and their prospects echo in empty space." It seemed utterly clear to him now that liberalism had a fatal flaw in it.

"The whole trend of liberal thought," he wrote during 1940, "has been to undermine faith in the absolute. . . . It has tried to make reason the judge . . . But since life is a changing process . . . the attempt to find a humanistic basis for keeping a promise, works logically with the conclusion, 'I can break it whenever I feel it convenient.'" He was now certain that he must renew that "faith in the absolute" which appeared to him to be the only possible ground for moral judgment. As he put it in a poem written a short time after visiting the Yorkville cinema:

> Either we serve the Unconditional
> Or some Hitlerian monster will supply
> An iron convention to do evil by.

So it was that he now began a search for, in the words of this same poem, "the vision that objectifies." He began to read some books of theology.

"The English intellectuals who now cry to Heaven against the evil incarnated in Hitler have no heaven to cry to: they have nothing to offer and their prospects echo in empty space."
—W. H. AUDEN

From *W. H. Auden: A Biography*, by Humphrey Carpenter. Copyright © 1981 by Humphrey Carpenter. Reprinted by permission of Felicity Bryan and the author.

QUESTIONS FOR THOUGHT AND DISCUSSION

1. The opening paragraph describes a memorable event in Auden's life during World War II. What happened that shocked him? What effect did this have on him?

2. Up until then, what had been Auden's belief system? What did this dogma say of human nature and the potential for humanity?

3. How were his beliefs challenged by the event in the cinema? Why does relativism not provide Auden a sufficient answer for Hitler? It is one thing to be shocked, but what was Auden's deeper need? Why does he suddenly feel he needs this?

4. What was the fatal flaw of liberalism for Auden?

5. Read the lines of poetry Auden wrote after the cinema experience. What does it mean? Is it so?

6. We are taught today to be "nonjudgmental" and repeatedly told that there are "no absolutes" by which to judge absolutely; yet in the face of real evil and inhumanity we make absolute condemnations anyway. What does that say of us?

7. What does an "ultimate condemnation" of evil imply of our view of the justice of the universe?

DEEDS THAT CRY OUT TO HEAVEN CRY OUT FOR HELL

The evidence that God existed "was the existence of Lenin and Trotsky, for whom a hell was needed."

—Winston Churchill to a colleague

"Deeds that cry out to heaven also cry out for hell. This is the point that was brought out very clearly in the debate over Eichmann's execution. Without going into the question of either the legality or the wisdom of the execution, it is safe to say that there was a very general feeling that 'hanging is not enough' in this case. But what would have been 'enough'? . . . No human punishment is 'enough' in the case of deeds as monstrous as these. These are deeds that demand not only condemnation, but *damnation* in the full religious meaning of the word—that is, the doer not only puts himself outside the community of men; he also separates himself in a final way from a moral order that transcends the human community, and thus invokes a retribution that is more than human."

—Peter Berger, *A Rumor of Angels*

TWO
A TIME FOR ANSWERS

THE SECOND STAGE IN THE QUEST FOR MEANING IS WHEN WE ACTIVELY SEEK ANSWERS to the specific questions and crises raised at the first stage—and are drawn toward the one we believe is the answer. In other words, we consider the available guides and maps and choose the one best suited to where we are and where we wish to go. The point of the second stage is easy to see but hard to follow. If searchers are constituted by their questions and sense of need, their automatic response— consciously or unconsciously—is to pursue answers. The respective founding leaders and truth-claims of various beliefs and worldviews will then prove attractive or unattractive according to their power to throw light on the issues in the seeker's heart and mind. Does this belief provide the best explanation of the troubling questions?

Five aspects of this second stage of the quest deserve underscoring. First, the search is conceptual. Hopes, fears, hurts, and other emotions play their part, but the second stage unashamedly has to do with ideas and beliefs and the difference they make. At first sight, this may not seem to fit the fact that ours is a pragmatic age, impatient with "mere words." But we need only remember that "ideas have consequences," beliefs influence behavior, and differences make a difference. Words are like maps, only paper representations, but they point to solid realities just as maps lead to very real places and very different destinations. Beliefs may seem unreal, but we need to remember the paradox of human history—that even the most solid, earthly powers vanish into dust while only the seemingly insubstantial things of words, thoughts, and spirit truly endure.

WANTED: AN UNPRACTICAL MAN

"There has arisen in our time a most singular fancy: the fancy that when things go very wrong we need a practical man. It would be far truer to say, that when things go very wrong we need an unpractical man.

79

Certainly, at least, we need a theorist. A practical man means a man accustomed to mere daily practice, to the way things commonly work. When things will not work, you must have the thinker, the man who has some doctrine about why they work at all."

—G. K. Chesterton, *What's Wrong with the World*

Second, the search is comparative. *Occasionally a searcher will be satisfied by the first answer encountered. But more often, especially today when so many guides and maps are being showcased, searchers "shop around" before settling on the answer that convinces them. In this process, contrast is the mother of clarity.*

Third, the search is conditional. *There is no uncertainty about the questions spurring this second stage of the search. Establishing that was the thrust of the first stage. But there obviously is uncertainty about the answer because it hasn't yet been found. So this stage of the inquiry has a strong air of the conditional. It is always a case of "If this proves to be what I'm looking for, then . . ."*

Fourth, the search is channeled. *It might appear that with so many answers clamoring to be heard and so many issues involved in listening to them, searching is futile unless one has three lifetimes and a bottomless bank account. But in fact, the specific questions and sense of need from the first stage provide a clear focus that makes the difference between a true searcher and a mere dilettante or a browser among ideas.*

UNRIDDLING LIFE

For me, "Christianity was the answer to a riddle, not the last truism uttered after a long talk."

—G. K. Chesterton, *Orthodoxy*

Fifth, the search is consequential. *Ideas, beliefs, claims, and counterclaims may appear merely as words, words, words—especially to spectators on the sidelines. But those searching earnestly know that ideas have consequences, beliefs affect behavior, and differences make a real difference—perhaps even an eternal difference. So the urgency stoked by the questions and needs of Stage One is reinforced by the issues and consequences raised at Stage Two.*

At stake at this second stage of the quest is the attractiveness *of different faiths—their appeal because of the light they throw and the difference they make. Those who have learned from experience to listen to their own questions know it is time to move on to look for answers.*

But what of the objection that there are simply too many possible faiths to check out? The fact is that, while there are a million and one beliefs in the world, there are only so many "families of faith." A family of faith refers to all the beliefs that share the same view of ultimate reality, which therefore have important family resemblances giving them points of unity across the obvious range of their very genuine diversity.

For all practical purposes, there are three leading families of faith in the modern world. First is the Eastern family of faiths, including Hinduism, Buddhism, and New Age thought, whose common view of ultimate reality is the "undifferentiated impersonal." Second is the Western secular family of faiths, including atheism, naturalism, and secular humanism, whose common view of ultimate reality is "matter plus time plus chance." And third is the biblical family of faiths, including Judaism, the Christian faith, and Islam, whose shared view of ultimate reality is an "Infinite, Personal God."

I am not saying that everyone is conscious of what they believe. Many are not. Nor that we are all consistent in living as we believe. None of us is. Nor am I denying that the differences within families of faith are important—for example, between Bhakti Hinduism and Zen Buddhism, or between Orthodox Judaism and Liberal Protestantism. But what reduces the search to a manageable size is the prominent differences between the families of faiths. It is these differences the seeker confronts and assesses first.

A LAPSED PAGAN

"Born and brought up among enlightened Pagans, their outlook, and their standards and values, are those which I first knew, by which I was first educated.

"In maturity I have found enlightened Paganism inadequate to explain life as I see it, inadequate to deal with it as I find it. The picture presented to me in youth has proved, so it seems to me, a misleading picture, the account of existence offered a false account; the key with which I was furnished unlocks no door.

"I have found that the Christian world-picture, world-story, explanation, does fit the world that I know and have to live in."

—Rosalind Murray, daughter of Gilbert Murray,
the classical scholar and humanist

POINT TO PONDER:

When Bad Things Happen to Good People

Whence? What? Why? Whither? *Even if we reduce to three the main families of faith to which we can pose the deep questions about human life, the scale is vast and the range encyclopedic. At the very least, thoughtful people will want to raise questions and pursue issues from such areas as the origins of the universe, the existence and character of God (if there is one), the nature and dignity of humanness, the dilemma of evil, the possibility of salvation or liberation, human prospects in the face of death, the destiny of the planet, and so on.*

Such a range of questions goes far beyond the scope of one book. More importantly, it is too burdensome to tax any individual seeker. But as we have seen, no seeker wants or needs to explore all these issues. Each seeker is driven by his or her own quest, central to which is the answer to one burning question tossed up by life.

But for the sake of illustration, let's take one issue—the dilemma of evil, suffering, and death—and explore in outline how the three main families of faith differ in viewing it.

Why, of all subjects, should we focus on the problem of evil and suffering? For one thing, we are within living memory of a half century of the most evil years in history—the years that saw two savage world wars, other wars, monstrous totalitarianisms of the right and left, brutal dictatorships such as Hitler's and Stalin's, and the genocides of Auschwitz and Cambodia.

For another, there is a huge gulf in modern society between the visibility of evil and the deficiency of intellectual and moral tools to deal with it.

For yet another, this topic raises the deepest and most agonizing questions to each of us. Our answers to these questions are the very closest we come as human beings to unriddling life.

Finally, each of the great philosophies of life is at its crux an answer to evil and suffering. In fact, the differences between the three families of faiths when it comes to this topic are strong. Clearly the differences here make a great difference—not only for individuals, but for whole societies.

Two things must be borne in mind in exploring the various answers in any area. First, each faith or philosophy of life deserves to speak for itself rather than being understood in the words of its opponents and outsiders. Second, each faith and philosophy must be understood in its best form rather than its worst.

The link between a belief and its outcome is important for the searcher to examine. Some bad behavior, however, is an accurate reflection of a belief, while other bad behavior is such a contradiction of its belief that it is no reflection at all.

ONLY JUDGE THE PEAKS

"It is no argument against a gospel that it is not lived up to; indeed, it is an argument in its favor, for a gospel must be higher than the prevailing standard. It is no argument against a law that it is broken: in that disobedience lies the reason for making and maintaining the law; the law which is never to be broken is never required."

—Andrew Carnegie, "The Best Friends for Philanthropy"

"One should not judge a doctrine through its by-products but through its peaks."

—Albert Camus

"If a way of life be judged by its misinterpreters, which way will stand?"

—Herman Wouk, *The Will to Live On*

The readings in this part set out some examples of different perspectives of the human dilemmas of evil, suffering, and death from the three most important families of faith—the Eastern, the Western secularist, and the biblical. As Dallas Willard points out, the issue is not just (as the title of the popular book suggests) "when bad things happen to good people." It also includes when bad things don't happen to good people, when bad things don't happen to bad people, and when good things happen to bad people. Arnost Lustig argues in the first reading that the capacity to confront evil is a test of maturity—and humanity.

Calvin and Hobbes © Watterson. Reprinted with permission of Universal Press Syndicate. All rights reserved.

❋ Arnost Lustig ❋

Arnost Lustig (born 1926) is a professor of literature at the American University in Washington, D.C. He was born in Prague and sent with his parents to Auschwitz, where his father was gassed. After the war, he and his mother went back to Prague, where he earned a reputation as a radio reporter, screenwriter, and novelist. He left Czechoslovakia after the Soviet invasion in 1968 and came to the United States in 1970. His books include Night and Hope, Darkness Casts No Shadows, and Diamonds of the Night. The following passage comes from his meditation, later published in 1998, aired on National Public Radio on the fiftieth anniversary of the Allied liberation of Auschwitz-Birkenau in January 1945. Lustig's moving meditation is a challenge to realism about human evil.

Is Lustig's proposal for a "test of maturity" a fair test? What exactly would be included in such a test? The proposal has been widely discussed in a variety of settings. Most people find it an eminently fair test, and for most it would have to include at least two challenges: to realism and to hope. First, in terms of realism, does a faith (or philosophy or worldview) have a realistic view of evil that allows its believers to look evil in the white of the eye and pronounce evil as evil? Second, in terms of hope, does a faith also allow its believers to respond actively to evil with some genuine hope of countering it, perhaps even overcoming it in some way?

WHERE IS MAN?

"Auschwitz is the largest cemetery in the world, one without gravestones."

—Camp survivor

One prisoner turns to another and asks, "Where is God?" The other replies, "Where is man?"

—a story from Auschwitz

"Visitor, observe the remains of this camp and consider: whatever country you come from, you are not a stranger. Act so that your journey is not useless, and our deaths not useless. For you and your sons, the ashes of Auschwitz hold a message. Act so that the fruit of hatred, whose traces you have seen here, bears no more seed, either tomorrow or for ever after."

—The words of survivor Primo Levi, inscribed at Auschwitz

Remembering Auschwitz ∞

To write of Auschwitz-Birkenau as it was—no one will do. There were written ten thousand books on Auschwitz-Birkenau till today and we still do not understand. Three writers, who survived it and wrote down what they had seen, committed suicide: Tadeusz Borowski, the greatest talent of Polish literature in our century, almost immediately after he had completed his description of that inferno. Jean Amery, the Austrian humanist and essayist, when he found that the experience would remain the source of explanation for much that was still to come. And Primo Levi, the best one of many, tried to deliver the message only to find out the impossibility to communicate it. Many people who survived Auschwitz-Birkenau went insane as soon as the war was over. Some survivors gave birth to insane children.

Nine out of ten survivors of Auschwitz-Birkenau gain safe distance from it during the day, but at night, when the world is suspended, they inevitably return to it. Auschwitz-Birkenau was not behind them, but with them, in them.

When I returned to Auschwitz-Birkenau recently, a new horror possessed me. Auschwitz-Birkenau as a museum commemorating human brutality does not evoke in one's imagination even a shadow of the fear, anxiety, and hopelessness that the single moment of this death factory induced while in full operation.

Sometimes I wish that all men and women, wherever they live on earth, would have to visit Auschwitz-Birkenau for a day, an hour or even a single second during the time when Hitler, Himmler, Eichmann, or Baldur von Schirah, the Hitler Youth Leader, swelled with pride at what they had commissioned German architects, planners, and builders to do.

This visit would be a test of maturity before they could receive a driver's license or be allowed to vote or get married, with a guarantee, of course, that nothing would happen to them. I believe that this peek into hell would ripen their image of the world, for only those who have seen how little is needed to peel what is human from us—to turn us again into animals—can understand the world into which we are born.

Auschwitz-Birkenau is at the beginning of all questions that torment us, and instead of providing answers, it can only lead to further questions.

I remember an afternoon in September '44, when I stood in the gypsy camp by the high voltage wires, surrounded by bare Polish plains and forests.

Sometimes I wish that all men and women, wherever they live on earth, would have to visit Auschwitz-Birkenau for a day, an hour or even a single second.

I believe that this peek into hell would ripen their image of the world, for only those who have seen how little is needed to peel what is human from us—to turn us again into animals—can understand the world into which we are born.

A thin, transparent fog enveloped the ground, the people. Everything stunk. The smoke became a cloud and slowly black lines of ashes dropped down. Like everyone else, I wished the wind would lift or the earth reverse its direction. The ashes had a bitter taste. They fell on us, mute, dead, relentless ashes, in which human breath, shrieks, and tears could be felt. I stood at a concrete fence post with white porcelain insulators, taking it all in like a hallucination. A tune from Johann Strauss's "Die Fledermaus" ran through my mind.

A couple of days earlier I had heard the tune at the cabaret with my father, in the attic of the fire station in Theresienstadt. Now my father was only material for soap. Ashes. Smoke tasting of bones. The fog, as white as swan's wings, turned black, and song, sky and ashes fused into one. The curve of the Strauss melody and the plait of the lyrics suddenly acquired a new meaning: *Glucklich ist, wer vergisst, was doch nicht an Andernist.* Happy the one who forgets what cannot be changed. I was singing. My friends dragged me into the barracks before prisoner count so I would live at least unto the next day.

It was exactly what the men of the S.S. wanted for those who still lived in Auschwitz-Birkenau: to feel as insane and lonely, as lost and helpless, as in a nightmare; to regard the absurd as normal and the normal as absurd. But the loneliness among the dead is still better than the loneliness of the living.

From an interview on "All Things Considered," National Public Radio, January 27, 1995, and "Auschwitz-Birkenau" by Arnost Lustig in *The Holocaust: Memories, Research, Reference* (Hayworth Press: New York, 1998). Reprinted by permission of the author.

THE END OF CIVILIZATION?

"And then came the Holocaust, which shook history and by its dimensions and goals marked the end of a civilization. Concentration-camp man discovered the anti-savior. . . . I remember the midnight arrival at Birkenau. Shouts. Dogs barking. Families together for the last time, families about to be torn asunder. A young Jewish boy walks at his father's side in the convoy of men; they walk and they walk and night walks with them toward a place spewing monstrous flames, flames devouring the sky. Suddenly an inmate crosses the ranks and explains to the men what they are seeing, the truth of the night: the future, the absence of future; the key to the secret, the power of evil.

"As he speaks, the young boy touches his father's arm as though to reassure him and whispers, 'This is impossible, isn't it? Don't listen to what he is telling us, he only wants to frighten us. What he says is impossible, unthinkable, it is all part of another age, the Middle Ages, not the twentieth century, not modern history. The world, Father, the civilized world would not allow such things to happen.'

"And yet the civilized world did know, and remained silent. Where was man in all this? And culture, how did it reach this nadir? All those spiritual leaders, those thinkers, those philosophers enamored of truth, those moralists drunk with justice—how was one to reconcile their teachings with Josef Mengele, the great master of selections in Auschwitz? I told myself that a grave, a horrible error had been committed somewhere—only, I knew neither its nature nor its author. When and where had history taken so bad a turn?"

—Elie Wiesel, *The Jew Today,*
describing his arrival at Auschwitz-Birkenau as a child in 1944

"God of forgiveness, do not forgive those murderers of Jewish children here. Remember the nocturnal processions of children and more children and more children, frightened, quiet, so quiet and so beautiful. If we could simply look at one, our hearts would break."

—prayer of Elie Wiesel at Crematorium II, fifty-one years later in 1995

QUESTIONS FOR THOUGHT AND DISCUSSION

1. What is the significance of Arnost Lustig's contrast of "day" and "night," "museum" and "death factory"?
2. What do you think of Lustig's proposal for a "test of maturity"? Is this a fair test?
3. What specific things would we look for in such a test? How would someone be changed by experiencing such evil?
4. What does he mean by "the loneliness among the dead is still better than the loneliness of the living"? What kinds of loneliness do you think he is describing?
5. Reflect on how different people you know, with different philosophies of life, would understand Auschwitz differently.
6. What gives one the basis to face the evil of Auschwitz and still come away with grounds for hope about human beings?

The Gospel of Buddha

Buddhism (from the Sanskrit for "enlightenment") is the religion inaugurated in the sixth century B.C. by Prince Siddhartha Gautama, called the Buddha. With its wide appeal in the West, it is an excellent example of the Eastern, or Asian, family of faiths. As the following story shows, the Buddha was born the son of a rajah in the Sakya tribe in Nepal, raised in luxury, and married to a beautiful cousin. But when he was twenty-nine he came face-to-face with the dilemmas of aging, disease, and death, and set out to find the secret of serenity in the face of suffering. After six years of asceticism, study, and meditation, he is said to have finally achieved enlightenment under a pipal tree at Bodh Gaya. In his first sermon to his five followers in the Deer Park near Benares, he outlined the Four Noble Truths and the Eightfold Path that became the foundations of Buddhism.

The Four Noble Truths are (1) Life is suffering; (2) The cause of suffering is craving or desire; (3) Suffering can be ended only by Nirvana, the extinguishing of desire; and (4) Nirvana can be accomplished by the Eightfold Path—right views, right intentions, right speech, right conduct, right livelihood, right effort, right mindfulness, and right meditation. Although Buddhism has considerable overlap with Hinduism, there are major differences—including its sophisticated atheistic tradition. Yet two doctrines that are vital to interpreting evil are common to both—samsara, the notion of the cycle of transmigration and rebirth that views suffering as part and parcel of the world of illusion and impermanence; and karma, the cosmic law of causality, according to which one's destiny is determined by one's actions in a past life. As evident here, suffering is seen as basic to human life in both Buddhism and Hinduism, and their broad, general response to it is detachment. After all, as Samuel Beckett remarked, "The major sin is the sin of being born."

GO EAST, YOUNG MAN

"Soon, in order to Westernize our kids properly, we will be sending them all to the East."

—Marshall McLuhan

"Orientation is to know where the Orient is."

—R. D. Laing

There is only one true purpose for everyone—"to seek one's self."

—Hermann Hesse

The Three Woes

The palace which the king had given to the prince was resplendent with all the luxuries of India; for the king was anxious to see his son happy.

All sorrowful sights, all misery, and all knowledge of misery were kept away from Siddhartha, for the king desired that no troubles should come nigh him; he should not know that there was evil in the world.

But as the chained elephant longs for the wilds of the jungles, so the prince was eager to see the world, and he asked his father, the king, for permission to do so.

And Suddhodana ordered a jewel-fronted chariot with four stately horses to be held ready, and commanded the roads to be adorned where his son would pass.

The houses of the city were decorated with curtains and banners, and spectators arranged themselves on either side, eagerly gazing at the heir to the throne. Thus Siddhartha rode with Channa, his charioteer, through the streets of the city, and into a country watered by rivulets and covered with pleasant trees.

There by the wayside they met an old man with bent frame, wrinkled face and sorrowful brow, and the prince asked the charioteer: "Who is this? His head is white, his eyes are bleared, and his body is withered. He can barely support himself on his staff."

The charioteer, much embarrassed, hardly dared speak the truth. He said: "These are the symptoms of old age. This same man was once a suckling child, and as a youth full of sportive life; but now, as years have passed away, his beauty is gone and the strength of his life is wasted."

Siddhartha was greatly affected by the words of the charioteer, and he sighed because of the pain of old age. "What joy or pleasure can men take," he thought to himself, "when they know they must soon wither and pine away!"

And lo! while they were passing on, a sick man appeared on the way-side, gasping for breath, his body disfigured, convulsed and groaning with pain.

The prince asked his charioteer: "What kind of man is this?" And the charioteer replied and said: "This man is sick. The four elements of his body are confused and out of order. We are all subject to such conditions: the poor and the rich, the ignorant and the wise, all creatures that have bodies, are liable to the same calamity."

And Siddhartha was still more moved. All pleasures appeared stale to him, and he loathed the joys of life.

All sorrowful sights, all misery, and all knowledge of misery were kept away from Siddhartha, for the king desired that no troubles should come nigh him; he should not know that there was evil in the world.

Siddhartha was greatly affected by the words of the charioteer, and he sighed because of the pain of old age. "What joy or pleasure can men take," he thought to himself, "when they know they must soon wither and pine away!"

The charioteer sped the horses on to escape the dreary sight, when suddenly they were stopped in their fiery course.

Four persons passed by, carrying a corpse; and the prince, shuddering at the sight of a lifeless body, asked the charioteer: "What is this they carry? There are streamers and flower garlands; but the men that follow are overwhelmed with grief!"

The charioteer replied: "This is a dead man: his body is stark; his life is gone; his thoughts are still; his family and the friends who loved him now carry the corpse to the grave."

And the prince was full of awe and terror: "Is this the only dead man," he asked, "or does the world contain other instances?"

With a heavy heart the charioteer replied: "All over the world it is the same. He who begins life must end it. There is no escape from death."

With bated breath and stammering accents the prince exclaimed: "O worldly men! How fatal is your delusion! Inevitably your body will crumble to dust, yet carelessly, unheedingly, ye live on."

With bated breath and stammering accents the prince exclaimed: "O worldly men! How fatal is your delusion! Inevitably your body will crumble to dust, yet carelessly, unheedingly, ye live on."

ALL IS ILLUSION

"The things of this samsaric world are all illusion, like a dream.
Where'er one looks, where is their substance?
Palaces built of earth and stone and wood,
Wealthy men endowed with food and dress and finery,
Legions of retainers who throng round the mighty—
These are like castles in the air, like rainbows in the sky.
And how deluded those who think of this as truth!
When uncles—nephews—brothers—sisters gather as kindred do,
When friends and neighbors gather in good fellowship—
These are like meetings of dream friends, like travelers sharing food with strangers.
And how deluded those who think of this as truth!
This phantom body grown in uterine water from a union of seed and blood—
Our habitual passions springing from the bad deeds of our past,
Our thoughts provoked by divers apparitions—
All are like flowers in autumn, clouds across the sky.
How deluded, O assembled birds, if you have thought of them as permanent.
The splendid plumage of the peacock with its many hues,
Our melodious words in which notes high and low are mingled,
The link of causes and effects which now have brought us here together—

They are like the sound of echoes, the sport of a game of illusion.

Meditate on this illusion, do not seize on them as truth!

Mists on a lake, clouds across a southern sky,

Spray blown by wind above the sea,

Lush fruits ripened by the summer sun—

In permanence they cannot last; in a trice they separate and fall away.

Meditate on their illusion, do not think of them as permanent!"

From the *Dharmapada* in *Buddhist Scriptures,* translated by Edward Conze (Penguin Classics, 1959). Copyright © 1959 by Edward Conze. Reproduced by permission of Penguin Books Ltd.

The charioteer observing the deep impression these sad sights had made on the prince, turned his horses and drove back to the city.

When they passed by the palaces of the nobility, Kisa Gotami, a young princess and niece of the king, saw Siddhartha in his manliness and beauty, and, observing the thoughtfulness of his countenance, said: "Happy the father that begot thee, happy the mother that nursed thee, happy the wife that calls husband this lord so glorious."

The prince hearing this greeting, said: "Happy are they that have found deliverance. Longing for peace of mind, I shall seek the bliss of Nirvana."

Then asked Kisa Gotami: "How is Nirvana attained?" The prince paused, and to him whose mind was estranged from wrong the answer came: "When the fire of lust is gone out, then Nirvana is gained; when the fires of hatred and delusion are gone out, then Nirvana is gained; when the troubles of mind, arising from blind credulity, and all other evils have ceased, then Nirvana is gained!" Siddhartha handed her his precious pearl necklace as a reward for the instruction she had given him, and having returned home looked with disdain upon the treasures of his palace.

His wife welcomed him and entreated him to tell her the cause of his grief. He said: "I see everywhere the impression of change; therefore, my heart is heavy. Men grow old, sicken, and die. That is enough to take away the zest of life."

The king, his father, hearing that the prince had become estranged from pleasure, was greatly overcome with sorrow and like a sword it pierced his heart.

"When the fire of lust is gone out, then Nirvana is gained; when the fires of hatred and delusion are gone out, then Nirvana is gained; when the troubles of mind, arising from blind credulity, and all other evils have ceased, then Nirvana is gained!"
—*SIDDHARTHA*

THE BODHISATVA'S RENUNCIATION

It was night. The prince found no rest on his soft pillow; he arose and went out into the garden. "Alas!" he cried, "all the world is full of darkness and ignorance; there is no one who knows how to cure the ills of existence." And he groaned with pain.

Siddhartha sat down beneath the great jambu-tree and gave himself to thought, pondering on life and death and the evils of decay. Concentrating his mind he became free from confusion. All low desires vanished from his heart and perfect tranquillity came over him.

In this state of ecstasy he saw with his mental eye all the misery and sorrow of the world; he saw the pains of pleasure and the inevitable certainty of death that hovers over every being; yet men are not awakened to the truth. And a deep compassion seized his heart.

While the prince was pondering on the problem of evil, he beheld with his mind's eye under the jambu-tree a lofty figure endowed with majesty, calm and dignified. "Whence comest thou, and who mayst thou be?" asked the prince.

In reply the vision said: "I am a samana. Troubled at the thought of old age, disease, and death I have left my home to seek the path of salvation. All things hasten to decay; only the truth abideth forever. Everything changes, and there is no permanency; yet the words of the Buddhas are immutable. I long for the happiness that does not decay; the treasure that will never perish; the life that knows of no beginning and no end. Therefore, I have destroyed all worldly thought. I have retired into an unfrequented dell to live in solitude; and, begging for food, I devote myself to the one thing needful."

"Can peace be gained in this world of unrest? I am struck with the emptiness of pleasure and have become disgusted with lust. All oppresses me, and existence itself seems intolerable."
—SIDDHARTHA

Siddhartha asked: "Can peace be gained in this world of unrest? I am struck with the emptiness of pleasure and have become disgusted with lust. All oppresses me, and existence itself seems intolerable."

The samana replied: "Where heat is, there is also a possibility of cold; creatures subject to pain possess the faculty of pleasure; the origin of evil indicates that good can be developed. For these things are correlatives. Thus where there is much suffering, there will be much bliss, if thou but open thine eyes to behold it. Just as a man who has fallen into a heap of filth ought to seek the great pond of water covered with lotuses, which is near by: even so seek thou for the great deathless lake of Nirvana to wash off the defilement of wrong. If the lake is not sought, it is not the fault of the lake. Even so when there is a blessed road leading the man held fast by wrong to the salvation of Nirvana, if the road is not walked upon, it is not the fault of the road, but of the person. And when a man who is oppressed with sickness, there being a physician who can heal him, does not avail himself of the physician's help, that is not the fault of the physician. Even so when a man oppressed by the malady of wrong-doing does not seek the spiritual guide of enlightenment, that is no fault of the evil-destroying guide."

The prince listened to the noble words of his visitor and said: "Thou bringest good tidings, for now I know that my purpose will be accomplished. My father advises me to enjoy life and to undertake worldly duties, such as will bring honor to me and to our house. He tells me that I am too young still, that my pulse beats too full to lead a religious life."

The venerable figure shook his head and replied: "Thou shouldst know that for seeking a religious life no time can be inopportune."

A thrill of joy passed through Siddhartha's heart. "Now is the time to seek religion," he said; "now is the time to sever all ties that would prevent me from attaining perfect enlightenment; now is the time to wander into homelessness and, leading a mendicant's life, to find the path of deliverance."

The celestial messenger heard the resolution of Siddhartha with approval.

"Now, indeed," he added, "is the time to seek religion. Go, Siddhartha, and accomplish thy purpose. For thou art Bodhisatva, the Buddha-elect; thou art destined to enlighten the world.

"Thou art the Tathagata, the great master, for thou wilt fulfill all right-eousness and be Dharmaraja, the king of truth. Thou art Bhagavat, the Blessed One, for thou art called upon to become the saviour and redeemer of the world.

"Fulfill thou the perfection of truth. Though the thunderbolt descend upon thy head, yield thou never to the allurements that beguile men from the path of truth. As the sun at all seasons pursues his own course, nor ever goes on another, even so if thou forsake not the straight path of righteousness, thou shalt become a Buddha.

"Persevere in thy quest and thou shalt find what thou seekest. Pursue thy aim unswervingly and thou shalt gain the prize. Struggle earnestly and thou shalt con-quer. The benediction of all deities, of all saints, of all that seek light is upon thee, and heavenly wisdom guides thy steps. Thou shalt be the Buddha, our Master, and our Lord; thou shalt enlighten the world and save mankind from perdition."

Having thus spoken, the vision vanished, and Siddhartha's heart was filled with peace. He said to himself:

"I have awakened to the truth and I am resolved to accomplish my pur-pose. I will sever all the ties that bind me to the world, and I will go out from my home to seek the way of salvation.

"Thou shouldst know that for seeking a religious life no time can be inopportune."

—*THE SAMANA*

"I have awakened to the truth and I am resolved to accomplish my purpose. I will sever all the ties that bind me to the world, and I will go out from my home to seek the way of salvation."

—*SIDDHARTHA*

"The Buddhas are beings whose words cannot fail: there is no departure from truth in their speech.

"For as the fall of a stone thrown into the air, as the death of a mortal, as the sunrise at dawn, as the lion's roar when he leaves his lair, as the delivery of a woman with child, as all these things are sure and certain—even so the word of the Buddhas is sure and cannot fail.

"Verily I shall become a Buddha."

The prince returned to the bedroom of his wife to take a last farewell glance at those whom he dearly loved above all the treasures of the earth. He longed to take the infant once more into his arms and kiss him with a parting kiss. But the child lay in the arms of his mother, and the prince could not lift him without awakening both.

There Siddhartha stood gazing at his beautiful wife and his beloved son, and his heart grieved. The pain of parting overcame him powerfully. Although his mind was determined, so that nothing, be it good or evil, could shake his resolution, the tears flowed freely from his eyes, and it was beyond his power to check their stream. But the prince tore himself away with a manly heart, suppressing his feelings but not extinguishing his memory.

The Bodhisatva mounted his noble steed Kanthaka, and when he left the palace, Mara stood in the gate and stopped him: "Depart not, O my Lord," exclaimed Mara. "In seven days from now the wheel of empire will appear, and will make thee sovereign over the four continents and the two thousand adjacent islands. Therefore, stay, my Lord."

The Bodhisatva replied: "Well do I know that the wheel of empire will appear to me; but it is not sovereignty that I desire. I will become a Buddha and make all the world shout for joy."

Thus Siddhartha, the prince, renounced power and worldly pleasures, gave up his kingdom, severed all ties, and went into homelessness. He rode out into the silent night, accompanied only by his faithful charioteer Channa.

Darkness lay upon the earth, but the stars shone brightly in the heavens.

From *The Gospel of Buddha*, translated by Paul Carus (Chicago: Open Court Publishing Co., 1917), pp. 14–25.

A talk given by Siddhartha Gautama (the Buddha, or "the Enlightened One") to his first five followers at the Isipatana Deer Park in Benares, soon after his enlightenment. For two and a half thousand years, Buddhists have revered this talk as the heart of his message and the defining moment of his mission.

SETTING IN MOTION THE WHEEL OF THE DHARMA

1. Thus have I heard. Once the 'One who Enjoys the Spoils of Victory' was staying at Isipatana near Benares.
2. He spoke to the group of five ascetics as follows: Monks, there are two extremes which one who has left the household life should not resort to.
3. What are they? One is devotion to sense desire and sense pleasure. It is demeaning. It is the way of ordinary folk. It is unworthy and unprofitable. The other is devotion to self mortification. It is painful and ignoble. It is not conducive to the real purpose of life. Giving up these extremes, the 'One who has Been There' has woken up to the middle way which provides insight and understanding and causes peace, wisdom, enlightenment and nirvana.
4. The Middle Way is the noble eight limb way of right view, right thought, right speech, right action, right livelihood, right effort, right mindfulness and right samadhi.
5. The noble truth of dukkha, affliction, is this: birth, old age, sickness, death, grief, lamentation, pain, depression, and agitation are dukkha. Dukkha is being associated with what you do not like, being separated from what you do like, and not being able to get what you want. In short, the five aggregates of grasping are dukkha.
6. The noble truth of samudaya, response to affliction, is this: it is thirst for self re-creation which is associated with greed. It lights upon whatever pleasures are to be found here and there. It is thirst for sense pleasure, for being and non-being.
7. The noble truth of nirodha, containment, is this: it is the complete capturing of that thirst. It is to let go of, be liberated from and refuse to dwell in the object of that thirst.
8. The noble truth of marga, the right track, is this: it is the noble eight-limb way, namely right view, right thought, right speech, right action, right livelihood, right effort, right mindfulness and right samadhi.

9. 'This is the noble truth of affliction'—this was the insight, understanding, wisdom, knowledge and clarity which arose in me about things I had not been taught.

 'Affliction should be understood to be a noble truth'—this was the insight, understanding, wisdom, knowledge and clarity which arose in me about things I had not been taught.

 'Full understanding of affliction as a noble truth has dawned'—this was the insight, understanding, wisdom, knowledge and clarity which arose in me about things I had not been taught.

10. 'This is the noble truth of response'—this was the insight, understanding, wisdom, knowledge and clarity which arose in me about things I had not been taught.

 'Response should be understood to be a noble truth'—this was the insight, understanding, wisdom, knowledge and clarity which arose in me about things I had not been taught.

 'Full understanding of response as a noble truth has dawned'—this was the insight, understanding, wisdom, knowledge and clarity which arose in me about things I had not been taught.

11. 'This is the noble truth of containment'—this was the insight, understanding, wisdom, knowledge and clarity which arose in me about things untaught.

 Containment should be understood to be a noble truth'—this was the insight, understanding, wisdom, knowledge and clarity which arose in me about things untaught.

 'Full understanding of containment as a noble truth has dawned'—this was the insight, understanding, wisdom, knowledge and clarity which arose in me about things untaught.

12. 'This is the noble truth of the path'—this was the insight, understanding, wisdom, knowledge and clarity which arose in me about things untaught.

 'This path should be understood to be a noble truth'—this was the insight, understanding, wisdom, knowledge and clarity which arose in me about things untaught.

 'Full understanding of the path as a noble truth has dawned'—this was the insight, understanding, wisdom, knowledge and clarity which arose in me about things untaught.

13. As long as I had not got a completely clear insight and understanding in all these three ways about each of these Four Noble Truths, I could not be sure that there was anyone in the world, divine or human, who

had woken up to the highest and most complete enlightenment.

14. However, when my insight and understanding had become completely clear in all these twelve turnings of the wheel, then I knew for sure that there was someone in the world who had woken up to the highest and most complete enlightenment. Then I knew that the liberation of my mind was unassailable. This is the last step. There is no further step.

15. When the Victorious One had said this, the five monks were filled with joy. In one of them, Kondañña, the pure Dharma Eye was completely opened. He saw that whatever can arise can be contained.

16. When the Victorious One had turned the wheel of the Dharma in this way the spirits of the earth cried out: Near Benares, in the Deer Park at Isipatana, the wheel of the highest Dharma has been turned and it cannot now be turned back by anyone, human or divine, anywhere in the world.

17, 18, 19. This cry resounded throughout the heavenly realms. The earth shook. An immeasurable light was now released into the world.

20. Then the Blessed One said: Venerable Kondañña has understood. And from that day on he was given the name 'He who understood'.

From *Saṁyutta-nikāya* 61.11, quoted in Appendix I *The Feeling Buddha*, by David Brazier (Fromm International Publishing Corp., 1998). Published by permission of Fromm.

TWELVE STEPS (MINUS ONE) TO THE END OF MISERY

On the complete fading out and cessation of ignorance ceases *karma*;
On the cessation of *karma* ceases consciousness;
On the cessation of consciousness cease name and form;
On the cessation of name and form cease the six organs of sense;
On the cessation of the six organs of sense ceases contact;
On the cessation of contact ceases sensation;
On the cessation of sensation ceases desire;
On the cessation of desire ceases attachment;
On the cessation of attachment ceases existence;
On the cessation of existence ceases birth;
On the cessation of birth cease old age and death, sorrow, lamentation, misery, grief, and despair. Thus does this entire aggregation of misery cease.

From *Saṁyutta-nikāya* 20.90, translated by H. C. Warren in *A Source Book in Indian Philosophy*, edited by Sarvepalli Radhakrishnan and Charles A. Moore (Princeton University Press, 1957). Reprinted by permission of Princeton University Press.

REALISTIC BUT DRASTIC

"Christ said, 'Seek first the kingdom and all these things shall be added unto you.' Buddha said, 'Seek first the kingdom and then you will need none of these things.'"

—G. K. Chesterton

"Buddhism is not a superficial palliative."

—David Brazier, *The Feeling Buddha*

QUESTIONS FOR THOUGHT AND DISCUSSION

1. What are the three woes that Siddhartha confronted? How does the charioteer describe each condition? How does Siddhartha react to each woe? What does this experience do to Siddhartha in light of the life of privileged diversion his father had given him?

2. Do these woes resonate with you in any way? Can you think of examples of this "reality check" in your own life? Did they elicit similar responses from you?

3. What prompts Siddhartha to "seek the bliss of Nirvana"? What is he seeing in the contrast of Nirvana with the suffering he has witnessed?

4. What is keeping him from Nirvana? What must he extinguish to reach it?

5. In the section, "The Bodhisatva's Renunciation," Siddhartha has a vision during a time of meditation. What does the samana in the vision say of truth and the everlasting? What is he seeking? How is he trying to obtain it?

6. After the vision, what does Siddhartha resolve to do? What things does he give up? What are the underlying themes of his departure and his future life? How does he see everyday experiences and pleasures?

7. Siddhartha's search is spurred by his encounters with old age, sickness, and death, but how do they fit in the perspective of his enlightenment?

8. Read the section, "Setting in Motion the Wheel of the Dharma." How does he describe affliction (dukkha)? What is the Buddha's answer to suffering? Does this worldview reckon with raw evil, like Auschwitz? What do you think of Buddha's proposed solution?

9. How would you relate this philosophy to Plato's parable of the cave?

10. What are the social and cultural consequences of this worldview? What would this way of thinking mean for our relationships?

BEYOND GOOD AND EVIL

"To the Buddhist good and evil are relative and not absolute terms."

—Christmas Humphreys, *Buddhism*

"The cultures of the East still differ from ours as they did then. They still belittle man as individual man. Under this runs an indifference to the world of the senses, of which the indifference to experienced fact is one face. Anyone who has worked in the East knows how hard it is there to get an answer to a question of fact."

—scientist Jacob Bronowski, *Science and Human Values*

Shirley MacLaine

Shirley MacLaine (born 1934) is an Oscar-winning stage and screen actress. Born in Richmond, Virginia, she attended high school in Washington, D.C., and took ballet lessons to prepare for her career in film. Her breakthrough came in the 1954 Broadway production of Pajama Game. *This led immediately to an Alfred Hitchcock film and then a whole raft of Hollywood successes, including* Terms of Endearment, *which won her an Oscar in 1984. In the 1960s MacLaine pursued many liberal causes, including Vietnam War protest, but she became even more controversial in the 1980s with her New Age books and television programs—promoting such ideas as reincarnation and trance channeling. The following passage comes from her book* It's All in the Playing *(1987). It describes her sharing at a New Year's party and illustrates well the New Age view of tackling human dilemmas. To be sure, there are more sophisticated arguments for the New Age philosophy, but MacLaine's popularity has made her an important gatekeeper introducing millions to the movement.*

GETTING GOOD AT PLAYING GOD

"We are as gods and might as well get good at it."

—cover of *Whole Earth Catalog*

It's All in the Playing

I began by saying that since I realized I created my own reality in every way, I must therefore admit that, in essence, I was the only person alive in my universe. I could feel the instant shock waves undulate around the table. I went on to express my feeling of total responsibility *and power* for all events that occur in the world because the world is happening only in my reality. *And* human beings feeling pain, terror, depression, panic, and so forth, were really only aspects of pain, terror, depression, panic, and so on, in *me!* If they were all characters in my reality, my dream, then of course they were only reflections of myself.

I was beginning to understand what the great masters had meant when they said "you are the universe." If we each create our own reality, then of course we are everything that exists within it. Our reality is a reflection of us.

Now, that truth can be very humorous. I could legitimately say that I created

> *I went on to express my feeling of total responsibility and power for all events that occur in the world because the world is happening only in my reality. And human beings feeling pain, terror, depression, panic, and so forth, were really only aspects of pain, terror, depression, panic, and so on, in me!*

the Statue of Liberty, chocolate chip cookies, the Beatles, terrorism, and the Vietnam War. I couldn't really say for sure whether anyone else in the world had actually experienced those things separately from me because these people existed as individuals only in my dream. I knew I had created the reality of the evening news at night. It was in my reality. But whether anyone else was experiencing the news *separately* from me was unclear, because *they* existed in my reality too. And if they reacted to world events, then I was creating them to react so I would have someone to interact with, thereby enabling myself to know me better.

My purpose in mentioning this on New Year's Eve was to project a hope that if I changed *my* conception of reality for the better in the coming year, I would in effect be contributing to the advancement of the world. Therefore, my New Year's resolution was to improve myself—which would in turn improve the world I lived in.

Most of the faces around the table looked scandalized. I created the Declaration of Independence and Marilyn Monroe and the fifty-five miles per hour speed limit? If I changed my reality, it would change the world? I had clearly gone too far. The discussion that ensued was a microcosm of the world itself. And while the others expressed their objections, I felt I *was creating them to object*, so that I could look at some things I hadn't resolved myself. In other words I *was* them. *They* were *me*. And all because I was creating them as characters in my play.

The classic question was asked: If what I was proposing were true, would it also be true that I did nothing for others, everything for myself?

And the answer is, essentially, yes. If I fed a starving child, and was honest about my motivation, I would have to say I did it for myself, because it made me feel better. Because the child was happier and more fulfilled, *I* would be. I was beginning to see that we each did whatever we did purely for self, and that was as it should be. Even if I had not created others in my reality and was therefore not responsible for them, I would feel responsible to my own feelings which desire to be positive and loving. Thus, in uplifting my own feelings I would uplift the feelings of my fellow human beings.

How do we change the world? By changing ourselves.

That was the gist of my New Year's projection.

I could legitimately say that I created the Statue of Liberty, chocolate chip cookies, the Beatles, terrorism, and the Vietnam War.

If I fed a starving child, and was honest about my motivation, I would have to say I did it for myself, because it made me feel better.

I LOVE YOU, NOT I AM YOU

"I *know* that I exist, therefore I AM.

I *know* that the God-source exists. Therefore IT IS.

Since I am part of that force, then I AM that I AM."

—Shirley MacLaine, *Dancing in the Light*

"I want to love my neighbor not because he is I, but precisely because he is not I. I want to adore the world, not as one likes a looking-glass, because it is one's self, but as one loves a woman, because she is entirely different. If souls are separate, love is possible. If souls are united love is obviously impossible."

—G. K. Chesterton

QUESTIONS FOR THOUGHT AND DISCUSSION

1. How would you describe Shirley MacLaine's philosophy? What is her "reality"? How do events and people fit into this reality?

2. How does MacLaine define evil? Is this a realistic view? Why or why not? Does she offer hope in the face of evil?

3. How is this tied into what we've been reading? Why do you think so many people today are attracted to New Age philosophy?

4. What would be the consequences of this worldview on society if it were followed more widely? What does it mean for good deeds as well as ill?

5. What are the similarities and differences between this New Age view and the perspectives of Buddhism and Hinduism?

6. What do you think of this New Age solution to the evil, suffering, and death in the world?

⁕ *Bertrand Russell* ⁕

Bertrand Arthur William, third Earl Russell (1872–1970), was one of the greatest twentieth-century philosophers as well as a mathematician and a controversial force in British politics and society. His Principles of Mathematics *(1903) and* Principia Mathematica *(with Alfred North Whitehead, 1910–1913), remain landmarks in the history of logic and mathematics. Russell taught at Cambridge University but his anti-war activities during World War I lost him his fellowship and landed him in prison.*

Thereafter Russell worked as a lecturer and a journalist; upon meeting Lenin and Trotsky he became one of the first left-leaning British intellectuals to become disillusioned with the Soviet experiment. He founded a progressive school and published books on education and marriage. As World War II began he renounced his pacifism; Cambridge returned his fellowship to him in 1944. He continued to express his controversial views in social, religious, and moral matters. He also became active in the nuclear disarmament movement and was arrested and imprisoned for taking part in a demonstration.

Russell was awarded the Nobel Prize for Literature in 1950. The following passage from his Why I Am Not a Christian *(1957) clearly expresses his atheism and humanism. Along with his life of indefatigably battling causes, it sets out his view of how a humanist confronts evil, suffering, and death. "A Free Man's Worship" is an excellent example of the Western secularist family of faiths, whose view of ultimate reality is "chance plus matter plus time." Written in 1902 at his brother-in-law Bernard Berenson's villa in Florence, it was published in 1910 and hailed at once as a tour de force.*

I AM—AND WHO BUT I?

"Man is the measure of all things."

—Protagoras, fifth century B.C.

"A man can do all things if he will."

—Leon Battista Alberti, fifteenth century A.D.

"Glory to man in the highest! For Man is the Master of Things."

—Algernon Swinburne, "Hymn of Man"

"Arise, your highness, great deeds are to be done."

—how Count Saint-Simon instructed his valet to wake him in the morning

"We must so live that we can say, 'Thus I willed it.'"

—Friedrich Nietzsche, *Ecce Homo*

"Man makes himself."

—archeologist Gordon Childe

"We see the future of man as one of his own making."

—geneticist H. J. Muller

"Today, in twentieth-century man, the evolutionary process is at last becoming conscious of itself. . . . Human knowledge worked over by human imagination, is seen as the basis to human understanding and belief, and the ultimate guide to human progress."

—Julian Huxley

"Our problems are man-made—therefore they can be solved by man. And man can be as big as he wants. No problem of human destiny is beyond human beings."

—John F. Kennedy, commencement address at American University

"I would give the greatest sunset in the world for one sight of New York's skyline. . . . The sky over New York and the will of man made visible. What other religion do we need?"

—Ayn Rand, *The Fountainhead*

"My personal life is a postscipt to my words; it consists of the sentence, *'And I mean it.'*"

—Ayn Rand

A Free Man's Worship 🦎

Amid such a world, if anywhere, our ideals henceforward must find a home. That man is the product of causes which had no prevision of the end they were achieving; that his origin, his growth, his hopes and fears, his loves and his beliefs, are but the outcome of accidental collocations of atoms; that no fire, no heroism, no intensity of thought and feeling, can preserve an individual life beyond the grave; that all the labors of the ages, all the devotion, all the inspiration, all the noonday brightness of human genius, are destined to extinction in the vast death of the solar system, and that the whole temple of man's achievement must inevitably be buried beneath the debris of a universe in ruins—all these things, if not quite beyond dispute, are yet so nearly certain that no philosophy which rejects them can hope to stand. Only within the scaffolding of these truths, only on the firm foundation of unyielding despair, can the soul's habitation henceforth be safely built. . . .

United with his fellow men by the strongest of all ties, the tie of a common doom, the free man finds that a new vision is with him always, shedding over every daily task the light of love. The life of man is a long march through the night, surrounded by invisible foes, tortured by weariness and pain, toward a goal that few can hope to reach, and where none may tarry long. One by one, as they march, our comrades vanish from our sight, seized by the silent orders of omnipotent death. Very brief is the time in which we can help them, in which their happiness or misery is decided. Be it ours to shed sunshine on their path, to lighten their sorrows by the balm of sympathy, to give them the pure joy of a never-tiring affection, to strengthen failing courage, to instill faith in hours of despair. Let us not weigh in grudging scales their merits and demerits, but let us think only of their need—of the sorrows, the difficulties, perhaps the blindnesses, that make the misery of their lives; let us remember that they are fellow sufferers in the same darkness, actors in the same tragedy with ourselves. And so, when their day is over, when their good and their evil have become eternal by the immortality of the past, be it ours to feel that, where they suffered, where they failed, no deed of ours was the cause; but wherever a spark of the divine fire kindled in their hearts, we were ready with encouragement, with sympathy, with brave words in which high courage glowed.

Brief and powerless is man's life; on him and all his race the slow, sure doom falls pitiless and dark. Blind to good and evil, reckless of destruction, omnipotent matter rolls on its relentless way; for man, condemned today to lose his dearest, tomorrow himself to pass through the gate of darkness, it remains only to cherish, ere yet the blow fall, the lofty thoughts that ennoble his little day; disdaining the coward terrors of the slave of Fate, to worship at the shrines that his own hands have built; undismayed by the empire of chance, to preserve a mind free from the wanton tyranny that rules his outward life; proudly defiant of the irresistible forces that tolerate, for a moment, his knowledge and his condemnation, to sustain alone, a weary but unyielding Atlas, the world that his own ideals have fashioned despite the trampling march of unconscious power.

The life of man is a long march through the night, surrounded by invisible foes, tortured by weariness and pain, toward a goal that few can hope to reach, and where none may tarry long. One by one, as they march, our comrades vanish from our sight, seized by the silent orders of omnipotent death.

Bertrand Russell, "A Free Man's Worship," in *Why I Am Not a Christian* (New York: Simon & Schuster, 1957), pp. 107, 115–116. Copyright © 1957 by George Allen & Unwin Ltd. First published in 1903. Reprinted by permission of Simon & Schuster, Routledge Ltd., and the Bertrand Russell Peace Foundation.

NOT SUCH GOOD NEWS AFTER ALL

"I wrote with passion & force, because I really thought I had a gospel. Now I am cynical about the gospel because it won't stand the test of life."

—Bertrand Russell, some years later

"I felt No, the man who wrote that is not the man Conrad sees now—the affection he gives is not now deserved—the man who would face a hostile universe rather than lose his vision has become a man who will creep into the first hovel to escape the terror & splendor of the night."

—Bertrand Russell, to his mistress on being
congratulated for his essay by Joseph Conrad

"The most drastic objection to humanism is that it is too bad to be true. The world is one vast tomb if human lives are ephemeral and human life itself doomed to ultimate extinction. . . . There is no end to hiding from the ultimate end of life, which is death. But it does not avail. On humanist assumptions, life leads to nothing, and every pretense that it does not is a deceit. If there is a bridge over a gorge which spans only half the distance and ends in mid-air, and if the bridge is crowded with human beings pressing on, one after another they fall into the abyss. The bridge leads nowhere, and those who are pressing forward to cross it are going nowhere. It does not matter where they think they are going, what preparations for the journey they may have made, how much they may be enjoying it all. The objection merely points out objectively that such a situation is a model of futility."

—H. J. Blackham, director of the British Humanist Association

"Atheism is a cruel, long-term business; I believe I have gone through it to the end."

—Jean-Paul Sartre, *Words*

"Conscious or not, agnosticism is the established church of modernity. By its somewhat bleak light, the educated and the rational conduct their immanent lives."

—George Steiner, *Errata*

QUESTIONS FOR THOUGHT AND DISCUSSION

1. In the first paragraph, Bertrand Russell lays out his worldview. What are its contours? Its origins? Is there meaning in the universe? Where are we going to end?

2. Continuing on, Russell describes the human life. What strikes you about the language he uses to describe the journey of atheism? What faith does he want to instill? What binds us together?

3. What is Russell's answer for evil and suffering?

4. What do you admire about and where do you disagree with Russell's views? Do you see any problems with how this worldview would work out practically? How does this apply ethically?

5. Read the box, "Not Such Good News After All." What do you think of these descriptions? What is H. J. Blackham's and Jean-Paul Sartre's view of the human condition?

6. What sort of person does this view appeal to? What would its impact be on different sectors of society—say, on political leaders, business people, and young people?

❈ Albert Camus ❈

Albert Camus (1913–1960) is one of the greatest and most widely read twentieth-century novelists and philosophers. A French writer, he is often paired with Jean-Paul Sartre as the French men of letters who did the most to popularize existentialism—the philosophy that sees no meaning in the universe and therefore puts a premium on human existence, action, and choice as the way to create our own meaning in life. Like Russell, Camus represents the Western secularist family of faiths, but in a form that many people have found warmer and more sympathetic.

Born in the French colony of Algeria, the son of a farm laborer, Camus studied philosophy at the University of Algiers. He worked as an actor, schoolmaster, playwright, and journalist in Algiers and Paris and during World War II was co-editor with Sartre of a left-wing Resistance newspaper. His international reputation began with his first novel, The Stranger *(sometimes translated* The Outsider*) in 1942. He broke with Sartre over ideological differences in 1948 and continued to write plays, novels, and essays. Among his other well-known writings are* The Plague *(1948),* The Fall *(1956), and the essays* The Myth of Sisyphus *(1942) and* The Rebel *(1951). He won the Nobel Prize for Literature in 1957. On January 4, 1960, he was killed in an auto accident on an icy French road returning to Paris from the south of France.*

The following reading is from The Plague. *The Algerian port of Oran is struck with an epidemic of bubonic plague (often interpreted as a metaphor of evil in the world). The courageous doctor Bernard Rieux represents those who, in the face of impossible odds, do what they can for the cause of human life and snatch what they can of occasional happiness. Jean Tarrou, a recent arrival in Oran, has become Rieux's friend during the plague.*

The Plague 🦎

"My question's this," said Tarrou. "Why do you yourself show such devotion, considering you don't believe in God? I suspect your answer may help me to mine."

His face still in shadow, Rieux said that he'd already answered: that if he believed in an all-powerful God he would cease curing the sick and leave that to Him. But no one in the world believed in a God of that sort; no, not even

Paneloux [the Catholic priest], who believed that he believed in such a God. And this was proved by the fact that no one ever threw himself on Providence completely. Anyhow, in this respect Rieux believed himself to be on the right road—in fighting against creation as he found it.

"Ah," Tarrou remarked. "So that's the idea you have of your profession?"

"More or less." The doctor came back into the light.

Tarrou made a faint whistling noise with his lips, and the doctor gazed at him.

"Yes, you're thinking it calls for pride to feel that way. But I assure you I've no more than the pride that's needed to keep me going. I have no idea what's awaiting me, or what will happen when all this ends. For the moment I know this; there are sick people and they need curing. Later on, perhaps, they'll think things over; and so shall I. But what's wanted now is to make them well. I defend them as best I can, that's all."

"Against whom?"

Rieux turned to the window. A shadow-line on the horizon told of the presence of the sea. He was conscious only of his exhaustion, and at the same time was struggling against a sudden, irrational impulse to unburden himself a little more to his companion; an eccentric, perhaps, but who, he guessed, was one of his own kind.

"I haven't a notion, Tarrou; I assure you I haven't a notion. When I entered this profession, I did it 'abstractedly,' so to speak; because I had a desire for it, because it meant a career like another, one that young men often aspire to. Perhaps, too, because it was particularly difficult for a workman's son, like myself. And then I had to see people die. Do you know that there are some who *refuse* to die? Have you ever heard a woman scream 'Never!' with her last gasp? Well, I have. And then I saw that I could never get hardened to it. I was young then, and I was outraged by the whole scheme of things, or so I thought. Subsequently I grew more modest. Only, I've never managed to get used to seeing people die. That's all I know. Yet after all—"

Rieux fell silent and sat down. He felt his mouth dry.

"After all—?" Tarrou prompted softly.

"After all," the doctor repeated, then hesitated again, fixing his eyes on Tarrou, "it's something that a man of your sort can understand most likely, but, since the order of the world is shaped by death, mightn't it be better for God if we refuse to believe in Him and struggle with all our might against death, without raising our eyes toward the heaven where He sits in silence?"

Tarrou nodded.

In this respect Rieux believed himself to be on the right road—in fighting against creation as he found it.

"Since the order of the world is shaped by death, mightn't it be better for God if we refuse to believe in Him and struggle with all our might against death, without raising our eyes toward the heaven where He sits in silence?"
—RIEUX

"Yes. But your victories will never be lasting; that's all."

Rieux's face darkened.

"Yes, I know that. But it's no reason for giving up the struggle."

"No reason, I agree. Only, I now can picture what this plague must mean for you."

"Yes. A never ending defeat."

Tarrou stared at the doctor for a moment, then turned and tramped heavily toward the door. Rieux followed him and was almost at his side when Tarrou, who was staring at the floor, suddenly said:

"Who taught you all this, Doctor?"

The reply came promptly:

"Suffering." . . .

[Tarrou himself contracts the plague and is on his deathbed.] At noon [Tarrou's] fever reached its climax. A visceral cough racked the sick man's body and he now was spitting blood. The ganglia had ceased swelling, but they were still there, like lumps of iron embedded in the joints. Rieux decided that lancing them was impracticable. Now and then, in the intervals between bouts of fever and coughing fits Tarrou still gazed at his friends. But soon his eyes opened less and less often and the glow that shone out from the ravaged face in the brief moments of recognition grew steadily fainter. The storm, lashing his body into convulsive movement, lit it up with ever rarer flashes, and in the heart of the tempest he was slowly drifting, derelict. And now Rieux had before him only a masklike face, inert, from which the smile had gone forever. This human form, his friend's, lacerated by the spear-thrusts of the plague, consumed by searing, superhuman fires, buffeted by all the raging winds of heaven, was foundering under his eyes in the dark flood of the pestilence, and he could do nothing to avert the wreck. He could only stand, unavailing, on the shore, empty-handed and sick at heart, unarmed and helpless yet again under the onset of calamity. And thus, when the end came, the tears that blinded Rieux's eyes were tears of impotence; and he did not see Tarrou roll over, face to the wall, and die with a short, hollow groan as if somewhere within him an essential cord had snapped.

The next night was not one of struggle but of silence. In the tranquil death-chamber, beside the dead body now in everyday clothing — here, too, Rieux felt it brooding, that elemental peace which, when he was sitting many nights before on the terrace high above the plague, had followed the brief foray at the gates. Then, already it had brought to his mind the silence brooding over the beds in which he had let men die. There as here it was the same solemn

pause, the lull that follows battle; it was the silence of defeat. But the silence
now enveloping his dead friend, so dense, so much akin to the nocturnal
silence of the streets and of the town set free at last, made Rieux cruelly aware
that this defeat was final, the last disastrous battle that ends a war and makes
peace itself an ill beyond all remedy. The doctor could not tell if Tarrou had
found peace, now that all was over, but for himself he had a feeling that no
peace was possible to him henceforth, any more than there can be an armistice
for a mother bereaved of her son or for a man who buries his friend. . . .

*This defeat was final, the
last disastrous battle that
ends a war and makes
peace itself an ill beyond
all remedy.*

He had lived at Tarrou's side, and Tarrou had died this evening without
their friendship's having had time to enter fully into the life of either. Tarrou
had "lost the match," as he put it. But what had he, Rieux, won? No more than
the experience of having known plague and remembering it, of having known
friendship and remembering it, of knowing affection and being destined one
day to remember it. So all a man could win in the conflict between plague and
life was knowledge and memories. But Tarrou, perhaps, would have called that
winning the match.

Another car passed, and Mme. Rieux stirred slightly. Rieux smiled toward
her. She assured him she wasn't tired and immediately added:

"You must go and have a good long rest in the mountains, over there."

"Yes, Mother."

Certainly he'd take a rest "over there." It, too, would be a pretext for memory. But if that was what it meant, winning the match — how hard it must be
to live only with what one knows and what one remembers, cut off from what
one hopes for! It was thus, most probably, that Tarrou had lived, and he realized the bleak sterility of a life without illusions. There can be no peace
without hope, and Tarrou, denying as he did the right to condemn anyone
whomsoever — though he knew well that no one can help condemning and
it befalls even the victim sometimes to turn executioner — Tarrou had lived
a life riddled with contradictions and had never known hope's solace. Did that
explain his aspiration toward saintliness, his quest of peace by service in the
cause of others? Actually Rieux had no idea of the answer to that question,
and it mattered little. The only picture of Tarrou he would always have would
be the picture of a man who firmly gripped the steering wheel of his car when
driving, or else the picture of that stalwart body, now lying motionless.
Knowing meant that: a living warmth, and a picture of death. . . .

Nonetheless, he knew that the tale he had to tell could not be one of a
final victory. It could be only the record of what had had to be done, and
what assuredly would have to be done again in the never ending fight against

terror and its relentless onslaughts, despite their personal afflictions, by all who, while unable to be saints but refusing to bow down to pestilences, strive their utmost to be healers.

HOPE AS REBELLION AGAINST ABSURDITY

Jean-Paul Sartre said that Camus needed someone to accuse, and "If it's not you, it will therefore be the universe." To which Camus replied that everyone needs to be innocent at any price, even if "one must accuse humankind and the sky."

—quoted in Camus's biography by Herbert R. Lottman

"The struggle towards the summits itself suffices to fill a man's heart."

—Albert Camus, inscription on his tombstone from *The Myth of Sisyphus*

"I rebel—therefore we exist."

—Albert Camus, *The Rebel*

"He who despairs because of the news is a coward, but he who sees hope in the human condition is mad."

—Albert Camus

"Camus continues to *think* despair, even to write it; but he *lives* hope."

—a friend of Camus

"His judgment pierced me like a sword and called in question my very right to exist. And it was true, I hadn't always realized that: I hadn't any right to exist. I had appeared by chance, I existed like a stone, a plant, a microbe. My life grew in a haphazard way and in all directions. Sometimes it sent me vague signals; at other times I could feel nothing but an inconsequential buzzing. I was just thinking . . . that here we are, all of us, eating and drinking, to preserve our precious existence, and that there's nothing, nothing, absolutely no reason for existing."

—Roquentin, in Jean-Paul Sartre's *Nausea*

"Hope is a good breakfast, but it is a bad supper."

—Francis Bacon

"I proclaim that I believe in nothing and that everything is absurd, but I cannot doubt the validity of my own proclamation and I am compelled to believe, at least, in my own protest."

—Albert Camus, *The Rebel*

"The greatest mystery is not that we have been flung at random among the profusion of the earth and the galaxy of the stars, but that in this prison we can fashion images of ourselves sufficiently powerful to deny our nothingness."

—French Minister of Culture André Malraux
in "The Walnut Trees of Attenberg"

"How great are the works of men, but how small the men themselves appear!"

—Max Weber, on crossing New York's Brooklyn Bridge
and viewing Wall Street

QUESTIONS FOR THOUGHT AND DISCUSSION

1. In the second paragraph, Dr. Rieux answers Tarrou's question of why he, not believing in God, helps people. What does he say? Why doesn't he believe in God? Is his view of the Catholic position fair?

2. What does Rieux mean that he is "fighting against creation as he found it"? How do you understand the word "creation" here?

3. Against whom or what is Rieux defending the victims of the plague? Does he see himself as successful? Are you attracted or repelled by Rieux's courage without hope?

4. Read the full paragraph starting "After all . . ." What strikes you about what he is saying? What has made him into this rebel against the world?

5. How would you describe Rieux's worldview? What does he believe about the meaning of life? Suffering? What is compelling him to help others?

6. Compare this active response to the passive Buddhist response entailed in pursuing Nirvana. Which do you think is more human? More practical?

7. How would you describe the differences between this worldview and Bertrand Russell's?

8. Do you think everyone is capable of such lonely heroism? How would most people react in such a lonely situation?

❧ C. S. Lewis ❧

C. S. Lewis was introduced earlier in part 1. A "lapsed atheist" who became a Christian, he is the twentieth century's most widely read spokesman for the biblical family of faiths, including Judaism and the Christian faith. The following essay is a tour de force demonstration of how differences in beliefs make a difference in behavior—both for individuals and societies. Lewis introduces here a key theme in the biblical response to evil and suffering—its bifocal vision or "blessedly two-edged character." Because of the twin truths of Creation and Fall, the biblical faiths—unlike the Eastern and secularist—view evil and suffering as alien and unnatural.

IN, BUT NOT OF

"It was within a Western Christian setting that our technological civilization came to birth, and this was no accident, because Christianity is both this-worldly and other-worldly."

—R. C. Zaehner, Spalding Professor of Eastern Religions, Oxford University

Some Thoughts ❧

At first sight nothing seems more obvious than that religious persons should care for the sick; no Christian building, except perhaps a church, is more self-explanatory than a Christian hospital.

At first sight nothing seems more obvious than that religious persons should care for the sick; no Christian building, except perhaps a church, is more self-explanatory than a Christian hospital. Yet on further consideration the thing is really connected with the undying paradox, the blessedly two-edged character, of Christianity. And if any of us were now encountering Christianity for the first time he would be vividly aware of this paradox.

Let us suppose that such a person began by observing those Christian activities which are, in a sense, directed towards this present world. He would find that this religion had, as a mere matter of historical fact, been the agent which preserved such secular civilization as survived the fall of the Roman Empire; that to it Europe owes the salvation, in those perilous ages, of civilized agriculture, architecture, laws, and literacy itself. He would find that this same religion has always been healing the sick and caring for the poor; that it has, more than any other, blessed marriage; and that arts and philosophy tend to flourish in its neighborhood. In a word, it is always either doing, or at least repenting with shame for not having done, all the things which secular humanitarianism enjoins. If our inquirer stopped at this point he would have no difficulty in classifying Christianity—giving it its place on a map of the "great religions." Obviously (he would say), this is one of the world-affirming religions like Confucianism or the agricultural religions of the great Mesopotamian city states.

But how if our inquirer began (as he well might) with quite a different series of Christian phenomena? He might notice that the central image in all Christian art was that of a Man slowly dying by torture; that the instrument of this torture was the world-wide symbol of the Faith; that martyrdom was almost a specifically Christian action; that our calendar was as full of fasts as of feasts; that we meditated constantly on the mortality not only of ourselves but of the whole universe; that we were bidden to entrust all our treasure to another world; and that even a certain disdain for the whole natural order (*contemptus mundi*) had sometimes been reckoned a Christian virtue. And here, once again, if he knew no more, the inquirer would find Christianity quite easy to classify; but this time he would classify it as one of the world-denying religions. It would be pigeon-holed along with Buddhism.

Either conclusion would be justified if a man had only the one or the other half of the evidence before him. It is when he puts both halves together and sees that Christianity cuts right across the classification he was attempting to make—it is then that he first knows what he is up against, and I think he will be bewildered.

Probably most of those who read this page have been Christians all their lives. If so, they may find it hard to sympathize with the bewilderment I refer to. To Christians the explanation of this two-edged character in their Faith seems obvious. They live in a graded or hierarchical universe where there is a place for everything and everything should be kept in its right place. The Supernatural is higher than the Natural, but each has its place; just as a man is higher than a dog, but a dog has its place. It is, therefore, to us not at all surprising that healing for the sick and provision for the poor should be less important than (when they are, as sometimes happens, alternative to) the salvation of souls; and yet very important. Because God created the Natural—invented it out of His love and artistry—it demands our reverence; because it is only a creature and not He, it is, from another point of view, of little account. And still more, because Nature, and especially human nature, is fallen it must be corrected and the evil within it must be mortified. But its essence is good; correction is something quite different from Manichaean repudiation or Stoic superiority. Hence, in all true Christian asceticism, that respect for the thing rejected which, I think, we never

In a word, it is always either doing, or at least repenting with shame for not having done, all the things which secular humanitarianism enjoins. If our inquirer stopped at this point he would have no difficulty in classifying Christianity—giving it its place on a map of the "great religions." Obviously (he would say), this is one of the world-affirming religions like Confucianism.

find in pagan asceticism. Marriage is good, though not for me; wine is good, though I must not drink it; feasts are good, though today we fast.

SILLY OLE BOMB

C. S. Lewis was asked by an interviewer during World War II what he would think if the Germans got the atom bomb, dropped one on England, and he saw it falling right on top of him. "If you only had time for one last thought, what would it be?" Lewis replied that he would look up at the bomb, stick out his tongue at it, and say, "Pooh! You're only a bomb. I'm an immortal soul."

This attitude will, I think, be found to depend logically on the doctrines of the Creation and the Fall. Some hazy adumbrations of a doctrine of the Fall can be found in Paganism; but it is quite astonishing how rarely outside Christianity we find—I am not sure that we ever find—a real doctrine of Creation. In Polytheism the gods are usually the product of a universe already in existence—Keats' *Hyperion,* in spirit, if not in detail, is true enough as a picture of pagan theogony. In Pantheism the universe is never something that God made. It is an emanation, something that oozes out of Him, or an appearance, something He looks like to us but really is not, or even an attack of incurable schizophrenia from which He is unaccountably suffering. Polytheism is always, in the long run, nature-worship; Pantheism always, in the long run, hostility to nature. None of these beliefs really leaves you free *both* to enjoy your breakfast *and* to mortify your inordinate appetites—much less to mortify appetites recognized as innocent at present lest they should become inordinate.

And none of them leaves anyone free to do what is being done in the Lourdes Hospital every day: to fight against death as earnestly, skillfully, and calmly as if you were a secular humanitarian while knowing all the time that death is, both for better and worse, something that the secular humanitarian has never dreamed of. The world, knowing how all our real investments are beyond the grave, might expect us to be less concerned than other people who go in for what is called Higher Thought and tell us that "death doesn't matter"; but we "are not high minded," [Psalm 131: 1] and we follow One who stood and wept at the grave of Lazarus—not surely, because He was grieved that Mary and Martha wept, and sorrowed for their lack of faith (though some thus interpret) but because death, the punishment of sin, is even more horrible in His eyes than in ours. The nature which He had created as God, the nature which He had assumed as Man, lay there before Him in its ignominy; a foul smell, food for worms. Though He was to revive it a moment later, He wept at the shame; if I may here quote a writer of my own communion, "I am not so much afraid of death as ashamed of it."

And that brings us again to the paradox. Of all men, we hope most of death; yet nothing will reconcile us to—well, its *unnaturalness*. We know that we were not made for it; we know how it crept into our destiny as an intruder; and we know Who has defeated it. Because Our Lord is risen we know that on one level it is an enemy already disarmed; but because we know that the natural level also is God's creation we cannot cease to fight against the death which mars it, as against all those other blemishes upon it, against pain and poverty, barbarism and ignorance. Because we love something else more than this world we love even this world better than those who know no other.

Of all men, we hope most of death; yet nothing will reconcile us to—well, its unnaturalness. We know that we were not made for it; we know how it crept into our destiny as an intruder; and we know Who has defeated it.

C. S. Lewis, "Some Thoughts," *God in the Dock* (Grand Rapids: William B. Eerdmans Publishing Company, 1983). Copyright © 1970 by C. S. Lewis Pte. Ltd. Reprinted by permission.

LIFE OUGHT TO BE OTHERWISE

"At the maddening center of despair is the insistent instinct—again, I can put it no other way—of a broken contract. Of an appalling and specific cataclysm. In the futile scream of the child, in the mute agony of the tortured animal, sounds the 'background noise' of a horror after creation, after being torn loose from the logic and repose of nothingness. Something—how helpless language can be—has gone hideously wrong. Reality should, could have been, otherwise. . . . The impotent fury, the guilt which master and surpass my identity carry with them the working hypothesis, the 'working metaphor,' if you will, of 'original sin.'"

—George Steiner, *Errata*

"Death makes me very angry. Premature death makes me angrier still."

—Larry Ellison, chairman of Oracle

"I first encountered the human implications of this belief many years ago through an older and wiser friend in Switzerland. We were together when he was told the news of a well-known Christian leader whose son was killed in a cycling accident. The leader had been devastated, but became the quiet admiration of all when he summoned up his strength, suppressed his grief, and preached eloquently on hope at his son's funeral. 'I trust he feels the same thing inside,' was my friend's quiet comment.

"Several weeks later my friend received a telephone call from the Christian leader. Could he come and talk to him? We welcomed him and he went in to talk with my friend, but after a few minutes the rest of us left the house altogether. The walls of chalets are thin and what we heard was not the hope of the preacher but the hurt of the father—pained and furious at God, dark and bilious in his blasphemy.

"My friend's response was not to rebuke him but to point him to the story told of Jesus at the tomb of his friend Lazarus. Three times it says in the account in the Gospel of John that Jesus was angry. One of the words used is the Greek term for 'furious indignation'—the word used by Aeschylus to describe war horses rearing up on their hind legs, snorting through their nostrils, and charging into battle. Face to face

> with death, Jesus of Nazareth utters no pieties about faith and hope. The world God had created good and beautiful and whole was now broken and in ruins. In moments he was going to do something, but Jesus' first response was outrage—instinctive, blazing outrage. Clearly, death was even worse in his eyes than ours. The world and life should have been otherwise, and those whose faith is too pious to feel outrage are too pious by half and harder on themselves than God is."
>
> —Os Guinness, *Long Journey Home*

QUESTIONS FOR THOUGHT AND DISCUSSION

1. Read the box, "In, But Not Of." What do you think of R. C. Zaehner's statement? Why would this be so?
2. What does C. S. Lewis mean by the "blessedly two-edged character, of Christianity"? What are the two edges?
3. What are the this-worldly, or "world-affirming," contributions of the Christian faith that Lewis lists? What are the other-worldly, or "world-denying," attributes? Do you agree?
4. What aspects of the world-affirming character of the Christian faith do you see in the history of your own country?
5. What are the biblical truths that lie behind this "two-edged character"? What are the practical consequences of the Christian faith being both this- and other-worldly?
6. Given the other-worldly concerns of Christians, how might others expect them to see and react to death?
7. Read the box, "Life Ought to Be Otherwise." What is the significance of Jesus' reaction to the death of Lazarus, even knowing he would live again? Compare Jesus' reaction to that of Camus's Dr. Rieux.
8. What do you think of Lewis's statement that in the Christian view death is unnatural? What difference would that make for facing it?
9. In your experience and among your friends, has the Christian faith, on balance, been a force for good or evil? If the latter, was the bad evidence a reflection or a contradiction of Christian beliefs?

THE PRACTICE OF TRUTH CUTS TWO WAYS

"By this all men will know that you are my disciples, if you love one another."

—Jesus, John 13:35

"If we would bring the Turks to Christianity, we must first be Christians."

—Erasmus

"Christianity must be divine, since it has lasted 1,700 years despite the fact that it is so full of villainy."

—Voltaire

"If men are so wicked with religion, what would they be without it?"

—Benjamin Franklin

"Every Stoic was a Stoic, but in Christendom, where is the Christian?"

—Ralph Waldo Emerson

"In truth there was only *one* Christian, and he died on the cross."

—Friedrich Nietzsche

"A Christian is one who believes the New Testament is a divinely inspired book admirably suited to the spiritual needs of his neighbor."

—Ambrose Bierce

"Christianity might be a good thing if anyone ever tried it."

—George Bernard Shaw

"The Christian ideal has not been tried and found wanting. It has been found difficult; and left untried."

—G. K. Chesterton

"If ever the book which I am not going to write is written, it must be the full confession by Christendom to Christendom's specific contribution to the sum of human cruelty and treachery. Large areas of the world will not hear us until we have publicly disowned much of our past. Why should they? We have shouted the name of Christ and enacted the service of Moloch."

—C. S. Lewis

"Take the case of a sour old maid, who is a Christian, but cantankerous. On the other hand, take some pleasant and popular fellow, but who has never been to Church. Who knows how much more cantankerous the old maid might be if she were *not* a Christian, and how much more likeable the nice fellow might be if he *were* a Christian? You can't judge Christianity simply by comparing the *product* in these two people; you would need to know what kind of raw material Christ was working on in both cases."

—C. S. Lewis, *God in the Dock*

"'I believe in the Holy Catholic Church,' and I only regret it does not exist."

—Archbishop William Temple

"For God's sake don't touch the Church of England! It is the only thing that stands between us and Christianity!"

—C. E. M. Joad, in his agnostic days

"Every day people are straying away from the church and going back to God."

—comedian Lenny Bruce

❋ C. S. Lewis ❋

This reading by C. S. Lewis is from his much loved, best-selling children's classic The Lion, the Witch, and the Wardrobe *(1950), which is the second of the seven-book series* The Chronicles of Narnia. *It captures a key aspect of the biblical view of evil: God cares and intervenes. In the story, the schoolboy Edmund, allured by the promises of the White Witch, has "joined her side" and betrayed his brother and sisters to her. In the passage below, Edmund has been rescued from the Witch by Aslan the lion, the Lord of the whole wood. The White Witch has come to claim vengeance against him.*

CLOSE AND CARING

"I have indeed seen the misery of my people in Egypt. I have heard them crying out because of their slave drivers, and I am concerned about their suffering. So I have come down to rescue them from the hand of the Egyptians."

—Exodus 3:7

"What other nation is so great as to have their gods near them the way the LORD our God is near us whenever we pray to him?"

—Deuteronomy 4:7

The Lion, the Witch, and the Wardrobe ✍

"You have a traitor there, Aslan," said the Witch. Of course everyone present knew that she meant Edmund. But Edmund had got past thinking about himself after all he'd been through and after the talk he'd had that morning. He just went on looking at Aslan. It didn't seem to matter what the Witch said.

"Well," said Aslan, "his offense was not against you."

"Have you forgotten the Deep Magic?" asked the Witch.

"Let us say I have forgotten it," answered Aslan gravely. "Tell us of this Deep Magic."

"Tell you?" said the Witch, her voice growing suddenly shriller. "Tell you what is written on that very Table of Stone which stands beside us? Tell you what is written in letters deep as a spear is long on the trunk of the World Ash Tree? Tell you what is engraved on the scepter of the Emperor-Beyond-the-Sea? You at least know the magic which the Emperor put into Narnia at the very beginning. You know that every traitor belongs to me as my lawful prey and that for every treachery I have a right to a kill."

"Oh," said Mr. Beaver. "So *that's* how you came to imagine yourself a Queen—because you were the Emperor's hangman. I see."

"Peace, Beaver," said Aslan, with a very low growl.

"And so," continued the Witch, "that Human creature is mine. His life is forfeit to me. His blood is my property."

"Come and take it then," said the Bull-with-the-man's-head in a great bellowing voice.

"Fool," said the Witch with a savage smile that was almost a snarl, "do you really think your master can rob me of my rights by mere force? He knows the Deep Magic better than that. He knows that unless I have blood as the Law says, all Narnia will be overturned and perish in fire and water."

"It is very true," said Aslan; "I do not deny it."

"Oh, Aslan!" whispered Susan in the Lion's ear. "Can't we—I mean, you won't, will you? Can't we do something about the Deep Magic? Isn't there something you can work against it?"

"Work against the Emperor's magic?" said Aslan, turning to her with something like a frown on his face. And nobody ever made that suggestion to him again. . . .

[That night, only Edmund's sisters, Susan and Lucy, follow Aslan to see how he will preserve Edmund's rescue.] When once Aslan had been tied (and tied so that he was really a mass of cords) on the flat stone, a hush fell on the crowd. Four hags, holding four torches, stood at the corners of the Table. The Witch bared her arms as she had bared them the previous night when it had been Edmund instead of Aslan. Then she began to whet her knife. It looked to the children, when the gleam of the torchlight fell on it, as if the knife were made of stone not of steel, and it was of a strange and evil shape.

At last she drew near. She stood by Aslan's head. Her face was working and twitching with passion, but his looked up at the sky, still quiet, neither angry nor afraid, but a little sad. Then, just before she gave the blow, she stooped down and said in a quivering voice,

"And now, who has won? Fool, did you think that by all this you would save the human traitor? Now I will kill you instead of him as our pact was, and

"You know that every traitor belongs to me as my lawful prey and that for every treachery I have a right to a kill."
—THE WITCH

"Fool, . . . do you really think your master can rob me of my rights by mere force? He knows the Deep Magic better than that. He knows that unless I have blood as the Law says, all Narnia will be overturned and perish in fire and water."
—THE WITCH

so the Deep Magic will be appeased. But when you are dead what will prevent me from killing him as well? And who will take him out of my hand *then*? Understand that you have given me Narnia forever, you have lost your own life, and you have not saved his. In that knowledge, despair and die."

The children did not see the actual moment of the killing. They couldn't bear to look and had covered their eyes. . . .

They walked to the eastern edge of the hill and looked down. The one big star had almost disappeared. The country all looked dark gray but beyond, at the very end of the world, the sea showed pale. The sky began to turn red. They walked to and fro more times than they could count between the dead Aslan and the eastern ridge, trying to keep warm; and oh, how tired their legs felt. Then at last, as they stood for a moment looking out toward to sea and Cair Paravel (which they could now just make out), the red turned to gold along the line where the sea and the sky met and very slowly up came the edge of the sun. At that moment they heard from behind them a loud noise—a great cracking, deafening noise as if a giant had broken a giant's plate.

"What's that?" said Lucy, clutching Susan's arm.

"I—I feel afraid to turn round," said Susan. "Something awful is happening."

"They're doing something worse to *him*," said Lucy. "Come on!" And she turned, pulling Susan round with her.

The rising of the sun had made everything look so different—all the colors and shadows were changed—that for a moment they didn't see the important thing. Then they did. The Stone Table was broken into two pieces by a great crack that ran down it from end to end; and there was no Aslan.

"Oh, oh, oh!" cried the two girls, rushing back to the Table.

"Oh, it's *too* bad," sobbed Lucy. "They might have left the body alone."

"Who's done it?" cried Susan. "What does it mean? Is it more magic?"

"Yes!" said a great voice behind their backs. "It is more magic." They looked round. There, shining in the sunrise, larger than they had seen him before, shaking his mane (for it had apparently grown again), stood Aslan himself.

"Oh, Aslan!" cried both the children, staring up at him, almost as much frightened as they were glad.

"Aren't you dead then, dear Aslan?" said Lucy.

"Not now," said Aslan.

"You're not—not a—?" asked Susan in a shaky voice. She couldn't bring herself to say the word *ghost*.

Aslan stooped his golden head and licked her forehead. The warmth of his breath and a rich sort of smell that seemed to hang about his hair came all over her.

"Do I look it?" he said.

"Oh, you're real, you're real! Oh, Aslan!" cried Lucy, and both girls flung themselves upon him and covered him with kisses.

"But what does it all mean?" asked Susan when they were somewhat calmer.

"It means," said Aslan, "that though the Witch knew the Deep Magic, there is a magic deeper still which she did not know. Her knowledge goes back only to the dawn of Time. But if she could have looked a little further back into the stillness and the darkness before Time dawned, she would have read there a different incantation. She would have known that when a willing victim who had committed no treachery was killed in a traitor's stead, the Table would crack and Death itself would start working backward."

BEARING IT

"In the picture the face is fearfully crushed by blows, swollen, covered with fearful, swollen, and blood-stained bruises, the eyes are open and squinting: the great wide-open whites of the eyes glitter with a sort of deathly, glassy light."

—Fyodor Dostoyevsky,
meditation on Hans Holbein's "Descent from the Cross,"
by which he came to faith through "the hell-fire of doubt"

"I do not know the answer to the problem of evil, but I do know love."

—Alyosha, in Dostoyevsky's *The Brothers Karamazov*

"All the other Distance
He hath traversed first—
No New Mile remaineth—."

—Emily Dickinson

"I have never thought that a Christian would be free of suffering, *umfundisi.* For our Lord suffered, not to save us from suffering, but to teach us how to bear suffering. For he knew that there is no life without suffering."

—Alan Paton, *Cry, The Beloved Country*

"I had an inkling of the reaction of the plague-stricken and dying sufferers in the sixteenth century. On this altar they saw their God, with the same suppurating ulcers as their own."

—Henri Nouwen, contemplating the Isenheimer Altar,
by Matthais Grünwald, in Colmar

QUESTIONS FOR THOUGHT AND DISCUSSION

1. What is the offense C. S. Lewis refers to in the opening paragraphs? Who was the offense against? Does the Witch deserve Edmund's life?

2. What does Lewis mean by "the Deep Magic" that puts Edmund irretrievably into the Witch's power?

3. What is the Law of the Deep Magic? Why can't Aslan get around the Law? What are the consequences should he try? What does he decide to do?

4. What is the deeper magic that the Witch did not know of? What did she think was going to happen? What did the deeper magic do?

5. What does the Table represent? What has been broken then, in the breaking of the Table?

6. How is the Law of the Deep Magic fulfilled?

7. Sacrifice is an alien notion to modern people. Do you find it repellent? How might it address dimensions of the power of evil that nothing else can reach?

8. What is Lewis saying by showing us Aslan's caring intervention?

Martin Luther King Jr.

The Rev. Dr. Martin Luther King Jr. (1928–1968) was the celebrated leader of the American civil rights movement in the mid-twentieth century. He was the son of a Baptist pastor, and earned his B.A. in sociology from Morehouse College and his Ph.D. in theology from Boston University. Thrust into prominence during the Alabama bus boycott, he had been leading his first pastorate in Montgomery for less than a year. One of the founders of the Southern Christian Leadership Conference in 1957, he inspired and supplied the philosophy of the nonviolent civil rights movement until his assassination in 1968.

King led the historic march on Washington, D.C., in 1963, where his "I Have a Dream" speech helped sway the nation against discrimination and segregation by invoking the highest ideals of America's founders. In 1964 he received the Nobel Peace Prize. President Jimmy Carter posthumously awarded him the nation's highest honor, the Medal of Freedom, and his birthday is commemorated as a national holiday.

The following reading is taken from a letter that Dr. King began to write on smuggled newspapers while jailed for civil disobedience in Birmingham, Alabama, on Good Friday, 1963. He was responding to a headline in The Birmingham News telling of fellow pastors who agreed with the aims of the civil rights movement, but as they expressed in a joint statement, not with the methods of nonviolent civil disobedience that Dr. King and those with him advocated. Going far beyond this limited point, King paints a view of the Christian faith that stirred his passion for justice and freedom.

WE SHALL NOT BE MOVED

"We will march through your dogs! And if you get some elephants, we'll march through them. And bring on your tigers and we'll march through them."

—comedian Dick Gregory, Mississippi, 1963

The opening sections looked like "a jumble of biblical phrases wrapped around pest control ads and garden club news."

—lawyer Clarence Jordan, describing King's first draft

"By degrees, King established a kind of universal voice, beyond time, beyond race. As both humble prisoner and mighty prophet, as father, harried traveler, and cornered leader, he projected a character of nearly unassailable breadth."

—Taylor Branch, *Parting the Waters*

Letter from Birmingham Jail ✎

April 16, 1963

My Dear Fellow Clergymen:

While confined here in the Birmingham city jail, I came across your recent statement calling my present activities "unwise and untimely." Seldom do I pause to answer criticism of my work and ideas. If I sought to answer all the criticisms that cross my desk, my secretaries would have little time for anything other than such correspondence in the course of the day, and I would have no time for constructive work. But since I feel that you are men of genuine good will and that your criticisms are sincerely set forth, I want to try to answer your statement in what I hope will be patient and reasonable terms.

I think I should indicate why I am here in Birmingham, since you have been influenced by the view which argues against "outsiders coming in." . . . More basically, I am in Birmingham because injustice is here. Just as the prophets of the eighth century B.C. left their villages and carried their "thus saith the Lord" far beyond the boundaries of their home towns, and just as the Apostle Paul left his village of Tarsus and carried the gospel of Jesus Christ to the far corners of the Greco-Roman world, so am I compelled to carry the gospel of freedom beyond my own home town. Like Paul, I must constantly respond to the Macedonian call for aid.

More basically, I am in Birmingham because injustice is here.

Moreover, I am cognizant of the inter-relatedness of all communities and states. I cannot sit idly by in Atlanta and not be concerned about what happens in Birmingham. Injustice anywhere is a threat to justice everywhere. We are caught in an inescapable network of mutuality, tied in a single garment of destiny. Whatever affects one directly, affects all indirectly. Never again can we afford to live with the narrow, provincial "outside agitator" idea. Anyone who lives inside the United States can never be considered an outsider anywhere within its bounds.

Injustice anywhere is a threat to justice everywhere. We are caught in an inescapable network of mutuality, tied in a single garment of destiny. Whatever affects one directly, affects all indirectly.

You deplore the demonstrations taking place in Birmingham. But your statement, I am sorry to say, fails to express a similar concern for the conditions that brought about the demonstrations. I am sure that none of you would want to rest content with the superficial kind of social analysis that deals merely with effects and does not grapple with underlying causes. It is unfortunate that demonstrations are taking place in Birmingham, but it is even more unfortunate that the city's white power structure left the Negro community with no alternative.

In any nonviolent campaign there are four basic steps: collection of the facts to determine whether injustices exist; negotiation; self-purification; and direct action. We have gone through all these steps in Birmingham. There can be no gainsaying the fact that racial injustice engulfs this community. Birmingham is probably the most thoroughly segregated city in the United States. Its ugly record of brutality is widely known. Negroes have experienced grossly unjust treatment in the courts. There have been more unsolved bombings of Negro homes and churches in Birmingham than in any other city in the nation. These are the hard brutal facts of the case. On the basis of these conditions, Negro leaders sought to negotiate with the city fathers. But the latter consistently refused to engage in good-faith negotiation. . . .

We have waited for more than 340 years for our constitutional and God-given rights. The nations of Asia and Africa are moving with jet-like speed toward gaining political independence, but we still creep at horse-and-buggy pace toward gaining a cup of coffee at a lunch counter. Perhaps it is easy for those who have never felt the stinging darts of segregation to say, "Wait." But when you have seen vicious mobs lynch your mothers and fathers at will and drown your sisters and brothers at whim; when you have seen hate-filled policemen curse, kick and even kill your black brothers and sisters; when you see the vast majority of your twenty million Negro brothers smothering in an airtight cage of poverty in the midst of an affluent society; when you suddenly find your tongue twisted and your speech stammering as you seek to explain to your six-year-old daughter why she can't go to the public amusement park that has just been advertised on television, and see tears welling up in her eyes when she is told that Funtown is closed to colored children, and see ominous clouds of inferiority beginning to form in her little mental sky, and see her beginning to distort her personality by developing an unconscious bitterness toward white people; when you have to concoct an answer for a five-year-old son who is asking "Daddy, why do white people treat colored people so mean?"; when you take a cross-country drive and find it necessary to sleep night after night in the uncomfortable corners of your automobile because no motel will accept you; when you are humiliated day in and day out by nagging signs reading "white" and "colored"; when your first name becomes "nigger," your middle name becomes "boy" (however old you are), and your last name becomes "John," and your wife and mother are never given the respected title "Mrs."; when you are harried by day and haunted by night by the fact that you are a Negro, living constantly at tiptoe stance, never quite knowing what to expect next, and are plagued with inner fears and outer resentments; when you

We have waited for more than 340 years for our constitutional and God-given rights. The nations of Asia and Africa are moving with jet-like speed toward gaining political independence, but we still creep at horse-and-buggy pace toward gaining a cup of coffee at a lunch counter.

There comes a time when the cup of endurance runs over, and men are no longer willing to be plunged into the abyss of despair.

are forever fighting a degenerating sense of "nobodiness"—then you will understand why we find it difficult to wait. There comes a time when the cup of endurance runs over, and men are no longer willing to be plunged into the abyss of despair. I hope, sirs, you can understand our legitimate and unavoidable impatience.

You express a great deal of anxiety over our willingness to break laws. This is certainly a legitimate concern. Since we so diligently urge people to obey the Supreme Court's decision of 1954 outlawing segregation in the public schools, at first glance it may seem rather paradoxical for us consciously to break laws. One may well ask: "How can you advocate breaking some laws and obeying others?" The answer lies in the fact that there are two types of laws: just and unjust. I would be the first to advocate obeying just laws. One has not only a legal but a moral responsibility to obey just laws. Conversely, one has a moral responsibility to disobey unjust laws. I would agree with St. Augustine that "an unjust law is no law at all."

Now, what is the difference between the two? How does one determine whether a law is just or unjust? A just law is a man-made code that squares with the moral law or the law of God. An unjust law is a code that is out of harmony with the moral law. To put it in the terms of St. Thomas Aquinas: An unjust law is a human law that is not rooted in eternal law and natural law. Any law that uplifts human personality is just. Any law that degrades human personality is unjust. All segregation statutes are unjust because segregation distorts the soul and damages the personality. It gives the segregator a false sense of superiority and the segregated a false sense of inferiority. . . .

A just law is a man-made code that squares with the moral law or the law of God. An unjust law is a code that is out of harmony with the moral law.

Of course, there is nothing new about this kind of civil disobedience. It was evidenced sublimely in the refusal of Shadrach, Meshach, and Abednego to obey the laws of Nebuchadnezzar, on the ground that a higher moral law was at stake. It was practiced superbly by the early Christians, who were willing to face hungry lions and the excruciating pain of chopping blocks rather than submit to certain unjust laws of the Roman Empire. To a degree, academic freedom is a reality today because Socrates practiced civil disobedience. In our own nation, the Boston Tea Party represented a massive act of civil disobedience. . . .

Human progress never rolls in on wheels of inevitability; it comes through the tireless efforts of men willing to be co-workers with God, and without this hard work, time itself becomes an ally of the forces of social stagnation.

Human progress never rolls in on wheels of inevitability; it comes through the tireless efforts of men willing to be co-workers with God, and without this hard work, time itself becomes an ally of the forces of social stagnation. We must use time creatively, in the knowledge that the time is always ripe to do right. Now is the time to make real the promise of democracy and transform our pending national elegy into a creative psalm of brotherhood. Now is the time to lift our national policy from the quicksand of racial injustice to the solid rock of human dignity. . . .

But though I was initially disappointed at being categorized as an extremist, as I continued to think about the matter I gradually gained a measure of satisfaction from the label. Was not Jesus an extremist for love: "Love your enemies, bless them that curse you, do good to them that hate you, and pray for them which despitefully use you, and persecute you." Was not Amos an extremist for justice: "Let justice roll down like waters and righteousness like an ever-flowing stream." Was not Paul an extremist for the Christian gospel: "I bear in my body the marks of the Lord Jesus." Was not Martin Luther an extremist: "Here I stand; I cannot do otherwise, so help me God." And John Bunyan: "I will stay in jail to the end of my days before I make a butchery of my conscience." And Abraham Lincoln: "This nation cannot survive half slave and half free." And Thomas Jefferson: "We hold these truths to be self-evident, that all men are created equal. . . ." So the question is not whether we will be extremists, but what kind of extremists we will be. Will we be extremists for hate or for love? Will we be extremists for the preservation of injustice or for the extension of justice? In that dramatic scene on Calvary's hill three men were crucified. We must never forget that all three were crucified for the same crime—the crime of extremism. Two were extremists for immorality, and thus fell below their environment. The other, Jesus Christ, was an extremist for love, truth, and goodness, and thereby rose above his environment. Perhaps the South, the nation, and the world are in dire need of creative extremists. . . .

There was a time when the church was very powerful—in the time when the early Christians rejoiced at being deemed worthy to suffer for what they believed. In those days the church was not merely a thermometer that recorded the ideas and principles of popular opinion; it was a thermostat that transformed the mores of society. Whenever the early Christians entered a town, the people in power became disturbed and immediately sought to convict the Christians for being "disturbers of the peace" and "outside agitators." But the Christians pressed on, in the conviction that they were "a colony of heaven," called to obey God rather than man. Small in number, they were big in commitment. They were too God-intoxicated to be "astronomically intimidated." By their effort and example they brought an end to such ancient evils as infanticide and gladiatorial contests. . . .

In those days the church was not merely a thermometer that recorded the ideas and principles of popular opinion; it was a thermostat that transformed the mores of society.

I hope the church as a whole will meet the challenge of this decisive hour. But even if the church does not come to the aid of justice, I have no despair about the future. I have no fear about the outcome of our struggle in Birmingham, even if our motives are at present misunderstood. We will reach the goal of freedom in Birmingham and all over the nation, because the goal of America is freedom. Abused and scorned though we may be, our destiny is tied up with America's destiny. Before the pilgrims landed at Plymouth, we were here. Before the pen of Jefferson etched the majestic words of the Declaration of Independence across the pages of history, we were here. For more than two centuries our forebears labored in this country without wages; they made cotton king; they built the homes of their masters while suffering gross injustice and shameful humiliation—and yet out of a bottomless vitality they continued to thrive and develop. If the inexpressible cruelties of slavery could not stop us, the opposition we now face will surely fail. We will win our freedom because the sacred heritage of our nation and the eternal will of God are embodied in our echoing demands. . . .

We will win our freedom because the sacred heritage of our nation and the eternal will of God are embodied in our echoing demands.

I wish you had commended the Negro sit-inners and demonstrators of Birmingham for their sublime courage, their willingness to suffer, and their amazing discipline in the midst of great provocation. One day the South will recognize its real heroes. They will be the James Merediths, with the noble sense of purpose that enables them to face jeering and hostile mobs, and with the agonizing loneliness that characterizes the life of the pioneer. They will be old, oppressed, battered Negro women, symbolized in a seventy-two-year-old woman in Montgomery, Alabama, who rose up with a sense of dignity and with her people decided not to ride segregated buses, and who responded with ungrammatical profundity to one who inquired about her weariness: "My feet is tired, but my soul is at rest." They will be the young high school and college students, the young ministers of the gospel, and a host of their elders, courageously and nonviolently sitting in at lunch counters and willingly going to jail for conscience' sake. One day the South will know that when these disinherited children of God sat down at lunch counters, they were in reality standing up for what is best in the American dream and for the most sacred values in our Judaeo-Christian heritage, thereby bringing our nation back to those great wells of democracy which were dug deep by the founding fathers in their formulation of the Constitution and the Declaration of Independence.

"My feet is tired, but my soul is at rest."
—*A MONTGOMERY WOMAN*

YOU CAN'T WIN

"This is what you get when you try to do something. You get it from both sides."

—Bishop James Carpenter,
one of those to whom the letter was addressed

QUESTIONS FOR THOUGHT AND DISCUSSION

1. What biblical precedents does Martin Luther King Jr. cite to explain his presence in Birmingham?

2. What are the four basic steps King takes in his campaigns of non-violence? How do they strike you?

3. Read the two paragraphs starting "You express a great deal of anxiety . . ." What reasoning does he give for civil disobedience? What are the two kinds of laws according to King? What do you think of this reasoning?

4. What biblical examples does King give for civil disobedience? Where did these people get the courage to go against the law?

5. King said, "the question is not whether we will be extremists, but what kind of extremists we will be." What does he mean? What biblical and historical models does he mention as examples of extremism? What do you think of his argument?

6. Do you think most Christians today are, in Dr. King's words, like "thermometers" or "thermostats"?

7. How does King's letter relate to Lewis's "two-edged character" of the Christian faith? What is King's approach to suffering? What does this say for how he sees life in this world? In the other world?

8. In looking back over the letter, how would you say King sees the connection between his faith and his activism?

POINT TO PONDER:

The Image and the Mirror Image

One problem of considering various answers through single readings is that we lose the sense of real life, of the unbreakable links between beliefs and behavior and between different faiths and the civilizations that are the fruit of their seeds.

A simple corrective is to look not only at the positive effects of faith in the life of a civilization but also at the negative effects of its disappearance. The consequences of its absence can be just as illuminating—and a great deal more compelling—than the consequences of its presence.

The next readings by Heinrich Heine and Friedrich Nietzsche illustrate this well. Neither was a Christian—Nietzsche in fact despised the Christian faith—but both had a clear picture of what happens when God "dies" for a civilization. In other words, they understand the effects when faith in God declines to the point at which it is no longer culturally compelling and authoritative.

Both are especially scornful of those who say "God is dead" and every-thing goes on as before—in Nietzsche's words, those "odious windbags of progressive optimism" who think it possible to have Christian morality with-out Christian faith.

PULLING OUT THE RUG

"They are rid of the Christian God and now believe all the more firmly that they must cling to the Christian morality. . . . When one gives up the Christian faith, one pulls the right to Christian morality out from under one's feet."

—Friedrich Nietzsche, *Twilight of the Idols*

It is often said that the twentieth century was one long footnote on Nietzsche's predictions. But the result of Heine's and Nietzsche's realism is a mirror-image witness to faith.

IF GOD IS "DEAD," IS EVERYTHING THE SAME?

God is "inconceivable" and immortality "unbelievable" but duty is nonetheless "peremptory and absolute."

—George Eliot

"The people I respect most behave as if they were immortal and as if society were eternal. Both assumptions are false: both of them must be accepted as true if we are to go on eating and working and loving, and are to keep open a few breathing holes for the human spirit."

—novelist and humanist E. M. Forster

"The Good Pagan is like the jealous lover who has killed his beloved to keep her all his own. He holds her body cold and inanimate, he is the master of the lifeless thing, but all that made her what she was has gone. He holds an empty likeness in his arms and soon even that will perish and putrefy."

—Rosalind Murray, *The Good Pagan's Failure*

"That is rather like the woman in the first war who said that if there were a bread shortage it would not bother her house because they always ate toast."

—C. S. Lewis

"God does not die on the day when we cease to believe in a personal deity, but we die on the day when our lives cease to be illumined by the steady radiance, renewed daily, of a wonder, the source of which is beyond all reason."

—Dag Hammarskjöld, *Markings*

❊ Heinrich Heine ❊

Heinrich Heine (1797–1856) was a German poet and essayist who was seminal to the Romantic movement in Germany. At seventeen he studied banking but later failed in his own trading business. At twenty-four he turned to law and earned his doctoral degree in 1825. His first love was poetry, however, and he earned great attention from the time of his first collection of poems, Gedichte (or "History"), in 1821. His revolutionary opinions prevented him from gaining official employment in Germany, but the social revolutions in Paris excited him and he traveled there in 1831, never to return to his homeland. Becoming more involved in politics than literature, he became the leader of the cosmopolitan democratic movement (the same movement that Victor Hugo portrayed in Les Misérables).

Heine was soberly realistic about just what a reawakening of paganism would mean. As you read this passage, remember that Heine was not a Christian believer and that he wrote these words more than a hundred years before the dark events of the twentieth century.

The Re-awakening of Paganism ❧

LAST RITES

"Do you hear the little bell tinkle? Kneel down—One brings the sacraments for a dying God."

—Heinrich Heine, 1832

And should ever that taming talisman break— the Cross—then will come roaring back the wild madness of the ancient warriors, with all their insane, Berserker rage.

It is to the great merit of Christianity that it has somewhat attenuated the brutal German lust for battle. But it could not destroy it entirely. And should ever that taming talisman break—the Cross—then will come roaring back the wild madness of the ancient warriors, with all their insane, Berserker rage, of whom our Nordic poets speak and sing. That talisman is now already crumbling, and the day is not far off when it shall break apart entirely. On that day, the old stone gods will rise from their long forgotten wreckage and rub from their eyes the dust of a thousand years' sleep. At long last leaping to life, Thor with his giant hammer will crush the gothic cathedrals. And laugh not at my forebodings, the advice of a dreamer who warns you away from the Kants and

Fichtes of the world, and from our philosophers of nature. No, laugh not at the visionary who knows that in the realm of phenomena comes soon the revolution that has already taken place in the realm of spirit. For thought goes before deed as lightning before thunder. There will be played in Germany a play compared to which the French revolution was but an innocent idyll.

Heinrich Heine, translated by Jeffrey Burke Satinover, in *The Empty Self: Gnostic Foundations of Modern Identity* (Boone, NC: Hamewith Books, 1994), pp. 32–33. Copyright © 1994 by Jeffrey Burke Satinover. Reprinted with permission.

No, laugh not at the visionary who knows that in the realm of phenomena comes soon the revolution that has already taken place in the realm of spirit. For thought goes before deed as lightning before thunder. There will be played in Germany a play compared to which the French revolution was but an innocent idyll.

CIVILIZATION BY EFFORT, CHAOS BY DEFAULT

"One of the most dangerous errors instilled into us by nineteenth-century progressive optimism is the idea that civilization is automatically bound to increase and spread. The lesson of history is the opposite; civilization is a rarity, attained with difficulty and easily lost. The normal state of humanity is barbarism, just as the normal surface of our planet is salt water."

—C. S. Lewis, *Rehabilitations*

QUESTIONS FOR THOUGHT AND DISCUSSION

1. What does Heinrich Heine see as the social influence of the Christian faith on the social fabric of Germany?

2. What does he see as the logic of barbarism? What was the "Beserker" world? How does Heine see Germany returning to that world?

3. What does he mean by "For thought goes before deed as lightning before thunder"? How do you understand his statement, "There will be played in Germany a play compared to which the French revolution was but an innocent idyll"?

4. What do you think of Heine's prediction, 100 years before Nazism and 110 years before the death camps? Where do you see the barbarism arising in the culture preceding Nazism?

5. Heine specifically mentions the gentling of European tribalism through the Cross. Can you think of other Christian truths that have been decisive in shaping European and North American civilization? What would happen if they were to disappear altogether?

6. Why do you think pagan gods reemerge when faith in the biblical God disappears in a culture?

Friedrich Nietzsche

Friedrich Wilhelm Nietzsche (1844–1900) was one of the most influential philosophers, writers, and iconoclasts of the nineteenth century. His influence is still profound a century later. He probably did as much as any thinker to overturn the foundations of Western civilization—natural law, the Christian faith, and liberal democracy—among intellectuals and pave the way for the more nihilistic philosophies of the twentieth century. Nietzsche was raised in Röcken, Saxony, where his father was a Lutheran pastor. A brilliant student at the universities of Bonn and Leipzig, he became professor of philology at the University of Basel at the age of twenty-four. He became a Swiss citizen and served in the Franco-Prussian War in 1870 but had to return to his university because of poor health.

Nietzsche became irreparably insane in 1889, but in the sixteen preceding years he wrote uncategorizable, unconventional works that, among other things, announced the "death of God" and explored unflinchingly and prophetically what all this meant for the Western world. Some of his major works are The Gay Science *(1882; sometimes translated as* The Joyful Wisdom*),* Thus Spake Zarathustra *(1883, which inspired composer Richard Strauss to create an orchestral piece, part of which became the well-known theme of the film* 2001: A Space Odyssey*),* Beyond Good and Evil *(1886), and in the last year of his sanity,* Twilight of the Idols *and* The Anti-Christ.

Nietzsche was a self-proclaimed "anti-Christ," yet he had no time for complacent middle-class thinking that could say, "God is dead" and go on living as before. If God was "dead" for Western culture, then nothing was the same. It was time to face the consequences.

WHY I AM A DESTINY

"I know my fate. One day there will be associated with my name the recollection of something frightful—of a crisis like no other before on earth, of the profoundest collision of conscience, of a decision evoked *against* everything that until then had been believed in, demanded, sanctified. I am not a man, I am dynamite. . . . I contradict as has never been contradicted and am none the less the opposite of a negative spirit. I am a *bringer of good tidings* such as there has never been, I know tasks from such a height that any conception of them has hitherto been lacking; only after me is it possible to hope again. With all that I am necessarily a man of fatality. For when truth steps into battle with the lie of millennia we shall have convulsions, an earthquake spasm, a transposition of valley and mountain such as has never been dreamed of. The concept politics has then become completely absorbed into a war of spirits, all the power-structures of the old society have been blown into the air—they one and all reposed on the lie: there will be wars such as there have never yet been on earth. Only after me will there be *grand politics* on earth."

—Friedrich Nietzsche, *Ecce Homo*, written only months before he went insane

The Parable of the Madman

Have you ever heard of the madman who on a bright morning lighted a lantern and ran to the market-place calling out unceasingly: "I seek God! I seek God!"—As there were many people standing about who did not believe in God, he caused a great deal of amusement. Why! is he lost? said one. Has he strayed away like a child? said another. Or does he keep himself hidden? Is he afraid of us? Has he taken a sea-voyage? Has he emigrated?—the people cried out laughingly, all in a hubbub. The insane man jumped into their midst and transfixed them with his glances. "Where is God gone?" he called out. "I mean to tell you! *We have killed him,*—you and I! We are all his murderers! But how have we done it? How were we able to drink up the sea? Who gave us the sponge to wipe away the whole horizon? What did we do when we loosened this earth from its sun?

"Whither does it now move? Whither do we move? Away from all suns? Do we not dash on unceasingly? Backwards, sideways, forwards, in all directions? Is there still an above and below? Do we not stray, as through infinite nothingness? Does not empty space breathe upon us? Has it not become colder? Does not night come on continually, darker and darker? Shall we not have to light lanterns in the morning? Do we not hear the noise of the grave-diggers who are burying God? Do we not smell the divine putrefaction?—for even Gods putrefy! God is dead! God remains dead! And we have killed him! How shall we console ourselves, the most murderous of all murderers? The holiest and the mightiest that the world has hitherto possessed, has bled to death under our knife,—who will wipe the blood from us? With what water could we cleanse ourselves? What lustrums, what sacred games shall we have to devise? Is not the magnitude of this deed too great for us? Shall we not ourselves have to become Gods, merely to seem worthy of it? There never was a greater event,—and on account of it, all who are born after us belong to a higher history than any history hitherto!"

"Where is God gone?" he called out. "I mean to tell you! We have killed him,—you and I! We are all his murderers! But how have we done it? How were we able to drink up the sea? Who gave us the sponge to wipe away the whole horizon? What did we do when we loosened this earth from its sun?"
—THE MADMAN

"The holiest and the mightiest that the world has hitherto possessed, has bled to death under our knife,—who will wipe the blood from us? With what water could we cleanse ourselves?"
—THE MADMAN

Here the madman was silent and looked again at his hearers; they also were silent and looked at him in surprise. At last he threw his lantern on the ground, so that it broke in pieces and was extinguished. "I come too early," he then said, "I am not yet at the right time. This prodigious event is still on its way, and is traveling,—it has not yet reached men's ears. Lightning and thunder need time, the light of the stars needs time, deeds need time, even after they are done, to be seen and heard. This deed is as yet further from them than the furthest star,—and yet *they have done it!*"—It is further stated that the madman made his way into different churches on the same day, and there intoned his *Requiem aeternam deo*. When led out and called to account, he always gave the reply: "What are these churches now, if they are not the tombs and monuments of God?"—

WHAT OUR CHEERFULNESS SIGNIFIES

The most important of more recent events—that "God is dead," that the belief in the Christian God has become unworthy of belief—already begins to cast its first shadows over Europe. To the few at least whose eye, whose suspecting glance, is strong enough and subtle enough for this drama, some sun seems to have set, some old, profound confidence seems to have changed into doubt: our old world must seem to them daily more darksome, distrustful, strange, and "old." In the main, however, one may say that the event itself is far too great, too remote, too much beyond most people's power of appreciation, for one to suppose that so much as the report of it could have reached them; not to speak of many who already knew what had taken place, and what must all collapse now that this belief had been undermined,—because so much was built upon it, so much rested on it, and had become one with it: for example our entire European morality.

Even we, the born riddle-readers, who wait as it were on the mountains posted 'twixt to-day and to-morrow, and engirt by their contradiction, we, the firstlings and premature children of the coming century into whose sight especially the shadows which must forthwith envelop Europe should already have come.

This lengthy, vast and uninterrupted process of crumbling, destruction, ruin, and overthrow which is now imminent: who has realized it sufficiently to-day to have to stand up as the teacher and herald of such a tremendous logic of terror, as the prophet of a period of gloom and eclipse, the like of which has probably never taken place on earth before? . . . Even we, the born riddle-readers, who wait as it were on the mountains posted 'twixt to-day and to-morrow, and engirt by their contradiction, we, the firstlings and premature children of the coming century into whose sight especially the shadows which must forthwith envelop Europe *should* already have come—how is it that even we, without genuine sympathy for this period of gloom, contemplate its advent without any *personal* solicitude or fear?

Are we still, perhaps too much under the *immediate effects* of the event—and are these effects, especially as regards *ourselves,* perhaps the reverse of what was to be expected—not at all sad and depressing, but rather like a new and indescribable variety of light, happiness, relief, enlivenment, encouragement, and dawning day? . . . In fact, we philosophers and "free spirits" feel ourselves irradiated as by a new dawn by the report that the "old God is dead"; our hearts overflow with gratitude, astonishment, presentiment, and expectation.

At last the horizon seems open once more granting even that it is not bright; our ships can at last put out to sea in face of every danger; every hazard is again permitted to the discerner; the sea, *our* sea, again lies open before us; perhaps never before did such an "open sea" exist.—

From Friedrich Nietzsche, "The Joyful Wisdom," Sections 125 & 343, in *A Casebook on Existentialism,* William V. Spamos (New York: Crowell, 1966).

At last the horizon seems open once more granting even that it is not bright; our ships can at last put out to sea in face of every danger; every hazard is again permitted to the discerner; the sea, our *sea, again lies open before us; perhaps never before did such an "open sea" exist.*

IDEAS HAVE CONSEQUENCES

"I am absolutely convinced that the gas chambers of Auschwitz, Treblinka, and Maidanek, were ultimately prepared not in some ministry or other in Berlin, but rather at the desks and in the lecture halls of nihilistic scientists and philosophers."

—Victor Frankl, *The Doctor and the Soul*

QUESTIONS FOR THOUGHT AND DISCUSSION

1. Friedrich Nietzsche's parable opens with a crowd mocking a madman seeking God. In his response to their laughter, what is the significance of the powerful images he uses—"drink up the sea," "wipe away the whole horizon," "infinite nothingness," "grave-diggers who are burying God"?

2. What does he mean by "who will wipe the blood from us? With what water could we cleanse ourselves?" What is he saying to the smug churchgoers of the day?

3. Read from "Shall we not ourselves have to become Gods . . ." to the end of the paragraph. How do you understand this? Why must this be so?

4. In the next paragraph, he says, "This deed is as yet further from them than the furthest star,—and yet *they have done it!*" What does the madman mean?

5. Why does Nietzsche view "the death of God" as cataclysmic? What does he have to say to the "riddle-readers" or philosophers of the day? What are the "benefits" he sees of having an "open sea"? What does he mean? What does this mean for society at large?

6. Think over the century since Nietzsche wrote of "the death of God" and the experience of North America as well as Europe. Who has been more accurate—the complacent who thought everything would go on as before, even without God, or Nietzsche who saw that nothing could ever be the same?

THREE
A TIME FOR EVIDENCES

THE THIRD STAGE IN THE QUEST FOR MEANING BEGINS WHEN WE ASK WHETHER THE answer we found so illuminating at the second stage is in fact true. The answer threw light on the problem, but does it have weight? Believing it to be true would make all the difference, but can we confirm it as true? Is there such solid evidence that we can check it out and verify it?

There are fancier names for this third stage—philosophers call it "verification" and lawyers "due diligence." But what is at stake is the everyday process of "checking it out." Evidence does not create faith; it confirms it or disconfirms it. Are there good and solid reasons to believe what we are being asked to believe? If this question is not answered, or—worse still—is not allowed, then the searcher may become a believer but will always be vulnerable to the doubt that faith is only a projection, a form of wish-fulfillment, an illusion, or a crutch. We would believe only because we need to believe—which at best is irrational and at worst is dishonest. The wisest way is to say, as Pascal does in Pensées, "We must look at this in detail, then. We must put evidence on the table."

What we believe is absolutely crucial, but why we believe what we believe is also of vital importance. The third stage of the quest is a time for confirmations that what we believe is true. At this point, the Christian faith has emerged as unique in satisfactorily answering life's questions. But the Christian faith is not true because it works; it works because it is true.

We do not believe because we need to believe. Rather, because we need something, we disbelieve what we believed before because of questions our previous beliefs could not answer. But then, after (1) disbelief and (2) the search for and discovery of a better answer, we then (3) take the time to check that the answer we have found is true.

One reminder is important: As we saw in the introduction, these readings are pointers, *not impersonal, ironclad* proofs. *They are for* participants, *not* spectators. *Like a child's drawing created by joining the dots on a page, our convictions as searchers grow clear and firm as we wrestle with the issues that the search prompts. We have to reach our own convictions; they are not always spelled out in the readings and, where they are, they are other people's beliefs, not ours. When it comes to the Christian faith, our convictions as believers are our own or they are nothing. They are more like a lover's reasons for accepting a marriage proposal than a student's reasons for accepting a mathematician's formula.*

Put differently, the sort of confirmations at stake in this third stage of the quest are not impersonal—like dazzling demonstrations of the kind traveling salespeople put on to seduce their clients. For one thing, we are not bystanders or browsers, we are searchers who are focused and involved; we know our own questions and needs after the first stage, and we want answers. For another thing, the evidence is not random or disconnected, it is framed; we have discovered the answers to our questions and found them illuminating at the second stage. Those answers provide a framework in which we can truly consider whether the evidence is compelling or not.

TIME FOR TRUTH

Philosophers are those with "no taste for falsehood; that is, they are completely unwilling to admit what's false but hate it, while cherishing the truth."

—Plato

"Truth! Truth! How the very marrow of my soul yearned for it."

—St. Augustine, *Confessions*

"My country is truth."

—Emily Dickinson

"Truth or nothing."

—Max Weber's motto

"Christianity claims to give an account of *facts*—to tell you what the real universe is like. Its account of the universe may be true, or it may not, and once the question is really before you, then your natural inquisitiveness must make you want to know the answer. If Christianity is untrue, then no honest man will want to believe it, however helpful it might be; if it is true, every honest man will want to believe it, even if it gives him no help at all."

—C. S. Lewis, *God in the Dock*

"Prefer truth to everything."

—Albert Camus

THE POINT IS TO TRAVEL

"When we are lost in the woods the sight of a signpost is a great matter. He who first sees it cries 'Look!' The whole party gathers round and stares. But when we have found the road and are passing signposts every few miles, we shall not stop and stare. They will encourage us and we will be grateful to the authority that set them up. But we shall not stop and stare, or not much; not on this road, though their pillars are of silver and their lettering of gold. 'We would be at Jerusalem.'"

—C. S. Lewis, *Surprised by Joy*

POINT TO PONDER:

The Prelude to Confirmation Is Disconfirmation

If all serious searching is constituted by a sense of questioning and need—as we saw at stage one of the quest—experience shows that there is a close link between confirmation and disconfirmation. If we become genuine seekers and look for answers to our questions, the search for the adequate answer is sharpened when other answers fail to satisfy and are shown to be inadequate or contradictory. These moments of truth that contradict some answers are a vital part of the quest.

The reason for this point is simple: While nothing is unarguable, there are thoughts that can be thought but not lived.

The following three short readings illustrate this one essential point. They are examples of experiences and insights that have had this disconfirming effect for many people in recent decades. In other words, the original incidents described are telling, but so also has been their effect on real people who were searching. Such disconfirmations sharpen even further the desire to see whether the Christian faith, by contrast, not only provides answers but also is true.

THOUGHTS THAT CAN BE THOUGHT BUT NOT LIVED

"Among great philosophers, Hume, who hung his nose as far as any over the nihilistic abyss, withdrew it sharply when he saw the psychological risks involved and advised dilution of metaphysics by playing backgammon and making merry with his friends. The conclusion of Hume's philosophizing was indeed a radical skepticism, which left no convincing logical grounds for believing anything natural, let alone supernatural, was there at all, and he saved his 'reason' or, as we might say, his 'philosophical personality' . . . by refusing to take the implications of his philosophy to heart."

—philosopher Kathleen Knott on David Hume, in *Objections to Humanism*

"In his own case, he provided himself with no means for getting out of the nihilism into which he plunged himself, precisely because it was a deliberate plunge over the edge. . . . He imprisoned himself within the chalked circle of his own metaphysical assumptions. . . . There are positions which can be thought but not lived, there are exploratory ventures from which there is no return. Nietzsche's thoughts were fascinated by unexplored regions of abysses, glaciers, and mountain peaks. One can look down into the bottom of an abyss refusing the possibility of throwing oneself over the edge, but one cannot explore the possibility by a tentative jump. One can examine in thought the possibility of nihilism . . . but if one is determined to will and to live the possibility of nihilism, then one no longer has any independent standpoint under one's feet. . . . One is actually sucked down and engulfed."

—philosopher H. J. Blackham on Friedrich Nietzsche,
in *Six Existentialist Thinkers*

"Peculiar people, psychologically, these scholars. They will set a fuse to the most daring ideas, apparently unaware or regardless of what they are doing. It is their successors who, in the fullness of time, realize the implications of their legacy. Meanwhile, they themselves cling to tradition."

—historian Paul Hazard, *The European Mind in the Eighteenth Century*

Robert M. Pirsig

Robert M. Pirsig is a writer best known for his critically acclaimed, philosophical bestseller Zen and the Art of Motorcycle Maintenance *(1974). Born in 1928, he earned an M.A. from the University of Minnesota and, like the book's narrator, taught writing at the universities of Montana and Illinois at Chicago and worked as a technical writer. He later moved with his family to Sweden and published a second philosophical novel,* Lila.

In this passage from Zen and the Art of Motorcycle Maintenance, *a character named Phaedrus (actually Pirsig himself) is on the road to the East—studying Oriental philosophy at Benares Hindu University—and is stopped in his tracks. His account has also had the effect of stopping many others. After a century that was the most murderous in human history, the question raised here is not trivial.*

Were Hiroshima and Nagasaki Illusory?

In all of the Oriental religions great value is placed on the Sanskrit doctrine of *Tat tvam asi,* "Thou art that," which asserts that everything you think you are and everything you think you perceive are undivided. To realize fully this lack of division is to become enlightened.

Logic presumes a separation of subject from object; therefore logic is not final wisdom. The illusion of separation of subject from object is best removed by the elimination of physical activity, mental activity, and emotional activity. There are many disciplines for this. One of the most important is the Sanskrit *dhyana,* mispronounced in Chinese as "Chan" and again mispronounced in Japanese as "Zen." Phaedrus never got involved in meditation because it made no sense to him. In his entire time in India "sense" was always logical consistency and he couldn't find any honest way to abandon this belief. That, I think, was creditable on his part.

But one day in the classroom the professor of philosophy was blithely expounding on the illusory nature of the world for what seemed the fiftieth time and Phaedrus raised his hand and asked coldly if it was believed that the atomic bombs that had dropped on Hiroshima and Nagasaki were illusory. The professor smiled and said yes. That was the end of the exchange.

Within the traditions of Indian philosophy that answer may have been correct, but for Phaedrus and for anyone else who reads newspapers regularly and is concerned with such things as mass destruction of human beings that answer was hopelessly inadequate. He left the classroom, left India and gave up.

Robert M. Pirsig, *Zen and the Art of Motorcycle Maintenance* (New York: William Morrow and Company, Inc., 1974), pp. 125-127. Reprinted by permission of HarperCollins Publishers and Random House Group Ltd.

Within the traditions of Indian philosophy that answer may have been correct, but for Phaedrus and for anyone else who reads newspapers regularly and is concerned with such things as mass destruction of human beings that answer was hopelessly inadequate. He left the classroom, left India and gave up.

QUESTIONS FOR THOUGHT AND DISCUSSION

1. What do Hindus mean by the undividedness of *Tat tvam asi*? How does Pirsig explain it? How does this philosophy relate to the thinking of Shirley MacLaine?

2. How would you explain "Zen" or *dhyana*? How does logic figure into "Zen" and "final wisdom" in this way of thinking? How is the final wisdom achieved?

3. What was the question Phaedrus posed to the Indian philosophy professor? What do you think was behind it?

4. What did the professor mean by answering "illusory"? Explain.

5. What is Pirsig's reaction to the professor's answer? Why can't Pirsig accept the answer? Do you think his reaction fair? Is he just a young American who doesn't understand the culture, or is his reaction innately human?

6. What is your reaction to the professor's response?

7. What are the consequences of this philosophy for a society?

❧ *Issa* ❧

The Japanese poet Issa (1762–1826) is perhaps the best loved of all Haiku poets because of the humanness of his writing. His own life was very sad—all five of his children died before he was thirty, and then his young wife died. After these deaths, he went to the Zen master and asked for an explanation for such suffering. The master reminded him that the world was dew. Just as the sun rises and the dew evaporates, so on the wheel of suffering sorrow is transient, life is transient, human beings are transient. Involvement in the passion of grief and mourning speaks of a failure to transcend the momentum of selfish egoism.

That the world was dew was his religious—or philosophical—answer. Yet on returning home, Issa wrote a poem in which the logic of Buddhism (and Hinduism) and the logic of his humanness go in contradictory directions. The former does not fit or fulfill the latter, and in the poignancy of the tension is a question that has caused many people to rethink their journey in this direction.

NO MOURNING HERE

"You have grieved for those who deserve no grief. . . . Neither for the living nor the dead do the wise grieve."

—Lord Krishna, *The Bhagavad-Gita*

"On desire depends attachment; on attachment depends existence; on existence depends birth; on birth depends old age and death, sorrow, lamentation, misery, grief, and despair. Thus does this entire aggregation of misery arise."

—a Buddhist doctrine

The World Is Dew ∾

Translated literally:

> This Dewdrop World
> a dewdrop world it is, and still,
> although it is . . .

Or more simply:

> The world is dew—
> The world is dew—
> And yet,
> And yet . . .

And yet, And yet . . .

In Harold G. Henderson, *An Introduction to Haiku* (New York: Doubleday Anchor, 1958).

QUESTIONS FOR THOUGHT AND DISCUSSION

1. The introduction gives the backdrop for Issa's poem. In the face of Issa's suffering and grief, what was the Zen master's explanation? Expand on what his answer means within the Buddhist framework.

2. How does this encounter of master and poet relate to the Haiku? What is Issa saying in the poem? What is the heart-cry of the poem? How does each translation strike you?

3. Do you think Issa's Haiku is a fair response to the master's teaching? What does the teaching mean for the reality of Issa's grief? What does his response mean for the practicality of the philosophy?

❊ Charles Darwin ❊

Charles Robert Darwin (1809–1892), naturalist and author of Origin of Species, *is known for the theory of evolution, which arguably changed the world's view of itself as much as any idea since the time of Christ. At the age of twenty-two Darwin was recommended as a naturalist to the* HMS Beagle, *which was about to begin a five-year, globe-encircling voyage. During the voyage, he made the observations and collected the data that nourished the rest of his professional career.*

A century and a half after his book, the terrain of discussion has altered beyond recognition. Science and religion are now often seen as allies rather than enemies, with many religious believers holding versions of theistic evolution, while evolutionary theory is under assault for scientific reasons. But the passages below show why many people have been troubled by Darwin's conclusions: He had apparently lost his faculty for comprehending anything apart from empirical data. His own naturalistic and reductionist philosophy had affected his mind as well as his theories in biology.

The Life and Letters of Charles Darwin 🐚

LETTER TO MR. J. FORDYCE, 1879

At the present day the most usual argument for the existence of an intelligent God is drawn from the deep inward conviction and feelings which are experienced by most persons.

Formerly I was led by feelings such as those just referred to (although I do not think that the religious sentiment was ever strongly developed in me), to the firm conviction of the existence of God, and of the immortality of the soul. In my Journal I wrote that whilst standing in the midst of the grandeur of a Brazilian forest, "it is not possible to give an adequate idea of the higher feelings of wonder, admiration, and devotion, which fill and elevate the mind." I well remember my conviction that there is more in man than the mere breath of his body. But now the grandest scenes would not cause any such convictions and feelings to rise in my mind. It may be truly said that I am like a man who has become color-blind, and the universal belief by men of the existence of redness makes my present loss of perception of not the least value as evidence. This argument would be a valid one if all men of all races had the same inward conviction of the existence of one God; but we know that this is very far from being the case. Therefore I cannot see that such inward convictions and feelings are of any weight as evidence of what really exists. The state of mind which grand scenes formerly excited in me, and which was intimately connected with a belief in God, did not essentially differ from that which is often called the sense of sublimity; and however difficult it may be to explain the genesis of this sense, it can hardly be advanced as an argument for the existence of God, any more than the powerful though vague and similar feelings excited by music. . . .

Another source of conviction in the existence of God, connected with the reason, and not with the feelings, impresses me as having much more weight. This follows from the extreme difficulty or rather impossibility of conceiving this immense and wonderful universe, including man with his capacity of looking far backwards and far into futurity, as the result of blind chance or necessity. When thus reflecting I feel compelled to look to a First Cause having an intelligent mind in some degree analogous to that of man; and I deserve to be called a Theist. This conclusion was strong in my mind about the time, as far as I can remember, when I wrote the *Origin of Species*; and it is since that time that it has very gradually, with many fluctuations, become weaker. But then arises the doubt, can the mind of man, which has, as I fully believe, been developed from a mind as low as that possessed by the lowest animals, be trusted when it draws such grand conclusions?

LETTER TO MR. W. GRAHAM, 1881

Nevertheless you have expressed my inward conviction, though far more vividly and clearly than I could have done, that the Universe is not the result of chance. But then with me the horrid doubt always arises whether the convictions of man's mind, which has been developed from the mind of the lower animals, are of any value or at all trustworthy. Would any one trust in the convictions of a monkey's mind, if there are any convictions in such a mind?

It may be truly said that I am like a man who has become color-blind, and the universal belief by men of the existence of redness makes my present loss of perception of not the least value as evidence.

But then with me the horrid doubt always arises whether the convictions of man's mind, which has been developed from the mind of the lower animals, are of any value or at all trustworthy. Would any one trust in the convictions of a monkey's mind, if there are any convictions in such a mind?

LETTER TO SIR J. D. HOOKER, 1868

I am glad you were at the "Messiah," it is the one thing that I should like to hear again, but I dare say I should find my soul too dried up to appreciate it as in old days; and then I should feel very flat, for it is a horrid bore to feel as I constantly do, that I am a withered leaf for every subject except Science. It sometimes makes me hate Science, though God knows I ought to be thankful for such a perennial interest, which makes me forget for some hours every day my accursed stomach.

Charles Darwin, *The Life and Letters of Charles Darwin,* volumes I and II, edited by Francis Darwin (New York: D. Appleton & Co., 1888, 1899).

FROM THE AUTOBIOGRAPHY

I have said that in one respect my mind has changed during the last twenty or thirty years. Up to the age of thirty, or beyond it, poetry of many kinds, such as the works of Milton, Gray, Byron, Wordsworth, Coleridge, and Shelley, gave me great pleasure, and even as a schoolboy I took intense delight in Shakespeare, especially in the historical plays. I have also said that formerly pictures gave me considerable, and music very great delight. But now for many years I cannot endure to read a line of poetry; I have tried lately to read Shakespeare, and found it so intolerably dull that it nauseated me. I have also almost lost my taste for pictures or music. Music generally sets me thinking too energetically on what I have been at work on, instead of giving me pleasure. I retain some taste for fine scenery, but it does not cause me the exquisite delight which it formerly did. . . . My mind seems to have become a kind of machine for grinding general laws out of large collections of facts.

My mind seems to have become a kind of machine for grinding general laws out of large collections of facts.

From *The Autobiography of Charles Darwin,* edited by Francis Darwin (New York: D. Appleton & Co., 1885).

QUESTIONS FOR THOUGHT AND DISCUSSION

1. In his "Letter to Mr. J. Fordyce," Charles Darwin describes how he has become "color-blind." What does he mean? What does this say of his naturalistic philosophy in comparison with his earlier religious belief?

2. What does he mean by his "horrid doubt" about the human mind? Does he have an answer to this?

3. Read the letter to Sir J. D. Hooker and the passage from his autobiography. What strikes you about how he describes himself and his interests? What is happening to him? What is behind the change? Are you surprised by his reactions to beauty and the arts?

4. In light of his having reduced all nature to empirical data, do you think this loss of interest is reasonable? Is he consistent with what he believes? Is this a rational transition, would you say?

5. Is your view of nature and the arts rich-hued or black-and-white?

6. Looking back over the stories in part 3 so far, which do you find the most compelling?

7. Do you think it should count against a worldview that a person cannot live on the basis of what it teaches? Why or why not?

POINT TO PONDER:

Truth—The New Obscenity

"What is truth?' said jesting Pilate and didn't stay for an answer." Francis Bacon's famous quip illustrates how claims to truth have always been controversial. Yet in an era that prizes tolerance, affirms diversity, and bends over backwards not to appear judgmental, serious claims to truth sound much like an obscenity—often prompting embarrassed looks, rising blood pressures, and even open hostility. Clearly a claim to truth marks one off as culturally gauche, politically most incorrect, or on the side of the fanatics and bomb throwers.

SKIPPING OVER THE TRUTH

Natural selection was so compelling a theory to Charles Darwin's brother Erasmus that the lack of evidence at crucial points didn't trouble him. "In fact the a priori reasoning is so entirely satisfactory to me that if the facts won't fit in, why so much worse for the facts is my feeling."

— **Erasmus Darwin,** after receiving a copy of Charles's *Origin of Species*

"I have absolutely no knowledge of atheism as an outcome of reasoning, still less an event; with me it is obviously instinct."

— **Friedrich Nietzsche**

"Men occasionally stumble over the truth, but most of them pick themselves up and hurry off as if nothing had happened."

— **Winston Churchill**

"It is not that the methods of science somehow compel us to accept a material explanation of the phenomenal world, but on the contrary that we are forced by our a priori adherence to material causes to create an apparatus or investigation and a set of concepts that produce material explanations, no matter how mystifying to the uninitiated. Moreover, that materialism is absolute, for we cannot allow a Divine Foot in the door."

— **Harvard biologist Richard Lewontin,** *New York Review of Books*

TRUE TO OUR TRUTHS

The Christian faith, however, unashamedly claims to be objectively true— not relatively, not subjectively, not pragmatically, but objectively true. And the claim is important for three reasons. First, the claim is true to the character of Christian truths. It does not come out of an ornery spirit or a perverse desire for sterile debate, but as the expression of central Christian doctrines. Christians hold that God, being personal, is trustworthy—and therefore true. God the Word speaks truly and his words can be checked—as true. God, the lord of history, enters his own created world—in all its gritty empirical reality. The cow dung at his manger smelled like all dung smells. The wine at the wedding reception he attended could be checked for alcoholic content. The cross on which he died was a rough Roman instrument of execution that could have given someone nasty splinters. The blood that flowed unstaunched from his wounds had his unique DNA pattern. The time at which he rose from the grave could be marked by an alarm clock just as the fact of the Resurrection was news hard enough for a Peter Jennings or Tom Brokaw.

SEVEN STANZAS AT EASTER
by John Updike

"Make no mistake: if He rose at all
    it was as His body;
    if the cells' dissolution did not reverse, the molecules
    reknit, the amino acids rekindle,
    the Church will fall.
It was not as the flowers,
    each soft Spring recurrent;
    it was not as His Spirit in the mouths and fuddled
    eyes of the eleven apostles;
    it was as His flesh: ours.
The same hinged thumbs and toes,
    the same valved heart
    that—pierced—died, withered, paused, and then
    regathered out of enduring Might
    new strength to enclose.
Let us not mock God with metaphor,
    analogy, sidestepping, transcendence;
    making of the event a parable, a sign painted in the
    faded credulity of earlier ages:
    let us walk through the door.
The stone is rolled back, not papier-mâché,

not a stone in a story,
    but the vast rock of materiality that in the slow
    grinding of time will eclipse for each of us
    the wide light of day.
And if we will have an angel at the tomb,
    make it a real angel,
    weighty with Max Planck's quanta, vivid with hair,
    opaque in the dawn light, robed in real linen
    spun on a definite loom.
Let us not seek to make it less monstrous,
    for our own convenience, our own sense of beauty,
    lest, awakened in one unthinkable hour, we are
    embarrassed by the miracle,
    and crushed by remonstrance."

AGAINST THE TIDE

A second reason for the importance of the claim to objective truth is that it sets off the Christian faith from muddled or inadequate modern positions. Christian claims are not pious make-believe, religious gobbledygook, or greeting-card sentiment. They are objective truth claims that are either true or false. There simply is no choice in-between.

But what is objective truth? How can truth be tested? How do we know that we know what we know? For all the controversies and complications surrounding truth, the notion of truth remains straightforward. In our ordinary speech, telling the truth is "telling it like it is." We can say, then, that a statement, an idea, or a belief is true if what it is about is as it is presented in the statement. Belief in something doesn't make it true; only truth makes a belief true. But without truth, a belief may be only speculation plus sincerity. Or perhaps, worse still, bad faith. True beliefs, then, are beliefs that correspond with reality. What they represent as new is in fact so. That is what we mean when we say that a belief is true.

Put differently, when the Christian faith claims to be objectively true, that declaration directly opposes those that are typically modern. Thus Christian faith is not a form of relativism—true only "for us." Being objectively true, it is true in a way that is independent of majority decisions and cultural perspectives. Nor is Christian faith subjectivism—true only because "we feel it." Feelings come and go, and thus are an unreliable ground for faith; truth is needed to ground feelings. Nor is Christian faith pragmatism—true simply "because it works." Rather it works because it is true. In sum, the Christian claim to objective truth means that truth is true even if nobody believes it; falsehood is false even if everybody believes it.

OBJECTIVE IS OBJECTIVE IS OBJECTIVE

1. The word objective in the phrase "objective truth" does not refer to an unemotional, detached or impersonal attitude. Truth is not an attitude. Truth is not how we know, truth is what we know.

2. Objective does not mean "known by all" or "believed by all." Even if everyone believes a lie, a lie is still a lie. "You don't find truth by counting noses."

3. Objective does not mean "publicly proved." An objective truth could be privately known—for example, the location of a hidden treasure. It could also be known without being proved; to know is one thing, to give good proofs or reasons for your knowledge is another.

What objective means in "objective truth" is "independent of the knower and his consciousness." "I itch" is a subjective truth; "Plato wrote the *Republic*" is an objective truth. "I don't want to be unselfish" is a subjective truth; "I ought to be unselfish whether I want to or not" is an objective truth.

—Peter Kreeft, Professor of Philosophy, Boston College

TRUE OR FALSE (OR BAD FAITH)

A third reason for emphasizing objective truth is that truth is the needed safeguard against "bad faith"—religion used dishonestly as a fiction to protect us against the terror of a world without meaning.

There are two powerful attacks on religion based on outrage against evil. One attack is against God himself. (As Fyodor Dostoyevsky's Ivan says in The Brothers Karamazov, "All the knowledge in the world is not worth a child's tears.") The other attack is against human believing. If faith's only ground is that the alternative to faith is the terror of meaninglessness, then faith is only a useful fiction, a helpful lie, a handy shield to ward off reality.

But there is a simple antidote to bad faith—truth. When wrestling with whether or not to believe, such considerations as happiness and usefulness are not a substitute for truth. "God exists, therefore you will be happier. . . . Trust in God and you will have peace. . . . Let our country return to God and we will have more law-abiding communities and enjoy greater prosperity." Such arguments from whatever religion are pernicious forms of bad faith, or what the Hebrew-Christian Scriptures relentlessly attack as "idolatry"—putting created things in the place of God and using God for ends less than himself. But we can counter them by an absolute emphasis on truth. There is finally only one reason to believe in the Christian faith—it is true. Our task as honest searchers is to conform our desires to truth, not truth to our desires.

YES OR NO, TRUE OR NOT

"Perhaps the essential malady of these religious arguments is the attempt to use criteria other than truth in dealing with questions of truth. Perhaps this malady is the heart of religious bad faith. Whatever religious propositions we take, we confront thereby a burning question of truth. 'God exists'—yes or no? Is the statement true or is it not? No other criterion but that of truth respects the dignity of such a proposition."

—Peter Berger

❧ *G. K. Chesterton* ❧

G. K. Chesterton was introduced earlier in part 1. The following passage is from Orthodoxy, *his famous defense of the Christian faith. He combines penetrating intelligence with keen observations and inimitable wit to counter the skeptics of his day, such as his friend George Bernard Shaw.*

Chesterton describes a "moment of discovery" in his own experience. Wrestling with whether human beings should be optimistic or pessimistic about life, he suddenly sees the significance that in the Christian view, both optimism *and* pessimism *are correct. Obviously the confirmation described here is a big-picture, broad-gauge kind. At stake is not a single historical fact (such as, "Did Jesus rise from the dead on the third day after his crucifixion?"), but the broad fit of Christian beliefs and worldview with the observable realities of human experience.*

BOTH/AND

"If I am asked, as a purely intellectual question, why I believe in Christianity, I can only answer . . . I believe in it quite rationally upon the evidence. But the evidence in my case . . . is not really in this or that alleged demonstration; it is in an enormous accumulation of small but unanimous facts."

—G. K. Chesterton, *Orthodoxy*

"Man is neither angel nor beast, and it is unfortunately the case that anyone trying to act the angel acts the beast."

—Blaise Pascal, *Pensées*

"Actually it seems to me that one can hardly say anything either bad enough or good enough about life."

—C. S. Lewis, *Letters of C. S. Lewis*

"Man is that being who invented the gas chambers of Auschwitz; however, he is also that being who entered those chambers upright, with the Lord's Prayer or the *Shema Yisrael* on his lips."

—Viktor Frankl, *Man's Search for Meaning*

The Flag of the World ✍

Then I remembered that it was actually the charge against Christianity that it combined these two things which I was wildly trying to combine. Christianity was accused, at one and the same time, of being too optimistic about the universe and of being too pessimistic about the world. The coincidence made me suddenly stand still.

An imbecile habit has arisen in modern controversy of saying that such and such a creed can be held in one age but cannot be held in another. Some dogma, we are told, was credible in the twelfth century, but is not credible in the twentieth. You might as well say that a certain philosophy can be believed on Mondays, but cannot be believed on Tuesdays. You might as well say of a view of the cosmos that it was suitable to half-past three, but not suitable to half-past four. What a man can believe depends upon his philosophy, not upon the clock or the century. If a man believes in unalterable natural law, he cannot believe in any miracle in any age. If a man believes in a will behind law, he can believe in any miracle in any age. Suppose, for the sake of argument, we are concerned with a case of thaumaturgic [miraculous] healing. A materialist of the twelfth century could not believe it any more than a materialist of the twentieth century. But a Christian Scientist of the twentieth century can believe it as much as a Christian of the twelfth century. It is simply a matter of a man's theory of things. Therefore in dealing with any historical answer, the point is not whether it was given in our time, but whether it was given in answer to our question. And the more I thought about when and how Christianity had come into the world, the more I felt that it had actually come to answer this question. . . .

Thus the ancient world was exactly in our own desolate dilemma. The only people who really enjoyed this world were busy breaking it up; and the virtuous people did not care enough about them to knock them down. In this dilemma (the same as ours) Christianity suddenly stepped in and offered a singular answer, which the world eventually accepted as *the* answer. It was the answer then, and I think it is the answer now.

This answer was like the slash of a sword; it sundered; it did not in any sense sentimentally unite. Briefly, it divided God from the cosmos. That transcendence and distinctness of the deity which some Christians now want to remove from Christianity, was really the only reason why any one wanted to be a Christian. It was the whole point of the Christian answer to the unhappy pessimist and the still more unhappy optimist. . . . And the root phrase for all Christian theism was this, that God was a creator, as an artist is a creator. A poet is so separate from his poem that he himself speaks of it as a little thing he has "thrown off." Even in giving it forth he has flung it away. This principle that all creation and procreation is a breaking off is at least as consistent through the cosmos as the evolutionary principle that all growth is a branching out. A woman loses a child even in having a child. All creation is separation. Birth is as solemn a parting as death.

It was the prime philosophic principle of Christianity that this divorce in the divine act of making (such as severs the poet from the poem or the mother from the new-born child) was the true description of the act whereby the absolute energy made the world. According to most philosophers, God in making the world enslaved it. According to Christianity, in making it, He set it free. God had written, not so much a poem, but rather a play; a play he had planned as perfect, but which had necessarily been left to human actors and stage-managers, who had since made a great mess of it. I will discuss the truth of this theorem later. Here I have only to point out with what a startling smoothness it passed the dilemma we have discussed in this chapter. In this way at least one could be both happy and indignant without degrading one's self to be either a pessimist or an optimist. On this system one could fight all the forces of existence without deserting the flag of existence. One could be at peace with the universe and yet be at war with the world. . . .

And then followed an experience impossible to describe. It was as if I had been blundering about since my birth with two huge and unmanageable machines, of different shapes and without apparent connection—the world and the Christian tradition. I had found this hole in the world: the fact that one must somehow find a way of loving the world without trusting it; somehow one must love the world without being worldly. I found this projecting feature of Christian theology, like a sort of hard spike, the dogmatic insistence that God was personal, and had made a world separate from Himself. The spike of dogma fitted exactly into the hole in the world—it had evidently been meant to go there—and then the strange thing began to happen.

When once these two parts of the two machines had come together, one after another, all the other parts fitted and fell in with an eerie exactitude. I could hear bolt after bolt over all the machinery falling into its place with a kind of click of relief. Having got one part right, all the other parts were repeating that rectitude, as clock after clock strikes noon. Instinct after instinct was answered by doctrine after doctrine.

Or, to vary the metaphor, I was like one who had advanced into a hostile country to take one high fortress. And when that fort had fallen the whole country surrendered and turned solid behind me. The whole land was lit up, as it were, back to the first fields of my childhood. All those blind fancies of boyhood which in the fourth chapter I have tried in vain to trace on the darkness, became suddenly transparent and sane. I was right when I felt that roses

When once these two parts of the two machines had come together, one after another, all the other parts fitted and fell in with an eerie exactitude. I could hear bolt after bolt over all the machinery falling into its place with a kind of click of relief.

were red by some sort of choice: it was the divine choice. I was right when I felt that I would almost rather say that grass was the wrong color than say it must by necessity have been that color: it might verily have been any other. My sense that happiness hung on the crazy thread of a condition did mean something when all was said: it meant the whole doctrine of the Fall.

Even those dim and shapeless monsters of notions which I have not been able to describe, much less defend, stepped quietly into their places like colossal caryatides of the creed. The fancy that the cosmos was not vast and void, but small and cozy, had a fulfilled significance now, for anything that is a work of art must be small in the sight of the artist; to God the stars might be only small and dear, like diamonds. And my haunting instinct that somehow good was not merely a tool to be used, but a relic to be guarded, like the goods from Crusoe's ship — even that had been the wild whisper of something originally wise, for, according to Christianity, we were indeed the survivors of a wreck, the crew of a golden ship that had gone down before the beginning of the world.

But the important matter was this, that it entirely reversed the reason for optimism. And the instant the reversal was made it felt like the abrupt ease when a bone is put back in the socket. I had often called myself an optimist, to avoid the too evident blasphemy of pessimism. But all the optimism of the age had been false and disheartening for this reason, that it had always been trying to prove that we fit in to the world. The Christian optimism is based on the fact that we do *not* fit in to the world. I had tried to be happy by telling myself that man is an animal, like any other which sought its meat from God. But now I really was happy, for I had learnt that man is a monstrosity. I had been right in feeling all things as odd, for I myself was at once worse and better than all things.

The Christian optimism is based on the fact that we do not fit in to the world.

The optimist's pleasure was prosaic, for it dwelt on the naturalness of everything; the Christian pleasure was poetic, for it dwelt on the unnaturalness of everything in the light of the supernatural. The modern philosopher had told me again and again that I was in the right place, and I had still felt depressed even in acquiescence. But I had heard that I was in the *wrong* place, and my soul sang for joy, like a bird in spring. The knowledge found out and illuminated forgotten chambers in the dark house of infancy. I knew now why grass had always seemed to me as queer as the green beard of a giant, and why I could feel homesick at home.

From *Orthodoxy* by G. K. Chesterton, chapter V (New York: Dodd, Mead & Co., 1908).

QUESTIONS FOR THOUGHT AND DISCUSSION

1. In the first paragraph, Chesterton searches for something that would combine optimism and pessimism. What does he recall? What does he mean by, "The coincidence made me suddenly stand still"? What is happening?

2. What "imbecile habit" that Chesterton sees has arisen in modern times? On what does he say a person's beliefs depend? Why is this significant?

3. How does Chesterton see the dilemma of the ancient world as similar to that of our age? What is the dilemma?

4. What does Chesterton say was the effect of the Christian faith on the world? Why? What are some of the images he uses to explain this phenomenon? What is "the whole point of the Christian answer"?

5. What does he mean by, "In this way at least one could be both happy and indignant without degrading one's self to be either a pessimist or an optimist"?

6. Read the paragraph, "And then followed an experience . . ." What imagery does he use to describe his experience? What are "the hole" and "the spike"? What does he mean by "loving the world without trusting it"?

7. How does the experience confirm for him the truth of the Christian faith?

8. How do you understand his statement that humans are "the survivors of a wreck, the crew of a golden ship that had gone down before the beginning of the world"?

9. Why does Chesterton think it is important to be able to explain both optimism and pessimism, both the glory and the wretchedness of humanity? What is he saying, "I really was happy, for I had learnt that man is a monstrosity"? What do you make of this? How could such a discovery be a comfort? Can you relate at all? How is the pleasure of the Christian different from the pleasure of the optimist? What does he mean by, "I could feel homesick at home"?

10. What elements do you see Chesterton wrestling with in the process of searching for the answers he seeks? Do you think his discovery of the "fit" is common to all seekers of the meaning of life?

✤ Eleonore Stump ✤

Eleonore Stump is Robert J. Henle Professor of Philosophy at St. Louis University. She is widely known for her work in medieval philosophy and the philosophy of religion and has written, cowritten, and edited many books in these fields. She has received several grants from the National Endowment for the Humanities and previously taught at the Virginia Polytechnic Institute and State University, as well as Oberlin College and the University of Notre Dame.

In this widely read essay, Stump shows how the problem of evil led her as a philosopher toward faith—not away from it. Her cogent but moving statement illustrates the growing prominence of faith among the most eminent contemporary philosophers.

THE EVIL WITHIN

"This view of human evil which I adopted unthinkingly as a young man I have come fundamentally to disbelieve. . . . A view which regards evil as the by-product of circumstances, which circumstances can, therefore, alter and even eliminate, has come to seem intolerably shallow.

"For I am not arguing so much as trying to describe a new way of looking at things, the truth of which was insistently borne in upon me by the events of the times. It was only later that it struck me that this new way of looking at things was only a very old way; was, in fact, the way which I had been taught in my childhood, namely, the Christian way. And with the conviction that mankind is in part evil—I am giving here the sequence of the stages of this conversion, if conversion it may be called, as they actually occurred—came a conviction of the evil in myself."

—philosopher C. E. M. Joad, describing
his conversion during World War II

The Mirror of Evil 🦋

There are different ways to tell the story of one's own coming to God. Straightforward autobiography has its merits, but, paradoxically, it can leave out the most important parts. I want to tell my story in a roundabout way that will, I hope, show directly what for me is and always has been the heart of the matter.

For reflective people, contemplation of human suffering tends to raise the problem of evil. If there is an omnipotent, omniscient, perfectly good God, how can it be that the world is full of evil? This response to evil is normal and healthy. I have discussed this problem myself in print and tried to find a solution to it. But there is another way to think about evil.

Consider just these examples of human suffering, which I take from my morning newspaper. Although the Marines are in Somalia, some armed Somalis are still stealing food from their starving neighbors, who are dying by the thousands. Muslim women and girls, some as young as ten years old, are being raped and tortured by Serb soldiers. In India, Hindus went on a rampage that razed a mosque and killed over 1,000 people. In Afghanistan gunmen fired into a crowded bazaar and shot ten people, including two children. Closer to home, the R. J. Reynolds company is trying to defend itself against charges that it is engaged in a campaign to entice adolescents to smoke. The recently defeated candidate for governor in my state, as well as lawyers and doctors employed by the state as advocates for disabled workers, are charged with stealing thousands of dollars from the fund designed for those workers. A high school principal is indicted on charges of molesting elementary and middle school boys over a period of twenty years. A man is being tried for murder in the death of a nine-year old boy; he grabbed the boy to use as a shield in a gun-fight. I could go on—racism, rape, assault, murder, greed and exploitation, war and genocide—but this is enough. By the time you read these examples, they will be dated, but you can find others just like them in your newspaper. There is no time, no part of the globe, free from evil. The crust of the earth is soaked with the tears of the suffering.

This evil is a mirror for us. It shows us our world; it also shows us ourselves. How could anyone steal at gunpoint food meant for starving children? How could anyone rape a ten-year-old girl? How could anyone bear to steal money from disabled workers or get rich by selling a product he knows will damage the health of thousands? But people do these things, and much worse things as well. We ourselves—you and I, that is—are members of the species that does such things, and we live in a world where the wrecked victims of this human evil float on the surface of all history, animate suffering flotsam and jetsam. The author of Ecclesiastes says, "I observed all the oppression that goes on under the sun: the tears of the oppressed with none to comfort them; and the power of their oppressors—with none to comfort them. Then I accounted those who died long since more fortunate than those who are still living" (4: 1–2).

Some people glance into the mirror of evil and quickly look away. They take note, shake their heads sadly, and go about their business. They work hard, they

For reflective people, contemplation of human suffering tends to raise the problem of evil. If there is an omnipotent, omniscient, perfectly good God, how can it be that the world is full of evil?

This evil is a mirror for us. It shows us our world; it also shows us ourselves.

Some people glance into the mirror of evil and quickly look away. They take note, shake their heads sadly, and go about their business.

worry about their children, they help their friends and neighbors, and they look forward to Christmas dinner. I don't want to disparage them in any way. Tolkien's hobbits are people like this. There is health and strength in their ability to forget the evil they have seen. Their good cheer makes them robust.

Some people look into the mirror of evil and can't shut out the sight.

But not everybody has a hobbit's temperament. Some people look into the mirror of evil and can't shut out the sight. You sit in your warm house with dinner on the table and your children around you, and you know that not far from you the homeless huddle around grates seeking warmth, children go hungry, and every other manner of suffering can be found. Is it human, is it decent, to enjoy your own good fortune and forget their misery? But it's morbid, you might say, to keep thinking about the evils of the world; it's depressive; it's sick. Even if that were true, how would you close your mind to what you'd seen once you'd looked into the mirror of evil?

Some people labor at obliviousness.

Some people labor at obliviousness. They drown their minds in drinking, or they throw themselves into their work. At certain points in his life, Camus seems to have taken this tack. He was at Le Chambon writing feverishly, and obliviously, while the Chambonnais were risking their lives rescuing Jews. Jonathan Swift, whose mordant grasp of evil is evident in his writings, was chronically afflicted with horror at the world around him; he favored violent exercise as an antidote. The success of this sort of strategy, if it ever really does succeed, seems clearly limited.

Some people believe that evil can be eliminated, that Eden on earth is possible.

Some people believe that evil can be eliminated, that Eden on earth is possible. Whatever it is in human behavior or human society that is responsible for the misery around us can be swept away, in their view. They are reformers on a global scale. The moral response to suffering, of course, is the Good Samaritan's: doing what we can to stop the suffering, to help those in need. Global reformers are different from Good Samaritans, though; global reformers mean to remove the human defects that produced the evil in the first place. The failure of the great communist social experiment is a sad example of the problems with this approach to evil. Every good family runs on the principle "from each according to his ability; to each according to his need." The extended human family in Eastern Europe intended to run on this principle and turned it instead into "from each according to his weakness; to each according to his greed." Ecclesiastes sums up the long-term prospects for global reform in this way: "I observed all the happenings beneath the sun, and I found that all is futile and pursuit of wind; a twisted thing that cannot be made straight, a lack that cannot be made good" (1: 14–15).

And don't reason and experience suggest that Ecclesiastes has the right of it? The author of Ecclesiastes says, "I set my mind to study and to probe with wisdom all that happens under the sun . . . and I found that all is futile . . . as wisdom grows, vexation grows; to increase learning is to increase heartache" (1: 13, 14, 18). This is a view that looks pathological to the hobbits of the world. But whether it *is* pathological depends on whose view of the world is right, doesn't it? A hobbit in a leper colony in a cheerful state of denial, oblivious to the disease in himself and others, wouldn't be mentally healthy either, would he? Ecclesiastes recognizes the goodness of hobbits. The author says over and over again, "eat your bread in gladness, and drink your wine in joy; . . . enjoy happiness with a woman you love all the fleeting days of life that have been granted to you under the sun" (9: 7, 9). But the ability to eat, drink, and be merry in this way looks like a gift of God, a sort of blessed irrationality. For himself, Ecclesiastes says, "I loathed life. For I was distressed by all that goes on under the sun, because everything is futile and pursuit of wind" (2: 17).

So, some people react with loathing to what they can't help seeing in the mirror of evil—loathing of the world, loathing of themselves. This malaise of spirit is more likely to afflict those living in some prosperity and ease, inhabitants of the court, say, or college students on scholarship. If you've just been fired or told you have six months to live or have some other large and urgent trouble, you're likely to think that you would be happy and life would be wonderful if only you didn't have *that* particular affliction. Given the attitude of Ecclesiastes, it's not surprising that the book was attributed to Solomon, who was as known for wealth and power as for wisdom.

Some people react with loathing to what they can't help seeing in the mirror of evil—loathing of the world, loathing of themselves.

The misery induced by the mirror of evil is vividly described by Philip Hallie in his book on Le Chambon. Hallie had been studying cruelty for years and was working on a project on the Nazis. His focus was the medical experiments carried out on Jewish children in the death camps. Nazi doctors broke and rebroke "the bones of six- or seven- or eight-year old Jewish children in order, the Nazis said, to study the processes of natural healing in young bodies." "Across all these studies," Hallie says, "the pattern of the strong crushing the weak kept repeating itself and repeating itself, so that when I was not bitterly angry, I was bored at the repetition of the patterns of persecution. . . . My study of evil incarnate had become a prison whose bars were my bitterness toward the violent, and whose walls were my horrified indifference to slow murder. Between the bars and the walls I revolved like a madman. . . . over the years I had dug myself into Hell."

Hallie shares with the author of Ecclesiastes an inability to look away from the loathsome horrors in the mirror of evil. The torment of this reaction to evil is evident, and it seems the opposite of what we expect from a religious spirit. It's no wonder that some people think Ecclesiastes has no place in the canonical Scriptures. To see why this view of Ecclesiastes is mistaken, we have to think not just about our reactive attitudes toward evil but also about our recognition of evil.

How does Hallie know— how do we know—that the torture of Jewish children by Nazi doctors is evil?

How does Hallie know—how do we know—that the torture of Jewish children by Nazi doctors is evil?

By reason, we might be inclined to answer. But that answer is not entirely right. It's true that our moral principles and our ethical theories rely on reason. But we build those principles and theories, at least in part, by beginning with strong intuitions about individual cases that exemplify wrongdoing, and we construct our ethical theories around those intuitions. We look for what the individual cases of wrongdoing have in common, and we try to codify their common characteristics into principles. Once the principles have been organized into a theory, we may also revise our original intuitions until we reach some point of reflective equilibrium, where our intuitions and theories are in harmony. But our original intuitions retain an essential primacy. If we found that our ethical theory countenanced those Nazi experiments on children, we'd throw away the theory as something evil itself.

But what exactly are these original intuitions? What cognitive faculty produces them? Not reason, apparently, since reason takes them as given and reflects on them. But equally clearly, not memory.

But what exactly are these original intuitions? What cognitive faculty produces them? Not reason, apparently, since reason takes them as given and reflects on them. But equally clearly, not memory: We aren't remembering that it is evil to torture children. And not sense perception either. When we say that we just see the wrongness of certain actions, we certainly don't mean that it's visible.

At this stage in our understanding of our own minds and brains, we don't know enough to identify the cognitive faculty that recognizes evil intuitively. But it would be a mistake to infer that there is no such faculty. . . . So I think it is clear that we have cognitive faculties that we don't understand much about but regularly and appropriately rely on, such as the ability to recognize people from their faces.

Our ability to recognize certain things as evil seems to me like this. We don't understand much about the faculty that produces moral intuitions in us, but we all regularly rely on it anyway. . . .

It also seems clear that this cognitive faculty can discern differences in kind and degree. For example, there is a great difference between ordinary wrongdoing and real wickedness.

It also seems clear that this cognitive faculty can discern differences in kind and degree. For example, there is a great difference between ordinary wrongdoing and real wickedness. A young Muslim mother in Bosnia was repeatedly raped in front of her husband and father, with her baby screaming on the floor beside her. When her tormentors seemed finally tired of her, she begged permission to nurse the child. In response, one of the rapists swiftly decapitated the baby and threw the head in the mother's lap. This evil is different, and we feel it immediately. We don't have to reason about it or think it over. As we read the story, we are filled with grief and distress, shaken with revulsion and incomprehension. The taste of real wickedness is sharply different from the taste of garden-variety moral evil, and we discern it directly, with pain.

What is perhaps less easy to see is that this faculty also discerns goodness. We recognize acts of generosity, compassion, and kindness, for example, without needing to reflect much or reason it out. And when the goodness takes us by surprise, we are sometimes moved to tears by it. Hallie describes his first acquaintance with the acts of the Chambonnais in this way: "I came across a short article about a little village in the mountains of southern France. . . . I was reading the pages with an attempt at objectivity . . . trying to sort out the forms and elements of cruelty and of resistance to it. . . . About halfway down the third page of the account of this village, I was annoyed by a strange sensation on my cheeks. The story was so simple and so factual that I had found it easy to concentrate upon *it*, not upon my own feelings. And so, still following the story, and thinking about how neatly some of it fit into the old patterns of persecution, I reached up to my cheek to wipe away a bit of dust, and I felt tears upon my fingertips. Not one or two drops; my whole cheek was wet." Those tears, Hallie says, were "an expression of moral praise"; and that seems right.

With regard to goodness, too, I think we readily recognize differences in kind and degree. We are deeply moved by the stories of the Chambonnais. People feel the unusual goodness of Mother Teresa and mark it by calling her a living saint. We sense something special in the volunteers who had been in Somalia well before the Marines came, trying to feed the starving. We don't have a single word for the contrary of wickedness, so "true goodness" will have to do. True goodness tastes as different from ordinary instances of goodness as wickedness does from ordinary wrongdoing; and we discern true goodness, sometimes, with tears.

Why tears, do you suppose? A woman imprisoned for life without parole for killing her husband had her sentence unexpectedly commuted by the governor, and she wept when she heard the news. Why did she cry? Because the news was good, and she had been so used to hearing only bad. But why cry at good news? Perhaps because if most of your news is bad, you need to harden your heart to it. So you become accustomed to bad news, and to one extent or another, you learn to protect yourself against it, maybe by not minding so much. And then good news cracks your heart. It makes it feel keenly again all

What is perhaps less easy to see is that this faculty also discerns goodness.

And then good news cracks your heart. It makes it feel keenly again all the evils to which it had become dull. It also opens it up to longing and hope, and hope is painful because what is hoped for is not yet here.

the evils to which it had become dull. It also opens it up to longing and hope, and hope is painful because what is hoped for is not yet here.

For the same reasons, we sometimes weep when we are surprised by true goodness. The latest tales of horror in the newspaper distress us but don't surprise us. We have all heard so many stories of the same sort already. But true goodness is unexpected and lovely, and its loveliness can be heartbreaking. The stories of the Chambonnais rescuing Jews even on peril of their own imprisonment and death went through him like a spear, Hallie says. Perhaps if he had been less filled with the vision of the mirror of evil, he would have wept less over Le Chambon.

Some people glimpse true goodness by seeing it reflected in other people, as Hallie did. Others approach it more indirectly through beauty, the beauty of nature or mathematics or music. But I have come to believe that ultimately all true goodness of the heartbreaking kind is God's. And I think that it can be found first and most readily in the traces of God left in the Bible.

Some people glimpse true goodness by seeing it reflected in other people, as Hallie did. Others approach it more indirectly through beauty, the beauty of nature or mathematics or music. But I have come to believe that ultimately all true goodness of the heartbreaking kind is God's. And I think that it can be found first and most readily in the traces of God left in the Bible.

The biblical stories present God as the glorious creator of all the beauty of heaven and earth, the majestic ruler and judge of the world. But Rebecca feels able to turn to Him when she doesn't understand what's happening in her womb, Hannah brings Him her grief at her childlessness, and Deborah trusts Him for victory in a pitched battle with her people's oppressors. Ezekiel presents Him at his most uncompromisingly angry, filled with righteous fury at human evil. But when God commands the prophet to eat food baked in human excrement as a sign to the people of the coming disasters, the shocked prophet tells Him, "I can't!", and almighty God rescinds His command (Ezekiel 4: 12–15). When His people are at their repellent moral worst, God addresses them in this way: "They say if a man put away his wife and she go from him and become another man's, shall he return to her again? . . . you have played the harlot with many lovers; yet return again to me, says the Lord" (Jeremiah 3: 1). And when we won't come to Him, He comes to us, not to rule and command, but to be despised and rejected, to bear our griefs and sorrows, to be stricken for our sake, so that we might be healed by His suffering.

There is something feeble about attempting to describe in a few lines the moving goodness of God that the biblical stories show us; and the attempt itself isn't the sort of procedure the biblical narratives encourage, for the same reason, I think, that the Bible is conspicuously lacking in proofs for the existence of God. Insofar as the Bible presents or embodies any method for comprehending the goodness of God or coming to God, it can be summed up in the Psalmist's invitation to individual listeners and readers: Taste and see that the Lord is good.

The Psalmist's mixed metaphor seems right. Whether we find it in the Chambonnais or in the melange of narrative, prayer, poetry, chronicle, and epistle that constitute the Bible, the taste of true goodness calls to us, wakes us up, opens our hearts. If we respond with surprise, with tears, with gratitude, with determination not to lose the taste, with commitment not to betray it, that tasting leads eventually to seeing, to some sight of or insight into God.

Hallie left his college office and his family and went seeking the villagers of Le Chambon. He concluded his study of the Chambonnais years later this way:

> We are living in a time, perhaps like every other time, when there are many who, in the words of the prophet Amos, "turn judgment to wormwood." Many are not content to live with the simplicities of the prophet of the ethical plumbline, Amos, when he says in the fifth chapter of his Book: "Seek good, and not evil, that ye may live: and so the Lord, the God of Hosts, shall be with you." . . . We are afraid to be "taken in," afraid to be credulous, and we are not afraid of the darkness of unbelief about important matters. . . . But perplexity is a luxury in which I cannot indulge. . . . For me, as for my family, there is the same *kind* of urgency as far as making ethical judgments about Le Chambon is concerned as there was for the Chambonnais when they were making their ethical judgments upon the laws of Vichy and the Nazis. . . . For me [the] awareness [of the standards of goodness] is my awareness of God. I live with the same sentence in my mind that many of the victims of the concentration camps uttered as they walked to their deaths: *Shema Israel, Adonoi Elohenu, Adonoi Echod.*

"For me [the] awareness [of the standards of goodness] is my awareness of God."
—PHILIP HALLIE

So, in an odd sort of way, the mirror of evil can also lead us to God. A loathing focus on the evils of our world and ourselves prepares us to be the more startled by the taste of true goodness when we find it and the more determined to follow that taste until we see where it leads. And where it leads is to the truest goodness of all—not to the boss of the universe whose word is moral law or to sovereignty that must not be dishonored, but to the sort of goodness of which the Chambonnais's goodness is only a tepid aftertaste. The mirror of evil becomes translucent, and we can see through it to the goodness of God. There are some people, then, and I count myself among them, for whom focus on evil constitutes a way to God. For people like this, Ecclesiastes is not depressing but deeply comforting.

If we taste and see the goodness of God, then the vision of our world that we see in the mirror of evil will look different, too.

If we taste and see the goodness of God, then the vision of our world that we see in the mirror of evil will look different, too. Start just with the fact of evil in the world, and the problem of evil presents itself forcefully to you. But start with a view of evil and a deep taste of the goodness of God, and you will know that there must be a morally sufficient reason for God to allow evil— not some legal and ultimately unsatisfying sort of reason, but the sort of reason that the Chambonnais would recognize and approve of, a reason in which true goodness is manifest. People are accustomed to say that Job got no answer to his anguished demand to know why God had afflicted him. But they forget that in the end Job says to God, "now I see you." If you could see the loving face of a truly good God, you would have an answer to the question why God had afflicted you. When you see the deep love in the face of a person you suppose has betrayed you, you know you were wrong. Whatever happened was done out of love for you by a heart that would never betray you and a mind bent on your good. To answer a mistaken charge of betrayal, someone who loves you can explain the misunderstanding or he can show his face. Sometimes showing his face heals the hurt much faster.

If a truly good God rules the world, then the world has a good mother, and life is under the mothering guidance of God. Even the most loathsome evils and the most horrendous suffering are in the hand of a God who is truly good. All these things have a season, as Ecclesiastes says, and all of them work together for good for those who love God—for those who are finding their way to the love of God, too, we might add.

Nothing in this thought makes evil less evil. Suffering remains painful; violence and greed are still execrable. We still have an obligation to lessen the misery of others, and our own troubles retain their power to torment us. But it makes a great difference to suppose that the sufferers of evil, maybe ourselves included, are in the arms of a mothering God.

Although, as Ecclesiastes is fond of saying, we often cannot understand the details of the reason why God does what He does in the world, when we have seen through the mirror of evil and taste the goodness of the Lord, we do understand the general reason, just as Job must have done when he said, "now I see you." Like a woman in childbirth, then, as Paul says, we feel our pains of the moment, but they are encircled by an understanding that brings peace and joy. . . .

For Hallie, for the author of Ecclesiastes, and for me, too, the ghastly vision in the mirror of evil becomes a means to finding the goodness of God, and with it peace and joy. I don't know any better way to sum it up than Habakkuk's. Habukkuk has the Ecclesiastes temperament. He begins his book this way: "How long, O Lord, shall I cry out and You not listen, shall I shout to You, 'Violence!' and You not save? Why do You make me see iniquity, why do You look upon wrong? Raiding and violence are before me, Strife continues and contention goes on. That is why decision fails and justice never emerges" (1: 1–4). But he ends his book this way. He presents the agricultural equivalent of nuclear holocaust: the worst sufferings imaginable to him, the greatest disaster for himself and his people. And he says this: "Though the fig tree does not bud, and no yield is on the vine, though the olive crop has failed, and the fields produce no grain, though sheep have vanished from the fold, and no cattle are in the pen, yet will I rejoice in the Lord, exult in the God who delivers me. My Lord God is my strength" (3: 17–19).

This is the best I can do to tell my story.

Excerpted from *God and the Philosophers: The Reconciliation of Faith and Reason*, edited by Thomas V. Morris. Copyright © 1994 by Thomas V. Morris. Reprinted by permission of Oxford University Press, Inc.

EVIL HARDENS, LOVE SOFTENS

"One day the tall priest caught him making one of those faces, and, believing the grimace was aimed at him, thought it right to enforce respect for the sacred character of his office; he called Jacques up before the whole assembly of children, and there, with his long bony hand, he hit him with all his strength. Jacques almost fell under the force of the blow. 'Now go back to your place,' the priest said. The child stared at him, without a tear (and for all his life it would be kindness and love that made him cry, never pain or persecution, which on the contrary only reinforced his spirit and his resolution), and returned to his bench."

—Albert Camus, in his autobiographical novel, *The First Man*

"The classic expositions of the doctrines that the world's miseries are compatible with its creation and guidance by a wholly good Being come from Boethius waiting in prison to be beaten to death and from St. Augustine meditating on the Sack of Rome."

—C. S. Lewis, *God in the Dock*

QUESTIONS FOR THOUGHT AND DISCUSSION

1. In her opening paragraphs, Eleonore Stump lays out the problem of evil in the world, then states, "This evil is a mirror for us." What do you think of her reasoning? How do different people react after looking

into this mirror? What are the marked differences of "global reformers" and "Good Samaritans"?

2. Why does she say that a "malaise of spirit is more likely to afflict those
living in some prosperity and ease, inhabitants of the court, say, or college students on scholarship"? Is this true? Why?

3. In answering the question "how do we know" evil, Stump argues that
reason by itself is insufficient. Why? Where does our understanding of
evil come from?

4. Stump says, "The taste of real wickedness is sharply different from the
taste of garden-variety moral evil, and we discern it directly, with pain."
Do you think this is true? What about her argument that we have a
similar faculty for discerning goodness and its varying degrees?

5. Why do you think people are hardened by evil but moved to tears by
true goodness? Do you agree or disagree with Stump, that "good news
cracks your heart"? Or do you think it is bad news that shocks the heart
open? What do you think most people would think? When have you
wept over goodness? What were you feeling?

6. What do you think of her argument that heartbreaking goodness is from
God? Is it true that "the Bible is conspicuously lacking in proofs for the
existence of God"? Why does Stump say that is so?

7. Do you find her movement from evil to faith as compelling for you as for
her? What do you think of her basing her faith on the character of God?
How is she discerning God's character? And how has this changed the
way she sees evil?

8. Stump's account of how evil jolted her toward faith has strong resemblances to earlier readings, such as W. H. Auden's experience in the
New York cinema. Why, contrary to common opinions, does evil lead
them *toward* faith rather than away? How does Stump line up on
Arnost Lustig's challenge?

9. Of Stump's description of reactions to evil, which comes closest to
describing where you are?

❧ C. S. Lewis ❧

C. S. Lewis was introduced earlier. In the essay below he examines the common view that Jesus was a great moral teacher but no more. What sounds moderately complimentary is in fact quite illogical, Lewis argues. Anyone who closely examines the life and claims of Jesus of Nazareth is left with a famous four-option question: In the light of his claims, was Jesus a liar, lunatic, legend, or Lord? Or as Lewis's celebrated argument is often expressed, was Jesus "mad, bad, or God"? As the life stories of both Lewis and his wife Joy Davidman show, this essay is not simply about a logical argument; it describes a defining moment in both their journeys to faith.

Lewis's argument highlights a distinctive feature of the Christian faith—the centrality of Jesus Christ. Christian beliefs are fundamentally centered on a person, not ideas. In the end, the best and final reason for believing that the Christian faith is true is Jesus himself.

SURPRISED BY TRUTH

"All my defenses—the walls of arrogance and cocksureness and self-love behind which I had hid from God—went down momentarily—and God came in . . . I must say I was the world's most surprised atheist."

—Joy Davidman

"If you look for truth, you may find comfort in the end: If you look for comfort you will not get either comfort or truth—only softsoap and wishful thinking to begin with and, in the end, despair."

—C. S. Lewis

What Are We to Make of Jesus Christ? ❧

What are we to make of Jesus Christ? This is a question which has, in a sense, a frantically comic side. For the real question is not what are we to make of Christ, but what is He to make of us? The picture of a fly sitting deciding what it is going to make of an elephant has comic elements about it. But perhaps the questioner meant what are we to make of Him in the sense of "How are we to

What are we to make of Jesus Christ? This is a question which has, in a sense, a frantically comic side. For the real question is not what are we to make of Christ, but what is He to make of us?

solve the historical problem set us by the recorded sayings and acts of this Man?" This problem is to reconcile two things. On the one hand you have got the almost generally admitted depth and sanity of His moral teaching, which is not very seriously questioned, even by those who are opposed to Christianity. In fact, I find when I am arguing with very anti-God people that they rather make a point of saying, "I am entirely in favor of the moral teaching of Christianity"—and there seems to be a general agreement that in the teaching of this Man and of His immediate followers, moral truth is exhibited at its purest and best. It is not sloppy idealism, it is full of wisdom and shrewdness. The whole thing is realistic, fresh to the highest degree, the product of a sane mind. That is one phenomenon.

The other phenomenon is the quite appalling nature of this Man's theological remarks. You all know what I mean, and I want rather to stress the point that the appalling claim which this Man seems to be making is not merely made at one moment of His career. There is, of course, the one moment which led to His execution. The moment at which the High Priest said to Him, "Who are you?" "I am the Anointed, the Son of the uncreated God, and you shall see Me appearing at the end of all history as the judge of the Universe."

But that claim, in fact, does not rest on this one dramatic moment. When you look into His conversation you will find this sort of claim running through the whole thing. For instance, He went about saying to people. "I forgive your sins." Now it is quite natural for a man to forgive something you do to *him*. Thus if somebody cheats *me* out of £5 it is quite possible and reasonable for me to say. "Well, I forgive him, we will say no more about it." What on earth would you say if somebody had done *you* out of £5 and I said, "That is all right, I forgive him"?

Now it is quite natural for a man to forgive something you do to him. *Thus if somebody cheats me* out of £5 *it is quite possible and reasonable for me to say. "Well, I forgive him, we will say no more about it." What on earth would you say if somebody had done* you *out of £5 and I said, "That is all right, I forgive him"?*

Then there is a curious thing which seems to slip out almost by accident. On one occasion this Man is sitting looking down on Jerusalem from the hill above it and suddenly in comes an extraordinary remark—"I keep on sending you prophets and wise men." Nobody comments on it. And yet, quite suddenly, almost incidentally, He is claiming to be the power that all through the centuries is sending wise men and leaders into the world. Here is another curious remark: in almost every religion there are unpleasant observances like fasting. This Man suddenly remarks one day, "No one need fast while I am here." Who is this Man who remarks that His mere presence suspends all normal rules? Who is the person who can suddenly tell the School they can have a half-holiday? Sometimes the statements put forward the assumption that He, the Speaker, is completely without sin or fault. This is always the attitude. "You, to whom I am talking are all sinners," and He never remotely suggests that this same reproach can be brought against Him. He says again, "I am begotten of the One God, before Abraham was, I am," and remember what the words "I am" were in Hebrew. They were the name of God, which must not be spoken by any human being, the name which it was death to utter.

Well, that is the other side. On the one side clear, definite moral teaching. On the other, claims which, if not true, are those of a megalomaniac, compared with whom Hitler was the most sane and humble of men. There is no half-way house and there is no parallel in other religions. If you had gone to Buddha and asked him "Are you the son of Brahma?" he would have said. "My son, you are still in the vale of illusion." If you had gone to Socrates and asked, "Are you Zeus?" he would have laughed at you. If you had gone to Mohammed and asked, "Are you Allah?" he would first have rent his clothes and then cut your head off. If you had asked Confucius, "Are you Heaven?", I think he would have probably replied, "Remarks which are not in accordance with nature are in bad taste." The idea of a great moral teacher saying what Christ said is out of the question. In my opinion, the only person who can say that sort of thing is either God or a complete lunatic suffering from that form of delusion which undermines the whole mind of man. If you think you are a poached egg, when you are looking for a piece of toast to suit you, you may be sane, but if you think you are God, there is no chance for you. We may note in passing that He was never regarded as a mere moral teacher. He did not produce that effect on any of the people who actually met Him. He produced mainly three effects—Hatred—Terror—Adoration. There was no trace of people expressing mild approval.

What are we to do about reconciling the two contradictory phenomena? One attempt consists in saying that the Man did not really say these things, but that His followers exaggerated the story, and so the legend grew up that He had said them. This is difficult because His followers were all Jews; that is, they belonged to that Nation which of all others was most convinced that there was only one God—that there could not possibly be another. It is very odd that this horrible invention about a religious leader should grow up among the one people in the whole earth least likely to make such a mistake. On the contrary we get the impression that none of His immediate followers or even of the New Testament writers embraced the doctrine at all easily.

Another point is that on that view you would have to regard the accounts of the Man as being *legends*. Now, as a literary historian, I am perfectly convinced that whatever else the Gospels are they are not legends. I have read a great deal of legend and I am quite clear that they are not the same sort of

On the one side clear, definite moral teaching. On the other, claims which, if not true, are those of a megalomaniac, compared with whom Hitler was the most sane and humble of men. There is no half-way house and there is no parallel in other religions.

It is very odd that this horrible invention about a religious leader should grow up among the one people in the whole earth least likely to make such a mistake.

thing. They are not artistic enough to be legends. From an imaginative point of view they are clumsy, they don't work up to things properly. Most of the life of Jesus is totally unknown to us, as is the life of anyone else who lived at that time, and no people building up a legend would allow that to be so. Apart from bits of the Platonic dialogues, there are no conversations that I know of in ancient literature like the Fourth Gospel. There is nothing, even in modern literature, until about a hundred years ago when the realistic novel came into existence. In the story of the woman taken in adultery we are told Christ bent down and scribbled in the dust with His finger. Nothing comes of this. No one has ever based any doctrine on it. And the art of *inventing* little irrelevant details to make an imaginary scene more convincing is a purely modern art. Surely the only explanation of this passage is that the thing really happened. The author put it in simply because he had *seen* it.

Then we come to the strangest story of all, the story of the Resurrection. It is very necessary to get the story clear. I heard a man say, "The importance of the Resurrection is that it gives evidence of survival, evidence that the human personality survives death." On that view what happened to Christ would be what had always happened to all men, the difference being that in Christ's case we were privileged to see it happening. This is certainly not what the earliest Christian writers thought. Something perfectly new in the history of the Universe had happened. Christ had defeated death. The door which had always been locked had for the very first time been forced open. This is something quite distinct from mere ghost-survival. I don't mean that they disbelieved in ghost-survival. On the contrary, they believed in it so firmly that, on more than one occasion, Christ had had to assure them that He was *not* a ghost. The point is that while believing in survival they yet regarded the Resurrection as something totally different and new. The Resurrection narratives are not a picture of survival after death; they record how a totally new mode of being has arisen in the Universe. Something new had appeared in the Universe: as new as the first coming of organic life. This Man, after death, does not get divided into "ghost" and "corpse." A new mode of being has arisen. That is the story. What are we going to make of it?

The question is, I suppose, whether any hypothesis covers the facts so well as the Christian hypothesis. That hypothesis is that God has come down into the created universe, down to manhood—and come up again, pulling it up with Him. The alternative hypothesis is not legend nor exaggeration nor the apparitions of a ghost. It is either lunacy or lies. Unless one can take the second alternative (and I can't) one turns to the Christian theory.

The question is, I suppose, whether any hypothesis covers the facts so well as the Christian hypothesis. That hypothesis is that God has come down into the created universe, down to manhood—and come up again, pulling it up with Him. The alternative hypothesis is not legend nor exaggeration nor the apparitions of a ghost. It is either lunacy or lies. Unless one can take the second alternative (and I can't) one turns to the Christian theory.

"What are we to make of Christ?" There is no question of what we can make of Him, it is entirely a question of what He intends to make of us. You must accept or reject the story.

The things He says are very different from what any other teacher has said. Others say, "This is the truth about the Universe. This is the way you ought to go," but He says, "*I* am the Truth, and the Way, and the Life." He says, "No man can reach absolute reality, except through Me. Try to retain your own life and you will be inevitably ruined. Give yourself away and you will be saved." He says, "If you are ashamed of Me, if, when you hear this call, you turn the other way, I also will look the other way when I come again as God without disguise. If anything whatever is keeping you from God and from Me, what-ever it is, throw it away. If it is your eye, pull it out. If it is your hand, cut it off. If you put yourself first you will be last. Come to Me everyone who is carrying a heavy load, I will set that right. Your sins, all of them, are wiped out, I can do that. I am Re-birth, I am Life. Eat Me, drink Me, I am your Food. And finally, do not be afraid, I have overcome the whole Universe." That is the issue.

From C. S. Lewis, "What Are We to Make of Jesus Christ?" *God in the Dock*, (Grand Rapids: William B. Eerdmans Publishing Company, 1983). Copyright © 1970 by C. S. Lewis Pte. Ltd. Reprinted by permission.

QUESTIONS FOR THOUGHT AND DISCUSSION

1. In tackling the question, "What are we to make of Jesus Christ?" what is the first feature of Jesus that C. S. Lewis examines? What of it? How do most people you know react to this aspect of Jesus?

2. What is the second feature of Jesus that Lewis addresses? What is the significance of Jesus' claims? How does Lewis highlight these claims as a theme running throughout Jesus' ministry? How do these singular claims undergird other statements Jesus made?

3. How does Lewis argue that the first feature of Jesus cannot be true if the second feature is not? What do you think of this step in his argument?

4. How does Lewis say that Jesus' claims differ from those of other great religious leaders?

5. According to Lewis, what options do we have about who Jesus Christ is? What is the view of each? What does he say is wrong with the argument that it is all legend and he never said what the Bible records him saying?

6. What is the resurrection of Jesus *not*, according to Lewis? What is it? What did Jesus' followers report? What is the "new mode of being"?

7. Lewis comes back to the initial question, "What are we to make of Christ?" How do you understand his response?

8. "Liar, lunatic, legend, or Lord?" Do you agree with Lewis's analysis of our possible responses? Which comes closest to the evidence as you investigate it?

❧ *The Gospel of Mark* ❧

The Gospel of Mark is usually taken as the earliest—and least challengeable—of the four Gospels. Like the others, its central focus is the person and work of Jesus of Nazareth. In a few bold strokes, Mark paints the setting for Jesus' entry onto the stage and then recounts one dramatic incident after another, each showing different aspects of his stunning, category-shattering claims and deeds.

The following account of the man let down through the roof is one such story. Spare in detail, it is rich in twists as those present suddenly grasp the immensity of what Jesus claims—and it backs his words by what he does. As one commentator notes, "No wonder the people wondered!"

Those first-century observers who eventually concluded that Jesus was not a liar or a lunatic, but Lord, did so, of course, on the basis of many such incidents. What sort of man could have done and said what he did? Such wonder—question-raising, objection-demolishing, framework-altering—eventually grew into faith in Jesus, as it has for millions throughout the centuries.

JESUS THE REASON

"The person and work of Christ are the rock upon which the Christian religion is built. . . . Take Christ from Christianity, and you disembowel it; there is practically nothing left. Christ is the center of Christianity; all else is circumference."

—John Stott, *Basic Christianity*

"Of course I had a deep respect, indeed a great reverence for the conventional Jesus Christ whom the church worshiped. But I was not at all prepared for the *unconventional* man revealed in these terse Gospels. No one could possibly have invented such a person: this was no puppet-hero built out of the imaginations of adoring admirers. 'This man Jesus' so briefly described, rang true, sometimes alarmingly true. I began to see now why the religious Establishment of those days wanted to get rid of him at all costs. He was sudden death to pride, pomposity, and pretense."

—J. B. Phillips, translator of the New Testament, in *The Ring of Truth*

A Man Through the Roof ❧

A few days later, when Jesus again entered Capernaum, the people heard that he had come home. So many gathered that there was no room left, not even outside the door, and he preached the word to them. Some men came, bringing to him a paralytic, carried by four of them. Since they could not get him to Jesus because of the crowd, they made an opening in the roof above Jesus and, after digging through it, lowered the mat the paralyzed man was lying on. When Jesus saw their faith, he said to the paralytic, "Son, your sins are forgiven."

Now some teachers of the law were sitting there, thinking to themselves, "Why does this fellow talk like that? He's blaspheming! Who can forgive sins but God alone?" Immediately Jesus knew in his spirit that this was what they were thinking in their hearts, and he said to them, "Why are you thinking these things? Which is easier: to say to the paralytic, 'Your sins are forgiven,' or to say, 'Get up, take your mat and walk'? But that you may know that the Son of Man has authority on earth to forgive sins. . . ." He said to the paralytic, "I tell you, get up, take your mat and go home." He got up, took his mat and walked out in full view of them all. This amazed everyone and they praised God, saying, "We have never seen anything like this!"

"Why does this fellow talk like that? He's blaspheming! Who can forgive sins but God alone?"
—THE TEACHERS OF THE LAW

"Which is easier: to say to the paralytic, 'Your sins are forgiven,' or to say, 'Get up, take your mat and walk'?"
—JESUS

Mark 2:1-12

QUESTIONS FOR THOUGHT AND DISCUSSION

1. What is the setting of this story? Where is Jesus and who is with him? What is he doing?
2. Why do the four friends let their paralytic friend down through the roof? What does such a dramatic act say of their expectations?
3. Which in fact is easier to say—"be healed" or "your sins are forgiven"? Why? To whom does Jesus direct his question? Why do you think the Pharisees were angry?
4. What would incidents like this one have done to the people around Jesus in terms of their coming to realize he was more than just a carpenter?
5. How does the evidence here bear on C. S. Lewis's argument that Jesus of Nazareth is either a liar, a lunatic, a legend, or what he claims to be—Lord?

FOUR
A TIME FOR COMMITMENT

THE FOURTH STAGE IN THE QUEST FOR MEANING IS WHEN WE BEGIN TO REACH CONCLU-
sions that come together and culminate in a step of commitment. In other words,
things so fall into place for us as seekers that we step forward to act on them, and
we can truly say we believe and that we have launched ourselves on our journey
home to God. Sometimes we are conscious of our part—the "step of faith"—and
sometimes of God's part—which Jesus spoke of as "being reborn from above." But
this stage of the quest actually overlaps with the experience of becoming a follower
of Christ, an initiatory step like a wedding that starts a marriage or the journey
of a thousand miles that begins with the first step.

A common mistake is to allow the lure of technique to intrude again at this
fourth stage. Far too often the seeker is confronted by people who are out to simplify
and sell the faith, reducing their understanding of the faith to a formula and their
promotion of their method to a franchise. The effect can be to shrink the "great
change" of conversion, as William Wilberforce called it, and reduce it to a simplis-
tic, stereotyped recipe that insults both the integrity and diversity of human beings
and the sovereign freedom of God.

There are, as stressed earlier, as many ways to faith as there are people who
come to faith. Such variety is as true of this fourth stage as of all the others. Conversion
may be gradual or sudden, quiet or dramatic, unmistakably evident to others or vir-
tually unnoticed. Such variations are infinite, but the reality of the experience is what
matters. It launches us on the journey home.

Yet two themes stand out in all the variety, themes which combine to make this
a time for commitment. The first is that Christian conversion entails an irreducible
component of personal responsibility in commitment. Even if someone has grown
up with the faith, it has to be chosen and entered into, not just inherited. Even if
awareness of faith has crept in on silent feet like the dawn, the daylight reality of

183

faith requires whole people and full participation. The good news of the gospel is a covenant agreement, a contract within a relationship that God offers to us. It is not enough for us only to see the need for what is offered (as we did in the first stage) or even the attractiveness and reliability of the terms (as we did in stages two and three). The covenant becomes binding only when it is signed, and our signature is the binding commitment that each of us gives as a whole person.

CLOSING THE DEAL

"He thought that the object of opening the mind is simply opening the mind. Whereas I am incurably convinced that the object of opening the mind, as of opening the mouth, is to shut it again on something solid."

—G. K. Chesterton (on H. G. Wells)

"[T]he word my Masai catechist, Paul, and I had used to convey faith was not a very satisfactory word in their language. It meant literally 'to agree to.' I, myself, knew the word had that shortcoming. He said 'to believe' like that was similar to a white hunter shooting an animal with his gun from a great distance. Only his eyes and his fingers took part in the act. We should find another word.

"He said for a man really to believe is like a lion going after its prey. His nose and eyes and ears pick up the prey. His legs give him the speed to catch it. All the power in his body is involved in the terrible death leap and single blow to the neck with the front paw, the blow that actually kills. And as the animal goes down the lion envelops it in his arms (Africans refer to the front legs of an animal as its arms), pulls it to himself, and makes it part of himself. This is the way a lion kills. This is the way a man believes. This is what faith is."

—a Western visitor to Kenya

"Who stands fast? Only the man whose final standard is not his reason, his principles, his conscience, his freedom, or his virtue, but who is ready to sacrifice all this when he is called to obedient and responsible action in faith and in exclusive allegiance to God—the responsible man, who tries to make his whole life an answer to the question and call of God."

—Dietrich Bonhoeffer

There is a second universal feature of the time for commitment: an unmistakable awareness that we start out searching, but we end up being discovered. We think we are looking for something, but we find we are found by someone. In the famous picture of Francis Thompson's poem, "the hound of heaven has tracked us down."

THE HOUND OF HEAVEN

"I should not have sought you unless you had first found me."

—Augustine

"You told us of the High God, how we must search for him, even leave our land and our people to find him. But we have not done this. We have not left our land. We have not searched for him. He has searched for us. He has searched us out and found us. All the time we think we are the lion. In the end, the lion is God."

—Masai tribesman

"At a moment of intense physical pain, while I was making the effort to love, although believing I had no right to give any name to the love, I felt, while completely unprepared for it (I had never read the mystics), a presence more personal, more certain, and more real than that of a human being. . . . Christ himself came down and took possession of me.

"In my arguments about the insolubility of the problem of God I had never foreseen the possibility of that, a real contact, person to person, here below, between a human being and God. . . . I had never read any mystical works because I had never felt any call to read them. God in his mercy had prevented me from reading the mystics, so that it should be evident to me that I had not invented this absolutely unexpected contact."

—Simone Weil

"Continue seeking Him with seriousness. Unless He wanted you, you would not be wanting Him."

—C. S. Lewis, in a letter

POINT TO PONDER:

Step, Leap, or Wager?

There are obvious reasons why such a commitment of faith is commonly diluted in the West today. With two thousand years of tradition, it easily becomes formal. With purely theoretical understandings of knowledge common, it easily becomes abstract and remote. With loose and inadequate descriptions of faith in circulation, it easily becomes weak and irrational. For example, one of the most common descriptions of faith is also the faultiest— when believers say their faith is "a leap in the dark," to suggest that it is blind or not based on reason at all.

True, C. S. Lewis uses the term of his own conversion, as we shall see, but in a very different sense. Skeptics use it justifiably to accuse believers of irrationality in faith, but many believers also use it as their preferred description of faith. A "leap in the dark" all too aptly describes how many believers actually come to believe irrationally, but does not properly describe what faith should be.

The term "leap of faith" was made popular by the nineteenth-century Danish philosopher Søren Kierkegaard, who used it to emphasize the passionate, personal nature of faith. But in his reaction to the excessive rationalism of his day, he—or at least his followers—toppled over into an equally exaggerated irrationality that does not do justice to the proper place of reason and truth in coming to faith.

The term "step of faith" is more apt than the phrase "leap in the dark." Christian commitment is more than naked reason. It is, after all, a whole person who makes the act of commitment, and whole people are far more than walking minds. But the commitment of faith is neither against reason nor, as we have seen in part 3, does it lack reason. It is thoroughly rational yet wholly personal too.

With all the confusion surrounding faith, it is worth emphasizing three vital aspects of Christian faith: Faith in Jesus Christ is knowledge that has grown into conviction that has grown into trust. Faith requires knowledge because we are not asked to trust someone about whom we know nothing. But it also requires conviction, because we not only know what faith is about, but are sure it is true. And finally it requires trust, for having faith is not merely being convinced of something, it is being committed to someone. Faith cannot stop short of commitment; it transfers reliance from ourselves to God. It

is not belief in a set of propositions, but trust in a person. Never in our lives
are we freer, more active, and more responsible than when we act on the decision to put our faith in God and set out on the journey home to him.

Having said that, we should underline that there is a proper moment of
choice to consider, a time of weighing things up, of making a decision — and
a vital element of this moment is openness. By the very nature of things, neither belief in God nor atheism can be proved conclusively with scientific rigor.
Isolate this moment, exaggerate the openness, put too glaring a spotlight on
the choice, and a searcher's decision can be burdened with anxiety. But understand the choice properly and it can be seen for what it is — a decision with
real openness yet real destiny at stake or, in Pascal's famous picture, a wager
with our lives on the line.

❧ Blaise Pascal ❧

Blaise Pascal was introduced in part 1. The following reading from Pensées outlines his celebrated argument "The Wager." Pascal was the most famous mathematician of his day as well as the inventor of a calculating machine that is the prototype of the modern computer. But in Pensées he does not attempt a cold, formal, mathematician's-style proof for God. Instead he uses his seasoned reflections on the mathematics of chance as he addresses the free-thinking leisured society of his day in a style appealing to gamblers and risk-takers.

After all, as stressed earlier, Pascal here is more a matchmaker than a mathematician. Anyone following his thought experiment comes face to face with the human calculations and choices that make up the step of faith. Life involves risk. History provides no safety nets. Society gives us no guarantees of success. Our very lives and health are not assured from one day to the next. So life is not only a series of choices, but an array of strategies for living that are actually calculated gambles. The very way we live now shows how we are either betting for or against God. Pascal's "The Wager," slightly shortened, is followed by helpful modern commentary by Peter Kreeft.

"The Wager" is often misunderstood. It is an argument for taking the step of faith, not an argument for the existence of God. Couched in gaming terms, it can easily be translated into the strategies and risks of investing. Either way it is a playful nudge with a deeply serious intent.

Peter Kreeft (born 1937) is a philosopher and author. Born in Paterson, New Jersey, he graduated from Calvin College, Yale University, and Fordham University. Since 1969 he has taught philosophy at Boston College. The author of more than twenty books, he is one of the ablest and most prolific advocates for the Christian faith today. He is a brilliant exponent of the art of Socratic dialogue and a writer with a wit and turn of phrase reminiscent of Chesterton. In the passage that follows, excerpts from Pascal's Pensées are in bold, and Kreeft's commentary is the indented text.

THE GAMBLER'S CHOICE

"If we must never take any chances . . . we should have nothing to do at all, for nothing is certain."

—Blaise Pascal

"Without any disrespect it must be said that Christianity is pre-eminently the gambler's religion. In no other religion are the stakes so high and the choices so momentous."

—Alan Watts

The Wager ❧

The Wager in a nutshell: We can be wrong in two ways: by "wagering" on God when there is no God or by "wagering" on there being no God when there is a God. The second mistake loses everything, the first loses nothing. The second is therefore the stupidest wager in the world, and the first is the wisest.

We can also be right in two ways: by wagering on God when there is a God or by wagering on no God when there is no God. If we are right in the first way, we gain everything; if we are right in the second way, we gain nothing, for there is nothing to gain. Therefore the first is the world's wisest wager and the second is the stupidest.

Let us now speak according to our natural lights. If there is a God, he is infinitely beyond our comprehension.

The most common criticism of the Wager is that it is selfish and does not lead you to true faith and love. This is perfectly true; it leads only to natural faith, selfishly motivated faith. It appeals not to the love of God but to the fear of Hell. But even this is a *beginning,* and one Jesus himself often appealed to. Should we be more "proper" than he was? God will of course not be *content* with this first step, but he will surely honor it and use it. Like a parent watching baby toddle, God our Father is "easy to please but hard to satisfy" (George Macdonald). . . .

Let us then examine this point, and let us say: "Either God is or he is not." But to which view shall we be inclined?

Objectively, there are only two possibilities: either God exists, or not. Subjectively, there are only two possibilities: either I believe, or not. Thus, combining the two sets of variables, we get four possibilities:
1. God exists and I believe in him.
2. God exists and I do not believe in him.
3. God does not exist and I believe in him.
4. God does not exist and I do not believe in him.

Reason cannot decide this question.

"The Wager in a nutshell: We can be wrong in two ways: by 'wagering' on God when there is no God or by 'wagering' on there being no God when there is a God."
—PETER KREEFT

"Let us then examine this point, and let us say: 'Either God is or he is not.' But to which view shall we be inclined?"
—BLAISE PASCAL

"If theoretical, objective, logical, scientific reason could decide this question, we would not need to 'wager.'"
—PETER KREEFT

If theoretical, objective, logical, scientific reason could decide this question, we would not need to "wager." If we had proof, we would not need to take a chance. The Wager is addressed only to those who are not convinced that reason can prove theism (God exists) or atheism (God does not exist).

Infinite chaos separates us.

The reason Pascal gives for reason's impotence is that "infinite chaos separates us." This "infinite chaos" is the infinite difference between our minds and God's, finitude and infinity; and also the infinite distance (and worse, divorce) between God's holiness and our sinfulness. According to Christianity, God has bridged both gaps. He has bridged the first "infinite chaos" by revealing himself, especially in the Incarnation; and the second (sin) by Christ's death.

At the far end of this infinite distance a coin is being spun which will come down heads or tails.

That is, at death we will find the coin of life coming down in one of two ways: either "heads"—you see God face to face—or "tails"—God's retreat, God's death, God's nonexistence. At death you will find out which of the two possibilities is true, atheism or theism.

How will you wager? Reason cannot make you choose either, reason cannot prove either wrong.

But now, before death, you must choose to believe one way or the other. Both theism and atheism are leaps of faith, bets, wagers, chances.

Thus neither atheists nor theists can be refuted and proved wrong. Thus both options remain open, and a "bet" is possible as well as necessary.

Do not then condemn as wrong those who have made a choice, for you know nothing about it. "No, but I will condemn them not for having made this particular choice, but any choice, for, although the one who calls heads and the other one are equally at fault, the fact is that they are both at fault: the right thing is not to wager at all."

In this paragraph, Pascal's imaginary objector defends a third possibility, neither atheism (which is betting against God) or theism (which is betting on

God) but agnosticism (which is not betting at all).

Although theoretically and objectively this is agnosticism, yet practically and existentially it is withdrawal, noncommitment, noninvolvement—something close to "indifference." Pascal's refutation of this "existential agnosticism" is simple and stunning and is repeated by nearly all later "existentialists," atheistic as well as theistic: "Yes, but you must wager." "Not to wager at all" is simply not an option any human being can live, though he can think it. The option of agnosticism is closed to us, not by thought but by life—or, rather, by death (as we shall see in the next note).

Yes, but you must wager. There is no choice, you are already committed.

"Not to wager at all' is simply not an option any human being can live, though he can think it. The option of agnosticism is closed to us, not by thought but by life—or, rather, by death."
—PETER KREEFT

We are "condemned to freedom" (to use Sartre's formula). "There is no choice," says Pascal; that is, we cannot choose whether or not we must choose. We *must* choose, though we are free to choose unbelief or belief.

Why can't we choose not to choose? Why can't we choose agnosticism?

Because we are "already committed," that is, "embarked" (*embarqué*), as on a ship. The ship is our life. The sea is time. We are moving, past a port that claims to be our true home. We can choose to turn and put in at this port (that is, to believe) or to refuse it (that is, to disbelieve), but we cannot choose to stay motionless out at sea. For we are not motionless; we are dying.

Our journey—and our fuel—is finite. Some day soon the fuel will run out, and we will no longer be *able* to choose to put in at the port of God, to believe, for we will have no more time. There is a point of no return.

In other words, to every possible question life presents three possible answers: Yes, No, and Evasion. Death removes the third answer.

This "home port," you see, is not just an *idea* (that God exists). It is a marriage proposal from this God. Not to say Yes is eventually to say No. Suppose Romeo proposes to Juliet, and she says neither Yes nor No, but Wait. Suppose the "wait" lasts and lasts—until she dies. Then her "wait" becomes No. Death turns agnosticism into atheism. For death turns "Tomorrow" into "Never."

Once this is clear, that a choice *must* be made, that there are only two alternatives, not three, the next step is easy. Once Pascal has you out of indifference and onto the battlefield, it becomes very clear which side is the wise one to choose. Not choosing sides is much more popular than choosing the wrong side; agnosticism is more respectable than atheism. Even though his refutation of atheism takes fifty sentences and his refutation of agnosticism takes only one, the crucial battle is here, in this one.

Which will you choose then? Let us see: since a choice must be made, let us see which offers you the least interest. You have two things to lose: the true and the good; and two things to stake: your reason and your will, your knowledge and your happiness; and your nature has two things to avoid: error and wretchedness.

We are all playing the same game (life) for the same two prizes. We all have two things we absolutely demand to win and not to lose: truth and happiness. No one wants to be deceived and no one wants to be miserable.

Imagine the two prizes we are playing for as blue chips (truth) and red chips (happiness). Now we cannot calculate our chances of winning the blue chips. Reason cannot prove the truth of either theism or atheism. Therefore we must calculate our chances of winning the red chips, happiness.

These are the two things everyone wants absolutely. No one wants to be a fool, stupid, ignorant, in error. "All men by nature desire to know. . . ." And no one wants to be wretched and miserable. . . . We seek truth with our reason and joy with our will, and these are the two things that raise us above the animal. That is why they are absolute and nonnegotiable to us: they are the fulfillment of our essence. If we attain them, we are a success, no matter how else we fail. If we fail at them, no other success can compensate for this loss. For "what does it profit a man if he gain the whole world and lose his own soul?" (Mark 8: 36 KJV).

Since you must necessarily choose, your reason is no more affronted by choosing one rather than the other. That is one point cleared up. But your happiness? Let us weigh up the gain and the loss involved in calling heads that God exists. Let us assess the two cases: if you win you win everything, if you lose you lose nothing.

"Let us weigh up the gain and the loss involved in calling heads that God exists. Let us assess the two cases: if you win you win everything, if you lose you lose nothing."
—BLAISE PASCAL

The red-chip calculation is as certain as the blue-chip calculation is uncertain. The only chance of winning the happiness we crave—adequate, total, eternal, unending, unlimited, infinite happiness—is the first of the four possibilities delineated [above], namely, the combination "God exists and I believe." And the only possibility of losing this happiness *and finding eternal unhappiness* is possibility number 2, "God exists and I do not believe." In possibilities number 3 and number 4, there is no God, and therefore no eternity, no Heaven and no Hell, no reward and no punishment, nothing to win and nothing to lose, no payoff for the wager.

Suppose you were offered a lottery ticket for free. Suppose you knew there was a 50 percent chance it was worth a million dollars, and a 50 percent chance it was worth nothing. Would it be reasonable to take the trouble to accept the gift, to *hope* at least in it, to trust the giver enough to accept the gift?

It would be obvious insanity not to.

Do not hesitate then; wager that he does exist.

To the objection that such "belief" is not yet true faith, the reply is: Of course not, but it is a step on the road to it. Even if it is sheer fear of God's justice in Hell, "the fear of the Lord is the beginning of wisdom" (Proverbs 1: 7). It is certainly not the end. Love is that. But "love stoops to conquer" and can use even fear as a beginning—like a loving parent shouting to a toddler to get out of the street.

True faith is not a wager but a relationship. But it can begin with a wager, just as a marriage can begin with a blind date.

"That is wonderful. Yes, I must wager, but perhaps I am wagering too much." Let us see: since there is an equal chance of gain and loss, if you stood to win only two lives for one you could still wager, but supposing you stood to win three?

You would have to play (since you must necessarily play) and it would be unwise of you, once you are obliged to play, not to risk your life in order to win three lives at a game in which there is an equal chance of losing and winning. But there is an eternity of life and happiness. That being so, even though there were an infinite number of chances, of which only one were in your favor, you would still be right to wager one in order to win two; and you would be acting wrongly, being obliged to play, in refusing to stake one life against three in a game, where out of an infinite number of chances there is one in your favor, if there were an infinity of infinitely happy life to be won.

Suppose you had to pay $2 for the lottery ticket that had a 50 percent chance of being worth $1,000,000. It would still be a great bet. Suppose I had to give up something if I became a Christian—adultery, for instance. It would still be a great exchange. Even if I had to pay $100 for a 50 percent chance of winning a million, it would be a good bet. In fact, anything less than half a million is a good risk for a 50 percent chance of winning a million.

"True faith is not a wager but a relationship. But it can begin with a wager, just as a marriage can begin with a blind date."
—PETER KREEFT

"Even if Romeo had
to give up Juliet to get
God, that would be like
giving up one cigarette
to get Juliet."
—PETER KREEFT

But here we are betting not on a million dollars but on infinite and eternal joy. Even if Romeo had to give up Juliet to get God, that would be like giving up one cigarette to get Juliet.

The objector may retort that Pascal leaves something out of this simple calculation. If we take the leap of faith and wager on God, we *may* gain something infinite, but we *will* have to give up something finite (which he calls "noxious pleasures"). The reply is that we also *will* gain something finite, namely, a moral meaning to life and the deep happiness of virtue. ("You will be faithful, honest, humble, grateful, full of good works, sincere, a true friend.") So even on the level of finite gain and loss, faith is a good bet. Converts are always happier as well as better after conversion. . . .

But here there is an infinity of infinitely happy life to be won, one chance of winning against a finite number of chances of losing, and what you are staking is finite. That leaves no choice; wherever there is infinity, and where there are not infinite chances of losing against that of winning, there is no room for hesitation, you must give everything. And thus, since you are obliged to play, you must be renouncing reason if you hoard your life rather than risk it for an infinite gain, just as likely to occur as a loss amounting to nothing.

This is conclusive and if men are capable of any truth this is it.

"Remember, it is not an
argument for the
existence of God but an
argument for faith. Its
conclusion is not
'Therefore God exists'
but 'Therefore you
should believe.'"
—PETER KREEFT

Remember, it is not an argument for the existence of God but an argument for *faith*. Its conclusion is not "Therefore God exists" but "Therefore you should believe."

"I confess, I admit it, but is there really no way of seeing what the cards are?" — "Yes. Scripture and the rest, etc."

Back to the blue chips. Can't we calculate with them at all? Pascal's answer is: Yes, we can. There are clues, there is evidence. But there is not proof, only probabilities. So even the blue-chip calculation leads to the same conclusion. If it is *probable* that the lottery ticket is a winner, it is reasonable to buy it.

—"Yes, but my hands are tied and my lips are sealed; I am being forced to wager and I am not free; I am being held fast and I am so made that I cannot believe. What do you want me to do then?"

Now the objector gets to the psychological root of the matter, and of his unbelief. The rational considerations all tell him to believe, yet he does not. So what holds him back then must not be rationality but irrationality; not reason but passion. . . .

—"That is true, but at least get it into your head that, if you are unable to believe, it is because of your passions, since reason impels you to believe and yet you cannot do so. Concentrate then not on convincing yourself by multiplying proofs of God's existence but by diminishing your passions. . . .

"I tell you that you will gain even in this life, and that at every step you take along this road you will see that your gain is so certain and your risk so negligible that in the end you will realize that you have wagered on something certain and infinite for which you have paid nothing."

What a deal! What good news this Gospel is! How could any bet be better? The next words, from the now-converted skeptic, may seem exaggerated or artificial to the uninvolved spectator, but they emerge inevitably and naturally from the lived movement of the argument.

"How these words fill me with rapture and delight!—"

"If my words please you and seem cogent, you must know that they come from a man who went down upon his knees before and after to pray this infinite and indivisible being, to whom he submits his own, that he might bring your being also to submit to him for your own good and for his glory: and that strength might thus be reconciled with lowliness."

Now Pascal lets the cat out of the bag and blows his cover. He is not a gambler but a matchmaker! The Wager is not a worldly calculation after all, but a divinely inspired fishnet to catch souls. . . .

The ultimate point, end, purpose, and goal of the Wager is God's glory—the same end as the end of all things.

"At least get it into your head that, if you are unable to believe, it is because of your passions, since reason impels you to believe and yet you cannot do so."
—BLAISE PASCAL

From Peter Kreeft, *Christianity for Modern Pagans: Pascal's* Pensées *Edited, Outlined, and Explained* (San Francisco: Ignatius Press, 1993). The selections from *Pensées* are translated by A. J. Krailsheimer (London: Penguin Classics, 1966). Copyright © 1966 by A. J. Krailsheimer. Reprinted by permission of Ignatius Press.

WHO HAS THE LAST WORD?

"Murry, on finding *le Bon Dieu*
Chose difficile à croire,
Illogically said 'Adieu'
But God said 'Au revoir.'"

—G. K. Chesterton,
on the meaning of Mr. Middleton Murry's *Farewell to God*

QUESTIONS FOR THOUGHT AND DISCUSSION

1. In the first two paragraphs, Peter Kreeft outlines Blaise Pascal's wager. How does he set up the argument? What are the terms?

2. Kreeft says the most common criticism of the Wager is that it is selfish, motivated by a fear of hell rather than a love of God. What do you think of this criticism? How might this be the beginning of something deeper? What is the meaning of God being "easy to please but hard to satisfy"?

3. Why does Pascal say "reason cannot decide this question" of God's existence? Does he mean that reason is useless, or that reason by itself is not enough?

4. What do you think of his argument against the stance of the agnostic—the person who says, "the right thing is not to wager at all"?

5. Why is agnosticism a form of practical atheism? Why can't we sit on the sidelines in life? In what sense are we "already committed" to choosing?

6. Once Pascal establishes that we have no choice but to choose, how does he set out the Wager? What do we have to lose and to gain? How do the odds stack up?

7. Is Pascal aiming to prove the existence of God? If not, what is this argument about?

8. At the final stage of the Wager, what does Pascal say might still be holding someone back from believing? What types of "passions" might he be referring to?

9. What does Pascal's picture of the Wager challenge us to see about human choices in life?

10. "The Wager" is a line of reasoning that appeals to some but leaves others cold. How about you?

11. Have you ever slowed down enough to reflect on destiny-affecting decisions such as Pascal advocates? What are the results?

✺ The Apostle Paul ✺

The apostle Paul, born as Saul of Tarsus in Cilicia in the first years of the Christian era, is "the Apostle to the Gentiles" and the greatest and most influential Christian thinker apart from Jesus. The son of a Jew from the tribe of Benjamin, he was brought up "a Pharisee of the Pharisees"—a top lawyer of Jewish law—and educated at Jerusalem where he studied under the famous Rabbi Gamaliel. As a Jew of the Dispersion, he was a Roman citizen who spoke and wrote Greek and was probably the best educated of all the New Testament writers.

The following reading recorded in the book of Acts is the celebrated account of the conversion of Saul of Tarsus. Within a few years of the crucifixion of Jesus, Saul came in contact with the new "Way" of the followers of Jesus. He joined in the intense persecution, including assisting at the stoning of Stephen, the first martyr. Saul becomes Paul after the experience described here, the account of his "Damascus Road experience" that has become influential as the prototype of Christian conversion. Not all conversions are such dramatic, all-at-once, complete about-turns as St. Paul's, but the elements of almost all conversions are here.

Saul Becomes Paul ✺

At this they covered their ears and, yelling at the top of their voices, they all rushed at [Stephen], dragged him out of the city and began to stone him. Meanwhile, the witnesses laid their clothes at the feet of a young man named Saul. . . .

Meanwhile, Saul was still breathing out murderous threats against the Lord's disciples. He went to the high priest and asked him for letters to the synagogues in Damascus, so that if he found any there who belonged to the Way, whether men or women, he might take them as prisoners to Jerusalem. As he neared Damascus on his journey, suddenly a light from heaven flashed around him. He fell to the ground and heard a voice say to him, "Saul, Saul, why do you persecute me?"

"Who are you, Lord?" Saul asked. "I am Jesus, whom you are persecuting,"

"Who are you, Lord?" Saul asked. "I am Jesus, whom you are persecuting," he replied.

he replied. "Now get up and go into the city, and you will be told what you must do."

The men traveling with Saul stood there speechless; they heard the sound but did not see anyone. Saul got up from the ground, but when he opened his eyes he could see nothing. So they led him by the hand into Damascus. For three days he was blind, and did not eat or drink anything.

In Damascus there was a disciple named Ananias. The Lord called to him in a vision, "Ananias!"

"Yes, Lord," he answered.

The Lord told him, "Go to the house of Judas on Straight Street and ask for a man from Tarsus named Saul, for he is praying. In a vision he has seen a man named Ananias come and place his hands on him to restore his sight."

"Lord," Ananias answered, "I have heard many reports about this man and all the harm he has done to your saints in Jerusalem. And he has come here with authority from the chief priests to arrest all who call on your name."

But the Lord said to Ananias, "Go! This man is my chosen instrument to carry my name before the Gentiles and their kings and before the people of Israel. I will show him how much he must suffer for my name."

Then Ananias went to the house and entered it. Placing his hands on Saul, he said, "Brother Saul, the Lord—Jesus, who appeared to you on the road as you were coming here—has sent me so that you may see again and be filled with the Holy Spirit." Immediately, something like scales fell from Saul's eyes, and he could see again. He got up and was baptized, and after taking some food, he regained his strength.

Acts 7:57-58; 9:1-19

QUESTIONS FOR THOUGHT AND DISCUSSION

1. How would you describe Saul's attitude to the new Christian faith at the beginning of this passage?

2. What is the watershed moment in this story? What are the elements of Saul's recognition of his interrupter? How do you know Saul is recognizing the truth? There is no surprise that as a Jew he says, "Lord," but what was the effect on him of hearing the "Lord" say "I am Jesus"?

3. What is the practical indication that there has been a turnaround? What was Ananias's fear? What is the significance of the blindness?

4. How does Paul's moment of truth relate to C. S. Lewis's argument about Jesus being a "liar, lunatic, legend, or Lord"?

5. Paul's story tells of a dramatic about-face. Why is this an important element in some conversions but not in others?

❦ C. S. Lewis ❦

C. S. Lewis was introduced earlier. This passage from Surprised by Joy *is his own account of his conversion—first from atheism to theism (on a double-decker bus) and later from theism to the Christian faith (on the way to Whipsnade Zoo). Notice, among other things, how his conversion fulfills his earlier experiences of joy that had acted as signals of transcendence and prompted his search.*

Surprised by Joy ❦

The odd thing was that before God closed in on me, I was in fact offered what now appears a moment of wholly free choice. In a sense, I was going up Headington Hill on the top of a bus. Without words and (I think) almost without images, a fact about myself was somehow presented to me. I became aware that I was holding something at bay, or shutting something out. Or, if you like, that I was wearing some stiff clothing, like corsets, or even a suit of armor, as if I were a lobster. I felt myself being, there and then, given a free choice. I could open the door or keep it shut; I could unbuckle the armor or keep it on. Neither choice was presented as a duty; no threat or promise was attached to either, though I knew that to open the door or to take off the corset meant the incalculable. The choice appeared to be momentous but it was also strangely unemotional. I was moved by no desires or fears. In a sense I was not moved by anything.

I felt myself being, there and then, given a free choice. I could open the door or keep it shut; I could unbuckle the armor or keep it on.

I chose to open, to unbuckle, to loosen the rein. I say, "I chose," yet it did not really seem possible to do the opposite. On the other hand, I was aware of no motives. You could argue that I was not a free agent, but I am more inclined to think that this came nearer to being a perfectly free act than most that I have ever done. Necessity may not be the opposite of freedom, and perhaps a man is most free when, instead of producing motives, he could only say, "I am what I do." Then came the repercussion on the imaginative level. I felt as if I were a man of snow at long last beginning to melt. The melting was starting in my back—drip-drip and presently trickle-trickle. I rather disliked the feeling. . . .

Really, a young Atheist cannot guard his faith too carefully. Dangers lie in wait for him on every side.

Really, a young Atheist cannot guard his faith too carefully. Dangers lie in wait for him on every side. You must not do, you must not even try to do, the will of the Father unless you are prepared to "know of the doctrine." All my acts, desires, and thoughts were to be brought into harmony with universal Spirit. For the first time I examined myself with a seriously practical purpose. And there I found what appalled me; a zoo of lusts, a bedlam of ambitions, a nursery of fears, a harem of fondled hatreds. My name was legion.

Of course I could do nothing—I could not last out one hour—without continual conscious recourse to what I called Spirit. But the fine philosophical distinction between this and what ordinary people call "prayer to God" breaks down as soon as you start doing it in earnest. Idealism can be talked, and even felt; it cannot be lived. It became patently absurd to go on thinking of "Spirit" as either ignorant of, or passive to, my approaches. Even if my own philosophy were true, how could the initiative lie on my side? My own analogy, as I now first perceived, suggested the opposite: if Shakespeare and Hamlet could ever meet, it must be Shakespeare's doing. Hamlet could initiate nothing. Perhaps, even now, my Absolute Spirit still differed in some way from the God of religion. The real issue was not, or not yet, there. The real terror was that if you seriously believed in even such a "God" or "Spirit" as I admitted, a wholly new situation developed. As the dry bones shook and came together in that dreadful valley of Ezekiel's, so now a philosophical theorem, cerebrally entertained, began to stir and heave and throw off its gravecloths, and stood upright and became a living presence. I was to be allowed to play at philosophy no longer. It might, as I say, still be true that my "Spirit" differed in some way from "the God of popular religion." My Adversary waived the point. It sank into utter unimportance. He would not argue about it. He only said, "I am the Lord"; "I am that I am"; "I am."

People who are naturally religious find difficulty in understanding the horror of such a revelation. Amiable agnostics will talk cheerfully about "man's search for God." To me, as I then was, they might as well have talked about the mouse's search for the cat. The best image of my predicament is the meeting of Mime and Wotan in the first act of *Siegfried; hier brauch' ich nicht Spärer noch Späher, Einsam will ich . . .* (I've no use for spies and snoopers. I would be private. . . .)

Remember, I had always wanted, above all things, not to be "interfered with." I had wanted (mad wish) "to call my soul my own." I had been far more anxious to avoid suffering than to achieve delight. I had always aimed at limited liabilities. The supernatural itself had been to me, first, an illicit dram, and then, as by a drunkard's reaction, nauseous. Even my recent attempt to live my philosophy had secretly (I now knew) been hedged round

Amiable agnostics will talk cheerfully about "man's search for God." To me, as I then was, they might as well have talked about the mouse's search for the cat.

by all sorts of reservations. I had pretty well known that my ideal of virtue would never be allowed to lead me into anything intolerably painful; I would be "reasonable." But now what had been an ideal became a command; and what might not be expected of one? Doubtless, by definition, God was Reason itself. But would He also be "reasonable" in that other, more comfortable, sense? Not the slightest assurance on that score was offered me. Total surrender, the absolute leap in the dark, were demanded. The reality with which no treaty can be made was upon me. The demand was not even "All or nothing." . . .

You must picture me alone in that room in Magdalen, night after night, feeling, whenever my mind lifted even for a second from my work, the steady, unrelenting approach of Him whom I so earnestly desired not to meet. That which I greatly feared had at last come upon me. In the Trinity Term of 1929 I gave in, and admitted that God was God, and knelt and prayed: perhaps, that night, the most dejected and reluctant convert in all England. I did not then see what is now the most shining and obvious thing; the Divine humility which will accept a convert even on such terms. The Prodigal Son at least walked home on his own feet. But who can duly adore that Love which will open the high gates to a prodigal who is brought in kicking, struggling, resentful, and darting his eyes in every direction for a chance of escape? The words *compelle intrare*, compel them to come in, have been so abused by wicked men that we shudder at them; but, properly understood, they plumb the depth of the Divine mercy. The hardness of God is kinder than the softness of men, and His compulsion is our liberation. . . .

It must be understood that the conversion . . . was only to Theism, pure and simple, not to Christianity. I knew nothing yet about the Incarnation. The God to whom I surrendered was sheerly non-human.

It may be asked whether my terror was at all relieved by the thought that I was now approaching the source from which those arrows of Joy had been shot at me ever since childhood. Not in the least. No slightest hint was vouchsafed me that there ever had been or ever would be any connection between God and Joy. If anything, it was the reverse. I had hoped that the heart of reality might be of such a kind that we can best symbolize it as a place; instead, I found it to be a Person. For all I knew, the total rejection of what I called Joy might be one of the demands, might be the very first demand, He would make upon me. There was no strain of music from within, no smell of eternal orchards at the threshold, when I was dragged through the doorway. No kind of desire was present at all.

My conversion involved as yet no belief in a future life. I now number

In the Trinity Term of 1929 I gave in, and admitted that God was God, and knelt and prayed: perhaps, that night, the most dejected and reluctant convert in all England.

It must be understood that the conversion . . . was only to Theism, pure and simple, not to Christianity. I knew nothing yet about the Incarnation.

it among my greatest mercies that I was permitted for several months, perhaps for a year, to know God and to attempt obedience without even raising that question. . . .

The last stage in my story, the transition from mere Theism to Christianity, is the one on which I am now least informed. Since it is also the most recent, this ignorance may seem strange. I think there are two reasons. One is that as we grow older we remember the more distant past better than what is nearer. But the other is, I believe, that one of the first results of my Theistic conversion was a marked decrease (and high time, as all readers of this book will agree) in the fussy attentiveness which I had so long paid to the progress of my own opinions and the states of my own mind. For many healthy extroverts self-examination first begins with conversion. For me it was almost the other way round. Self-examination did of course continue. But it was (I suppose, for I cannot quite remember) at stated intervals, and for a practical purpose; a duty, a discipline, an uncomfortable thing, no longer a hobby or a habit. To believe and to pray were the beginning of extroversion. I had been, as they say, "taken out of myself." If Theism had done nothing else for me, I should still be thankful that it cured me of the time-wasting and foolish practice of keeping a diary. (Even for autobiographical purposes a diary is nothing like so useful as I had hoped. You put down each day what you think important; but of course you cannot each day see what will prove to have been important in the long run.)

As soon as I became a Theist I started attending my parish church on Sundays and my college chapel on weekdays; not because I believed in Christianity nor because I thought the difference between it and simple Theism a small one, but because I thought one ought to "fly one's flag" by some unmistakable overt sign. I was acting in obedience to a (perhaps mistaken) sense of honor. The idea of churchmanship was to me wholly unattractive. I was not in the least anti-clerical, but I was deeply anti-ecclesiastical. . . .

But though I liked clergymen as I liked bears, I had as little wish to be in the Church as in the zoo. It was, to begin with, a kind of collective; a wearisome "get-together" affair. I couldn't yet see how a concern of that sort should have anything to do with one's spiritual life. To me, religion ought to have been a matter of good men praying alone and meeting by twos and threes to talk of spiritual matters. And then the fussy, time-wasting botheration of it all! The bells, the crowds, the umbrellas, the notices, the bustle, the perpetual arranging and organizing. Hymns were (and are) extremely disagreeable to me. Of all musical instruments I liked (and like) the organ least. I have, too, a sort of spiritual *gaucherie* which makes me unapt to participate in any rite. . . .

For many healthy extroverts self-examination first begins with conversion. For me it was almost the other way round. . . . To believe and to pray were the beginning of extroversion.

I was by now too experienced in literary criticism to regard the Gospels as myths. They had not the mythical taste. And yet the very matter which they set down in their artless, historical fashion—those narrow, unattractive Jews, too blind to the mythical wealth of the Pagan world around them—was precisely the matter of the great myths. If ever a myth had become fact, had been incarnated, it would be just like this. And nothing else in all literature was just like this. Myths were like it in one way. Histories were like it in another. But nothing was simply like it. And no person was like the Person it depicted; as real, as recognizable, through all that depth of time, as Plato's Socrates or Boswell's Johnson (ten times more so than Eckermann's Goethe or Lockhart's Scott), yet also numinous, lit by a light from beyond the world, a god. But if a god—we are no longer polytheists—then not a god, but God. Here and here only in all time the myth must have become fact; the Word, flesh; God, Man. This is not "a religion," nor "a philosophy." It is the summing up and actuality of them all. . . .

And nothing else in all literature was just like this. Myths were like it in one way. Histories were like it in another. But nothing was simply like it. And no person was like the Person it depicted.

I know very well when, but hardly how, the final step was taken. I was driven to Whipsnade one sunny morning. When we set out I did not believe that Jesus Christ is the Son of God, and when we reached the zoo I did. Yet I had not exactly spent the journey in thought. Nor in great emotion. "Emotional" is perhaps the last word we can apply to some of the most important events. It was more like when a man, after long sleep, still lying motionless in bed, becomes aware that he is now awake. . . .

I know very well when, but hardly how, the final step was taken. . . . When we set out I did not believe that Jesus Christ is the Son of God, and when we reached the zoo I did.

Freedom, or necessity? Or do they differ at their maximum? At that maximum a man is what he does; there is nothing of him left over or outside the act. As for what we commonly call Will, and what we commonly call Emotion, I fancy these usually talk too loud, protest too much, to be quite believed, and we have a secret suspicion that the great passion or the iron resolution is partly a put-up job.

They have spoiled Whipsnade since then. Wallaby Wood, with the birds singing overhead and the bluebells underfoot and the Wallabies hopping all round one, was almost Eden come again.

But what, in conclusion, of Joy? For that, after all, is what the story has mainly been about. To tell you the truth, the subject has lost nearly all interest for me since I became a Christian. I cannot, indeed, complain, like Wordsworth, that the visionary gleam has passed away. I believe (if the thing were at all worth recording) that the old stab, the old bittersweet, has come to me as often and as sharply since my conversion as at any time of my life whatever. But I now know that the experience, considered as a state of my own mind, had never had the kind of importance I once gave it. It was valuable only as a pointer to something other and outer. While that other was in doubt, the pointer naturally loomed large in my thoughts. When we are lost in the woods the sight of a signpost is a great matter. He who first sees it cries, "Look!" The whole party gathers round and stares. But when we have found the road and are passing signposts every few miles, we shall not stop and stare. They will encourage us and we shall be grateful to the authority that set them up. But we shall not stop and stare, or not much; not on this road, though their pillars are of silver and their lettering of gold. "We would be at Jerusalem."

C. S. Lewis, *Surprised by Joy* (New York: Harcourt, Brace & Company, 1955), pp. 211–224. Copyright © 1956 by C. S. Lewis. Pte. Ltd. and renewed 1984 by Arthur Owen Barfield. Reprinted by permission of Harcourt Inc. and C. S. Lewis Pte. Ltd.

NO INTERFERENCE PLEASE

"Rendering back one's will which we have so long claimed for our own, is, in itself, extraordinarily painful. To surrender a self-will inflamed and swollen with years of usurpation is a kind of death."

—C. S. Lewis, *The Problem of Pain*

QUESTIONS FOR THOUGHT AND DISCUSSION

1. In the first paragraph, C. S. Lewis describes his feeling of God pressing in, but having a choice. How was this so? Do you think this true to all human experience or unique to Lewis? What do you make of his terminology—"corsets," "armor," "lobster"? How does this describe the first universal theme: our full responsibility in believing? What is the process of his response?

2. What does Lewis mean by "a young Atheist cannot guard his faith too carefully"?

3. Lewis says, "I was to be allowed to play at philosophy no longer." What does he mean? What is happening to him? What light does this throw on the second universal theme: "we are found" more than "we find"?

4. Lewis had wanted not to be "interfered with" and considered "man's search for God" to be like a mouse's search for the cat. How do you understand this? Can you relate at all or do you know others with whom this would resonate? What are the consequences of his belief?

5. On the road from theism to the Christian faith, what changes occurred in Lewis's life? What do you think of his honesty? Do you think his reaction to church is unusual? What is the significance of his "flying his flag"?

6. How does Lewis explain what happened to his stabs of joy, once he came to faith?

7. How would you describe Lewis's coming to faith? In comparison with St. Paul's dramatic, once-for-all conversion, does Lewis's *progressive* conversion add to our understanding of the process of coming to faith or contradict it? How so?

POINT TO PONDER:

Always Two Options

One point we have seen repeatedly is that the journey toward faith is as endlessly varied as the people who take it. No cookie-cutter formula can describe it. At the same time, the outcome of the journey is not predetermined. Many snares, pitfalls, bypaths, and diversions line the way—immortalized by Homer's "lotus eaters" and "Scylla and Charybdis" as well as John Bunyan's "slough of despond" and "Vanity Fair."

But even at this fourth stage there is no inevitability. The truth may be pressing and conclusions may be compelling, but we are still free people and there are two options: to fall on our knees or turn on our heels. In other words, there is a moment that tests and exposes the honesty of our search as seekers. For all our good resolutions, we each come face to face with the same intellectual and moral challenge: Either we may seek to conform our desires to the truth, which leads to conviction, or we may seek to conform the truth to our desires, which leads to evasion.

The next series of readings illustrate the second possibility. There is a moment when searchers may see the truth but evade its logic and sidestep its force. Like a boxer cornered but bouncing off the ropes, they duck the issue and put out a smokescreen of evasions and excuses—often highly contradictory.

Nietzsche used the words "danger point" of people who knew the desperate truth of nihilism—that there is no meaning in life—but would not face it squarely. Instead, he said, they twist and turn "as soon as they touch the danger point." Awareness of such danger points, illustrated in these readings, is rare, but sobering and illuminating.

YOU CAN'T HAVE IT BOTH WAYS

"One accusation against Christianity was that it prevented men, by morbid tears and terrors, from seeking joy and liberty in the bosom of Nature. But another accusation was that it comforted men with a fictitious providence, and put them in a pink-and-white nursery. One great agnostic asked why Nature was not beautiful enough, and why it was hard to be free. Another great agnostic objected that Christian optimism, 'the garment of make-believe woven by pious hands,' hid from us the fact that Nature was ugly, and that it was impossible to be free. One rationalist had hardly done calling Christianity a nightmare before another began to call it a fool's paradise. This puzzled me; the charges seemed inconsistent."

—G. K. Chesterton, *Orthodoxy*

"Very often, however, this silly procedure is adopted by people who are not silly, but who, consciously or unconsciously, want to destroy Christianity. Such people put up a version of Christianity suitable for a child of six and make that the object of their attack. When you try to explain the Christian doctrine as it is really held by an instructed adult, they then complain that you are making their heads turn round and that it is all too complicated and that if there really were a God they are sure He would have made 'religion' simple, because simplicity is so beautiful, etc. You must be on your guard against these people, for they will change their ground every minute and only waste your time. Notice, too, their idea of God 'making religion simple': as if 'religion' were something God invented, and not His statement to us of certain quite unalterable facts about His own nature."

—C. S. Lewis, *Mere Christianity*

"I was at this time living, like so many atheists or anti-theists, in a whirl of contradictions. I maintained that God did *not* exist. I was also very angry with God for not existing. I was equally angry with him for creating a world."

—C. S. Lewis, *Surprised by Joy*

❀ M. Scott Peck ❀

Morgan Scott Peck (born 1936) is a psychiatrist and best-selling author. Educated at Harvard and Case Western Reserve universities, he served in the Army Medical Corps from 1963 to 1972 and practiced privately from 1972 to 1983. His first book, The Road Less Traveled (1978), remained on the top ten best-seller lists for over ten years.

The following reading is from People of the Lie: The Hope for Healing Human Evil, a ground-breaking description of true evil. It tells of a rare moment of candor in his long and difficult dealings with a woman called Charlene, from whom he learned much about the nature of evil.

Charlene: A Teaching Case ❧

Toward the end of therapy the problem was elucidated theologically as well as psychologically.

"Everything seems meaningless," Charlene complained to me one day.

"What is the meaning of life?" I asked her with seeming innocence.

"How should I know?" she replied with obvious irritation.

"You're a dedicated religious person," I responded. "Surely your religion must have something to say about the meaning of life."

"You're trying to trap me," Charlene countered.

"That's right," I acknowledged. "I am trying to trap you into seeing your problem clearly. What does your religion hold to be the meaning of life?"

"I am not a Christian," Charlene proclaimed. "My religion speaks of love, not of meaning."

"Well, what do Christians say as to the meaning of life? Even if it isn't what you believe, at least it's a model."

"I'm not interested in models."

"You were raised in the Christian Church. You spent almost two years as a professional teacher of Christian doctrine," I went on, goading her. "Surely you're not so dumb as to be unaware of what Christians say is the meaning of life, the purpose of human existence."

"We exist for the glory of God," Charlene said in a flat, low monotone, as

> "Everything seems meaningless."
> —CHARLENE

if she were sullenly repeating an alien catechism, learned by rote and extracted from her at gunpoint. "The purpose of our life is to glorify God."

"Well?" I asked.

"I cannot do it. There's no room for me in that. That would be my death. . . . I don't want to live for God. I will not. I want to live for me. My own sake!"
—CHARLENE

There was a short silence. For a brief moment I thought she might cry—the one time in our work together. "I cannot do it. There's no room for *me* in that. That would be my death," she said in a quavering voice. Then, with a suddenness that frightened me, what seemed to be her choked-back sobs turned into a roar. "I don't want to live for God. I will not. I want to live for me. My own sake!"

It was another session in the middle of which Charlene walked out. I felt a terrible pity for her. I wanted to cry, but my own tears would not come. "Oh, God, she's so alone," was all I could whisper.

QUESTIONS FOR THOUGHT AND DISCUSSION

1. What was Charlene's theological problem that came out in therapy with M. Scott Peck? What answer did her religion have for the problem?
2. As a former teacher of Christian doctrine and one who grew up in the church, Charlene was well aware of what the Christian faith had to say in regard to her problem. How does she sum up the doctrine? How does Peck describe her attitude in giving him an answer?
3. What is Charlene's reaction to the Christian meaning of life? At the heart, what are her problems with it?
4. Peck feels pity and sadness for Charlene. What is your reaction to her declarations?
5. Why do you think Charlene sees everything as meaningless?

Kenneth Clark

Kenneth MacKenzie Clark (1903–1983) was an eminent English art historian and television writer. Educated at Trinity College, Oxford, and privately wealthy, he worked in Florence with Bernard Berenson and became an authority on the Italian Renaissance. A professor at various art schools and director of the National Gallery in London, he was a major cultural influence in British life. The most brilliant lecturer of his day, he also wrote many books, but is best known for the BBC television series and book Civilization *(1969).*

The following reading comes from Clark's The Other Half, *the second of two autobiographical accounts of his life. His background was quite non-religious, but the impetus toward faith came from three impulses that mattered to him supremely: nature, art, and civilization. As this passage shows, he had no doubt the religious experiences were real. Yet at this stage of his life he brushed them aside, only to turn back and commit himself to faith in the last year of his life.*

INSPIRED, BUT BY WHOM?

"While writing *The Nude*, Kenneth Clark had what seems to have been a moment of divine inspiration. He had been working in his hotel room in Aldeburgh and had just finished a passage on Rubens when he realized that he was shaking and had to walk along the sea-front to calm himself. Perhaps it was the examination of such inspired works as Rubens's *Venus and Area*, or *Three Graces*, that had produced in him a sudden vivid awareness of the mysterious origins of creation. Perhaps it was the moment of true inner vision described by Walkter Pater and John Ruskin, or what Bernard Berenson meant when he spoke of 'IT-ness', an insight into the mystery of existence.

"After Somerset Maugham read a copy of his lecture, 'Moments of Vision' (given at Oxford in 1954, following this experience), he wrote to say how such an experience resembled the flashes of illumination experiences by the Spanish mystics. Inspiration and spiritual illumination: perhaps they were interchangeable ideas. As Kenneth Clark walked unsteadily along the sea-front at Aldeburgh, his bafflement was complete. If one accepted the idea of inspiration, one would have to believe in a source. However he, though an admirer of the church, was no convert. Such tricks of the mind could be explained as transparent wish-fulfillments. Or could they? At about this time he began having some other strange experiences which he believed were mystical in origin."

—Meryle Secrest, *Kenneth Clark*

In San Lorenzo ✍

This state of mind lasted for several months, and, wonderful though it was, it posed an awkward problem in terms of action. My life was far from blameless: I would have to reform.

I lived in solitude, surrounded by books on the history of religion, which have always been my favorite reading. This may help to account for a curious episode that took place on one of my stays in the villino. I had a religious experience. It took place in the Church of San Lorenzo, but did not seem to be connected with the harmonious beauty of the architecture. I can only say that for a few minutes my whole being was irradiated by a kind of heavenly joy, far more intense than anything I had known before. This state of mind lasted for several months, and, wonderful though it was, it posed an awkward problem in terms of action. My life was far from blameless: I would have to reform. My family would think I was going mad, and perhaps after all, it was a delusion, for I was in every way unworthy of receiving such a flood of grace. Gradually the effect wore off, and I made no effort to retain it. I think I was right; I was too deeply embedded in the world to change course. But that I had "felt the finger of God" I am quite sure, and, although the memory of this experience has faded, it still helps me to understand the joys of the saints.

I was too deeply embedded in the world to change course.

From *The Other Half,* by Kenneth Clark. Copyright © 1977 by Kenneth Clark. Reprinted by permission of John Murray (Publishers) Ltd.

QUESTIONS FOR THOUGHT AND DISCUSSION

1. What is the "religious experience" that Kenneth Clark describes? How long did it last? How do you understand what was going on?
2. What "awkward problem" did this experience pose for Clark? What are the sorts of consequences that he knew he was facing?
3. What ultimately did Clark decide to do? What does he mean by "I was too deeply embedded in the world to change course"? What does this episode say about deciding to believe or not believe? About our "worthiness" for such an experience?
4. What do you think of this experience overall and Clark's reaction to it?

BETTER LATE THAN NEVER

"The news [of Clark's conversion] emerged obliquely during a lengthy memorial service at St. James Piccadilly in the autumn of 1983. It was a very grand affair, attended by members of the intellectual and cultural élite as well as representatives of the Queen, Queen Mother and Princess Margaret, who braved a deluge of rain and packed the church. Among them was the architectural historian, biographer and diarist James Mees-Milne. He wrote, 'At the very end of the service an Irish Roman Catholic priest, whom I had noticed officiating . . . gave a second address. . . . He claimed that a week before he died K asked for him, made his confession, received the Sacraments and so was received into the Church of Rome. . . . The priest said, "This great man then said to me, 'Thank you, Father! You have done for me what I have long been wanting'," or words to this effect.' The news which had not been made public in typical Clarkian deference to others' opinions, caused a considerable stir, despite Lady Clark's explanation that her late husband's religious commitment was of long standing."

—Meryle Secrest, *Kenneth Clark*

❧ Aldous L. Huxley ❧

Aldous Leonard Huxley (1894–1963), the English novelist and essayist, is best known for his internationally best-selling novel, Brave New World. *He was the great-nephew of cultural critic Matthew Arnold, grandson of Thomas Huxley ("Darwin's bulldog"), and brother of biologist Julian Huxley. Huxley is well known for his interest in science and mysticism, believing that mysticism and the Eastern religions were the answer to the crisis of Western civilization. But his earlier work was very different.*

Earlier novels, such as Point Counter Point *(1928) and* Eyeless in Gaza *(1936), included witty, despairing portrayals of life in the 1920s and 1930s. The following reading appears in an early book,* Ends and Means, *in which he makes a candid admission. His rejection of the Christian faith, he reveals, was not dis-interested. His philosophy of meaninglessness was an instrument of liberation. Confronted with a choice between truth and desire, he rejected truth and chose desire. Sadly, his later turn to Eastern mysticism — at D. H. Lawrence's urging — came because he admitted that these early choices of meaninglessness had led him to despair. Huxley's admission is a clear example of the fact that we humans are not only truth-seekers, but truth-twisters.*

WHAT PRICE TRUTH?

"The truth is a snare; you cannot have it without being caught. You cannot have the truth in such a way that you catch it, but only such a way that it catches you."

—Søren Kierkegaard, *The Last Years*

Ends and Means 🐝

I had motives for not wanting the world to have a meaning; consequently assumed that it had none, and was able without any difficulty to find satisfying reasons for this assumption.

For, like so many of my contemporaries, I took it for granted that there was no meaning. This was partly due to the fact that I shared the common belief that the scientific picture of an abstraction from reality was a true picture of reality as a whole; partly also to other, non-intellectual reasons. I had motives for not wanting the world to have a meaning; consequently assumed that it had none, and was able without any difficulty to find satisfying reasons for this assumption.

Most ignorance is vincible ignorance. We don't know because we don't want to know. It is our will that decides how and upon what subjects we shall use our intelligence. Those who detect no meaning in the world generally do so because, for one reason or another, it suits their books that the world should be meaningless. . . .

No philosophy is completely disinterested. The pure love of truth is always mingled to some extent with the need, consciously or unconsciously felt by even the noblest and the most intelligent philosophers, to justify a given form of personal or social behavior, to rationalize the traditional prejudices of a given class or community. The philosopher who finds meaning in the world is concerned, not only to elucidate that meaning, but also to prove that it is most clearly expressed in some established religion, some accepted code of morals. The philosopher who finds no meaning in the world is not concerned exclusively with a problem in pure metaphysics. He is also concerned to prove that there is no valid reason why he personally should not do as he wants to do, or why his friends should not seize political power and govern in the way that they find most advantageous to themselves. The voluntary, as opposed to the intellectual, reasons for holding the doctrines of materialism, for example, may be predominantly erotic, as they were in the case of Lamettrie (see his lyrical account of the pleasures of the bed in *La Volupté* and at the end of *L'Homme Machine*), or predominantly political, as they were in the case of Karl Marx. . . .

For myself as, no doubt, for most of my contemporaries, the philosophy of meaninglessness was essentially an instrument of liberation. The liberation we desired was simultaneously liberation from a certain political and economic system and liberation from a certain system of morality. We objected to the morality because it interfered with our sexual freedom; we objected to the political and economic system because it was unjust. The supporters of these systems claimed that in some way they embodied the meaning (a Christian meaning, they insisted) of the world. There was one admirably simple method of confuting these people and at the same time justifying ourselves in our political and erotic revolt: we could deny that the world had any meaning whatsoever.

Those who detect no meaning in the world generally do so because, for one reason or another, it suits their books that the world should be meaningless.

For myself as, no doubt, for most of my contemporaries, the philosophy of meaninglessness was essentially an instrument of liberation.

There was one admirably simple method of confuting these people and at the same time justifying ourselves in our political and erotic revolt: we could deny that the world had any meaning whatsoever.

YOUR SLIP IS SHOWING

"We repudiated entirely customary morals, conventions, and traditional wisdom. As a philosophy, ours was a very good one to grow up under."

—John Maynard Keynes,
on the "immoralism" of the Bloomsbury Group

"I never see anything in it, except a metaphysical justification for doing what you like and what other people disapprove of."

—Beatrice Webb,
on the philosophy of the Bloomsbury Group

QUESTIONS FOR THOUGHT AND DISCUSSION

1. How do you understand Aldous Huxley's "other, non-intellectual reasons" for assuming that the world had no meaning? Are most people similarly aware or honest about it?

2. Huxley charges that "Most ignorance is vincible ignorance. We don't know because we don't want to know." Are educated people more committed to truth or just more sophisticated in their rationalizations?

3. Does Huxley believe in a "pure love of truth"? How does he see this affecting finding meaning—or not—in the world? What does he say are the deeper concerns of those who find no meaning in the world? What do you think?

4. How did he and his contemporaries use "the philosophy of meaninglessness" as "an instrument of liberation"? How would you describe his assessment of what they were doing?

5. Looking back over the last three stories, what are the common links in the inner debates going on?

6. Have you ever witnessed people who face their own "danger point" and then resort to various strategies to duck the truth?

POINT TO PONDER:

Journeying to Arrive

As we come to the close of these readings on the journey of life and the quest for meaning, one further point deserves pondering: People make two equal but opposite errors about the journey of life and the search for faith.

On one side, usually at the less educated level, are those who prematurely speak as if they have arrived. They properly emphasize the certainties and triumphs of faith but minimize the uncertainties and tragedies. Having come to faith, they speak and live as if they have arrived. All truths are clear-cut, all hopes materialized, all conclusions foregone—and all sense of journeying is reduced to the vanishing point. There are seemingly no risks, trials, dangers, setbacks, or disasters on their horizon.

Sadly for them, such people forget that life is a "pilgrim's progress." As the celebrated Rabbi Kotzker said, "He who thinks he is finished is finished."

On the other side, usually at the more educated level, are those who are so conscious of the journey that journeying without end becomes their passion and their way of life. To them it is unthinkable ever to arrive, and the ultimate gaucherie is to claim to have found a way or reached a conclusion. The journey itself is all. Questions, inquiry, searching, and conquering become an end in themselves. Ambiguity is everything.

Sadly for them, such people become seekers who refuse to find what they are looking for. As Daniel Boorstin, the Librarian of Congress, remarked, "We have come from seeking meaning to finding meaning in seeking."

Thoughtful people in the modern world are more prone to this second problem of journeying without end. There have always been insatiable seducers, such as Don Juan, and insatiable searchers, such as Faust. But never has eternal restlessness been so common as it is today—especially when it is stoked by consumerism. When we are moving, we dream of rest; when we rest, we dream of moving again. When we have little, we dream of more; when we have much, we dream of even more. The grammar of our forward-thrusting desires has no periods or paragraph endings, only commas and an endless series of "howevers" and "on the other hand."

Traditional societies were often trapped by the past into succumbing to stagnation. We modern people are lured by the future into yielding to the restlessness of perpetual craving. Like the story of the Flying Dutchman, we are compelled to roam the seas under a perpetual, self-inflicted damnation. We

Kudzy by Doug Marlette.
© 2000. Dist. by Los Angeles Times
Syndicate. Reprinted by permiss.on.

rightly celebrate free inquiry and open-ended thinking while we drown out the problem of our loss of home, our loss of a rudder, and our loss of maps.

NO AIM, NO END

"There is nothing worse for mortal men than wandering."

—Homer, *Odyssey*

"I cannot rest from travel, I will drink
Life to the lees. . . .
I am become a name;
For always roaming with a hungry heart."

—Alfred Lord Tennyson, "Ulysses"

A TIME WITHOUT TIME

"A young king of the East, anxious on his ascent of the throne to rule his kingdom justly, sent for the wise men of his country and ordered them to gather the wisdom of the world in books so that he might read them and learn how best to conduct himself. They went away and after thirty years returned with a string of camels laden with five thousand tomes. Here, they told him, is collected everything that wise men have learnt of the history and destiny of man. But the king was immersed in affairs of state and could not read so many books, so he bade them go and condense this knowledge into a smaller number. Fifteen years later they returned and their camels carried but five hundred works. In these volumes, they told the king, you will find all the wisdom of the world. But there were still too many and the king sent them away again. Ten years passed and they came back and now they brought no more than fifty books. But the king was old and tired. He had no time now even to read so few and he ordered his wise men once more to reduce their number and in a single volume give him an epitome of human knowledge so that he might learn at last what it was so important for him to know. They went away and set to work and in five years returned. They were old men when for the last time they came and laid the result of their labors in the king's hands, but now the king was dying and he had no time any more to read even the one book they brought him."

—retold by W. Somerset Maugham in *The Summing Up*

Again, the Christian faith maintains an extraordinary balance. We are on a journey, so we are truly travelers with all the attendant costs, risks, and dangers of the journey. Never in this life can we say we have arrived. But we know why we have lost our original home and, more importantly, we know the home to which we are going. And we know not only the one who awaits us there who makes it home, but the one who goes with us on the journey.

To those who say, "The search itself is its own reward" or "Better to travel hopefully than to arrive," followers of Christ see it differently. A journey is only meaningful if it has a destination; traveling hopefully is only possible if we are traveling homeward. So all who are followers of Jesus are wayfarers, but not wanderers. They have not arrived, but they have found the way—and in knowing the one who navigated this journey first, they have found not only the way, but the truth and the life. In the words of St. Augustine, such followers of the way down the centuries and across the continents are "a society of pilgrims of all languages." Thus, as these last quotations and the final reading show, there is a final contrast to consider: the contrast between journeying as eternal restlessness and journeying as finishing well in traveling home.

THE JOURNEY'S END

"Suppose we were wanderers who could not live in blessedness except at home, miserable in our wandering and desiring to end it and to return to our native country. We would need vehicles for land and sea which could be used to help us to reach our homeland, which is to be enjoyed. But if the amenities of the journey and the motion of the vehicles itself delighted us, and we were led to enjoy those things which we should use, we should not wish to end our journey quickly, and, entangled in a perverse sweetness, we should be alienated from our country, whose sweetness would make us blessed."

—St. Augustine, *On Christian Doctrine*

"For you have formed us for yourself, and our hearts are restless until they find their rest in you."

—St. Augustine, *Confessions*

"For there is a hope to attain a journey's end when there is a path which stretches between the traveler and his goal. But if there is no path, or if a man does not know which way to go, there is little use in knowing the destination. As it is, there is one road, and one only, well secured against the possibility of going astray; and this road is provided by one who is himself both God and man. As God, he is the goal; as man, he is the way."

—St. Augustine, *The City of God*

"Pioneers and empire builders were filled with hope and courage because, to do them justice, most of them . . . were in search of something, and not merely in search of searching. They consciously conceived an end of travel and not endless traveling. . . . For it is a sin against reason to tell men that to travel hopefully is better than to arrive; and when once they believe it, they travel hopefully no longer."

—G. K. Chesterton, *The Outline of Sanity*

"We shall not cease from exploration;
And the end of all our exploring
Will be to arrive where we started
And know the place for the first time."

—T. S. Eliot, *Four Quartets*

Helmuth James von Moltke

Helmuth James, Graf von Moltke (1907–1945) was a German lawyer, nobleman, and statesman who was tried and condemned by the Nazis just weeks before the defeat of Hitler and the end of World War II. The reading below is the count's last letter to his wife, written as he awaited his execution.

Various factors make the letter extremely moving—the count's beautiful relationship with his wife and children, the revealing grounds of the charge, the poignancy of the timing just days before his murderer-judges' own destruction, and so on. But the letter is also stirring because it is a window into the soul of a man's last day on the journey home, with only "a hard bit on the road ahead of me." Few of us will have such a sense of our last hour, but we can appreciate and use this letter to reflect on our own finishing the journey well.

Letters to Freya

Tegel, January 10, 1945

My dear heart, first I must say that quite obviously the last twenty-four hours of life are in no way different from any others. I always imagined that one would only feel shock, that one would say to oneself: Now the sun sets for the last time for you, now the clock only goes to twelve twice more, now you go to bed for the last time. None of that is the case. I wonder if I am a bit high, for I can't deny that my mood is positively elated. I only beg the Lord in Heaven that he will keep me in it, for it is surely easier for the flesh to die like that. How merciful the Lord has been to me! Even at the risk of sounding hysterical: I am so full of gratitude that there is hardly room for anything else. He guided me so firmly and clearly these two days: the whole room could have roared like Herr Freisler and all the walls could have shaken, it would have made no difference to me; it was truly as it says in Isaiah 43:2: When thou passest through the waters, I will be with thee; and through the rivers, they shall not overflow thee; when thou walkest through the fire, thou shalt not be burned; neither shall the flame kindle upon thee.—That is: your soul. When I was called upon for my final statement I almost felt like saying: There is only one thing I want to mention in my defense: *nehmen sie den Leib, Gut, Ehr, Kind*

I always imagined that one would only feel shock, that one would say to oneself: Now the sun sets for the last time for you, now the clock only goes to twelve twice more, now you go to bed for the last time. None of that is the case. I wonder if I am a bit high, for I can't deny that my mood is positively elated.

und Weib, lass fahren dahin, sie haben's kein Gewinn, das Reich muss uns doch bleiben [From Martin Luther's hymn, "A Mighty Fortress": "And though they take our life, / Goods, honor, children, wife, / Yet is their profit small, / These things shall vanish all, / The city of God remaineth."]. But that would have harmed the others. So I only said: I don't intend to say anything more, Herr Präsident.

Now there is still a hard bit of road ahead of me, and I can only pray that the Lord will continue as gracious to me as he has been. . . . Thanks also to yourself, my love, for your intercessions, thanks to all the others who prayed for us and for me. Your husband, your weak, cowardly, "complicated," very average husband, was allowed to experience all this. If I were to be reprieved now—which under God is no more likely or unlikely than a week ago—I must say that I should have to find my way all over again, so tremendous was the demonstration of God's presence and omnipotence. He can demonstrate them to us, and quite unmistakably, when he does precisely what doesn't suit us. Anything else is rubbish.

Thus I can only say this, dear heart: may God be as gracious to you as to me, then even a dead husband doesn't matter at all. He can, after all, demonstrate his omnipotence even while you make pancakes for the boys or clean them up, though that is, I hope, a thing of the past. I should probably take leave of you—I cannot do it; I should probably deplore and lament your daily toil—I cannot do it; I should probably think of burdens which now fall on you—I cannot do it. I can only tell you one thing: if you get the feeling of absolute protectedness, if the Lord gives it to you, which you would not have without this time and its conclusion, then I bequeath to you a treasure that cannot be confiscated, and compared with which even my life weighs nothing. These Romans, these miserable creatures of Schulze and Freisler and whatever the whole pack may be called: they couldn't even grasp how little they can take away!

I shall write more tomorrow, but since one never knows what will happen, I wanted to touch on every subject in the letter. Of course I don't know if I'll be executed tomorrow. It may be that I'll be interrogated further, beaten up, or stored away. Please scratch at the doors: perhaps it will keep them from beating me up too badly. Although after today's experience I know that God can also turn this beating to naught, even if there is no whole bone left in my body before I am hanged, although at the moment I have no fear of it, I'd rather avoid it.—So, good night, be of good cheer and undismayed. J.

[P.S.] Hercher, who really is a dear fellow, was a bit shocked at my good spirits; so you see that they were quite irrepressible.

Now there is still a hard bit of road ahead of me, and I can only pray that the Lord will continue as gracious to me as he has been.

I can only tell you one thing: if you get the feeling of absolute protectedness, if the Lord gives it to you, which you would not have without this time and its conclusion, then I bequeath to you a treasure that cannot be confiscated, and compared with which even my life weighs nothing.

[Continued] January 11, 1945

. . . The decisive phrase of the trial was: "Herr Graf, one thing Christianity and we National Socialists have in common, and only one: we demand the whole man." I wonder if he realized what he was saying? Just think how wonderfully God prepared this, his unworthy vessel. At the very moment when there was danger that I might be drawn into active preparations of a putsch—it was in the evening of the 19th that Stauffenberg came to Peter—I was taken away, so that I should be and remain free from all connection with the use of violence.—Then he planted in me my socialist leanings, which freed me, as big landowner, from all suspicion of representing interests.—Then he humbled me as I have never been humbled before, so that I had to lose all pride, so that at last I understand my sinfulness after thirty-eight years, so that I learn to beg for his forgiveness and to trust to his mercy.—Then he lets me come here, so that I can see you standing firm and I can be free of thoughts of you and the little sons, that is, of cares; he gives me time and opportunity to arrange everything that can be arranged, so that all earthly thoughts can fall away.—Then he lets me experience to their utmost depth the pain of parting and the terror of death and the fear of hell, so that all that should be over, too.—Then he endows me with faith, hope, and love, with a wealth of these that is truly overwhelming.— . . . and then your husband is chosen, as a Protestant, to be above all attacked and condemned for his friendship with Catholics, and therefore he stands before Freisler not as a Protestant, not as a big landowner, not as a nobleman, not as a Prussian, not as a German—all that was explicitly excluded in the trial, thus for instance Sperr: "I thought what an astonishing Prussian"—, but as a Christian and nothing else. "The fig leaf is off." says Herr Freisler. Yes, every other category was removed—"a man whom others of his class are naturally bound to reject," says Schulze. For what a mighty task your husband was chosen: all the trouble the Lord took with him, the infinite detours, the intricate zigzag curves, all suddenly find their explanation in one hour on the 10th of January 1945. Everything acquires its meaning in retrospect, which was hidden. . . .

And now, dear heart, I come to you. I have not mentioned you anywhere, because you, my love, occupy a wholly different place from all the others. For you are not a means God employed to make me who I am, rather you are myself. You are my 13th chapter of the First Letter to the Corinthians. Without this chapter no human being is human. Without you I would have accepted love as a gift, as I accepted it from Mami, for

"One thing Christianity and we National Socialists have in common, and only one: we demand the whole man."
—Freisler

Your husband is chosen . . . not as a Protestant, not as a big landowner, not as a nobleman, not as a Prussian, not as a German—all that was explicitly excluded in the trial . . . but as a Christian and nothing else.

For you are not a means God employed to make me who I am, rather you are myself. You are my 13th chapter of the First Letter to the Corinthians. Without this chapter no human being is human.

instance, thankful, happy, grateful as one is for the sun that warms one. But without you, my love, I would have "had not charity." I don't even say that I love you; that wouldn't be right. Rather, you are the part of me that, alone, I would lack. It is good that I lack it; for if I had it as you have it, this greatest of all gifts, my love, I could not have done a lot of things, I would have found it impossible to maintain consistency in some things, I could not have watched the suffering I had to see, and much else. Only together do we constitute a human being. We are, as I wrote a few days ago, symbolically, created as one. That is true, literally true. Therefore, my love, I am certain that you will not lose me on this earth, not for a moment. And we were allowed finally to symbolize this fact by our shared Holy Communion, which will have been my last.

I just wept a little, not because I was sad or melancholy, not because I want to return, but because I am thankful and moved by this proof of God's presence. It is not given to us to see him face to face, but we must needs be moved intensely when we suddenly see that all our life he has gone before us as a cloud by day and a pillar of fire by night and that he permits us to see it suddenly in a flash. Now nothing more can happen. . . .

It is not given to us to see him face to face, but we must needs be moved intensely when we suddenly see that all our life he has gone before us as a cloud by day and a pillar of fire by night and that he permits us to see it suddenly in a flash.

Dear heart, my life is finished and I can say of myself: He died in the fullness of years and of life's experience. This doesn't alter the fact that I would gladly go on living and that I would gladly accompany you a bit further on this earth. But then I would need a new task from God. The task for which God made me is done. If he has another task for me, we shall hear of it. Therefore by all means continue your efforts to save my life, if I survive this day. Perhaps there is another task.

The task for which God made me is done. If he has another task for me, we shall hear of it.

I'll stop, for there is nothing more to say. I mentioned nobody you should greet or embrace for me; you know yourself who is meant. All the texts we love are in my heart and in your heart. But I end by saying to you by virtue of the treasure that spoke from me and filled this humble earthen vessel:

*The Grace of our Lord Jesus Christ
and the love of God and the fellowship
of the Holy Spirit be with you all.*
                        Amen.

J.

QUESTIONS FOR THOUGHT AND DISCUSSION

1. How would you describe Count von Moltke's frame of mind in what he sees as his last twenty-four hours? What is the significance of the date? What do you find most striking in this moving description?

2. What did von Moltke hear in the Prosecutor's statement, "we demand the whole man"? How did it affect his response? How does he see that he has been uniquely prepared for this moment of reckoning? What did he mean when he said he stood before the Nazis "as a Christian and nothing else"? Why was this important to him?

3. How do you find his relationship to his wife and his parting words to her about their marriage?

4. Von Moltke writes, "I shall write more tomorrow, but since one never knows what will happen, I wanted to touch on every subject in the letter." In what sense is this not knowing the future true of everyone? How might living as if every day were the last change the way you live?

5. Find all the references to life as a journey in the letter ("Now there is still a hard bit of road ahead of me.") How do they bear on his faith in this supreme crisis?

6. If you were given a glimpse into your own "last hour," what would you like your view back over the journey of life and your view forward to be?

7. How would you have to live now to be able to write a paragraph like the last one by von Moltke?

HOME AT LAST

"There shall we rest and see, see and love, love and praise. This is what we shall be in the end without end. For what other end do we propose to ourselves than to attain to the kingdom of which there is no end?"

—St. Augustine, *The City of God*

"After this, it was noised abroad, that Mr. *Valiant-for-Truth* was taken with a summons by the same post as the other; and had this for a token that the summons was true, *That his pitcher was broken at the fountain.* When he understood it, he called for his friends, and told them of it. Then, said he, I am going to my Father's, and tho' with great difficulty I am got hither, yet now I do not repent me of all the trouble I have been at to arrive where I am. *My Sword* I give to him that shall succeed me in my Pilgrimage, and my *Courage* and *Skill* to him that can get it. My *marks* and *scars* I carry with me, to be a witness for me, that I have fought His battles, who now will be my Rewarder. When the day that he must go hence was come, many accompany'd him to the River-side, into which as he went, he said, *Death, where is thy Sting?* And as he went down deeper, he said, *Grave, where is thy Victory?* So he passed over, and all the Trumpets sounded for him on the other side."

—John Bunyan, *The Pilgrim's Progress*

In one of his letters Vincent van Gogh describes a painting he had seen of John Bunyan's "Pilgrim's Progress." A sandy path leads over the hills to a mountain, on top of which is the Heavenly City. On the road is a pilgrim who wants to go into the city. But he is tired and turns to a woman standing beside the road, and asks:

> "Does the road go uphill all the way?" "Yes, to the very end."
> "And will the journey take all day long?"
> "Yes, from morn till night, my friend."

"Truly," van Gogh concluded, "it is not a picture, but an inspiration."

❧ *For Further Reading* ❧

For those who desire to read further on the quest for meaning, the following is a short list of books that are both helpful and accessible.

Blaise Pascal, "The Wager and other selections from the *Pensées*," with commentary by Peter Kreeft. *The Trinity Forum Reading,* Fall 1995.

John R. W. Stott, *Basic Christianity* (Grand Rapids: Eerdmans, 1958). This is a clear and simple introduction to the Christian faith by the chaplain of the Queen of England.

Michael Green, *The Day Death Died* (Downers Grove, IL: InterVarsity, 1982). On the evidence for the resurrection of Jesus.

Os Guinness, *Long Journey Home* (Colorado Springs, CO: WaterBrook/ Doubleday, 2001).

C. S. Lewis, *Mere Christianity* (New York: Macmillan, 1958). The classic twentieth-century introduction to the Christian faith for thinking people.

James Sire, *The Universe Next Door: a basic world view catalog,* second edition, updated and expanded (Downers Grove, IL: InterVarsity, 1988). A clear comparison of worldviews.

F. F. Bruce, *Are the New Testament Documents Reliable?* 4th edition (Grand Rapids: Eerdmans, 1954).

READER'S GUIDE

Using This Book in a Discussion Group

THE FOLLOWING SMALL-GROUP GUIDE OFFERS A FORMAT FOR LEADING EIGHT NINETY-minute discussions of *The Journey*. Ideally, participants will read about forty pages of the book before each group meeting. However, it's possible for people to participate even if they have not had time to read the material beforehand.

The goals of this discussion group are to help participants:

- Become aware that they have questions about life, that either they have never thought about life's big questions, or something in their experience has made them realize that their current answers aren't good enough
- Address questions of life's meaning, such as: Who are we? Where have we come from? Why are we here? Where are we going? How should we live in light of these answers? What diversions can hinder us from grappling with these questions and living by the answers that seem most true to us?
- Seek answers to the crucial questions they're asking—explore a variety of philosophies to see how adequate their answers seem to participants
- Investigate whether the Christian, Buddhist, materialist, or other answers to life's questions are not just appealing to one's taste, but actually likely to be true
- Understand what's involved in committing oneself to a particular view of life, as opposed to merely giving it intellectual assent
- Draw conclusions about whether they are prepared to commit their lives to a particular view of the world

227

The eight group sessions break down as follows. The names listed are generally those of the author of a reading. In addition to the main readings marked here, you will sometimes discuss the short quotations that are scattered throughout the book.

1. A Time for Questions: Why Thinking Through One's Worldview Is Important (Introduction, Plato, Frankl)
2. A Time for Questions, continued: What Keeps Us from Asking the Big Questions, and What Prompts Us to Ask Them (Pascal, Goethe, Lewis, Berger, Chesterton, Auden)
3. A Time for Answers: Big Answers to the Problem of Evil from Three Main "Families of Faith" (Lustig, Buddha, Russell, Camus)
4. A Time for Answers, continued (Lewis, King, Heine, Nietzsche)
5. A Time for Evidences: Disconfirmation as a Part of Confirmation (Pirsig, Issa, Darwin)
6. A Time for Evidences, continued: A Look at the Christian Faith (Stump, Lewis, the Gospel of Mark)
7. A Time for Commitment: Three Perspectives on the Commitment of Faith (Pascal, St. Paul, Lewis)
8. A Time for Commitment, continued (Peck, Clark, Huxley, von Moltke)

In these readings, the biblical family of faiths (the Jewish and Christian faiths) receives more scrutiny than alternatives such as the Eastern or the secularist. The biblical faiths are the single strongest animating force in Western civilization and still the majority faith today. However, participants are encouraged to bring additional information about other faiths and philosophies to the conversation. This small group is intended to allow a robust airing of divergent views with an especially close examination of the Christian view to see how well it holds up. Participants who know something about Buddhism, Hinduism, atheism, existentialism, or other views of life will greatly enrich the discussion.

The Leader's Role

You don't need any special background in order to lead this discussion group effectively. The readings in this book include background information about the writers and their ideas. This reader's guide offers help in small group leadership. The format of the group will be discussion, not lecture, so you will not be expected to teach or answer questions. Any background you have (in history, philosophy, political science, and so on) will enrich the group, but your knowledge will not be the group's focus.

Your role is:

- To begin and end the meeting on time
- To introduce each reading
- To ask people to read aloud key portions of each reading
- To keep the group moving from reading to reading at a reasonable pace
- To select the questions that are most important for the group to discuss
- To ask questions
- To listen closely to answers and ask follow-up questions as appropriate
- To express your opinions at appropriate moments
- To set a tone of respect and free exchange of ideas
- To make sure that everyone who wants to speak gets adequate air time
- To help the group keep track of the big picture that the readings are sketching

Beginning and ending on time is a way of respecting participants. Latecomers won't mind if you start without them, and doing so rewards those who come on time. Likewise, even if you're in the middle of a great discussion, people will thank you if you cut it off when the time is up. Those who need to leave can leave, and if your host permits, others can stay and continue the conversation informally.

Each reading is preceded by a brief introduction about the author and the context. As you come to each reading, begin by summarizing this introduction in a few sentences. Then, ask someone to read aloud a portion of the reading that relates to the first question you want to ask. (This guide will suggest portions to be read aloud.) Reading aloud and asking questions will set the rhythm of the discussion. Reading aloud refreshes everyone's memory and involves people who may not have read the material ahead of time. (However, be aware that some people are uncomfortable reading aloud. You may want to ask people ahead of time how they feel about doing so.)

After twenty minutes or so, summarize the discussion about that reading and introduce the next one.

Most groups function better with two cofacilitators than with one. It's helpful to take turns guiding discussions on the different readings, or to let one person guide the discussion while the other keeps track of the time.

The Group's Emphasis

Some small groups emphasize the sharing of personal experiences and feelings. Many groups don't challenge people to think deeply. This series addresses whole people, the understanding as well as the feeling parts of them. Your task is to help the group think, understand, and draw conclusions together. However, the conversation will not be banter about airy notions. The questions are designed to be practical. The issues raised are relevant to the nitty-gritty lives of each person in your group. Ideally, people will leave each meeting with new thoughts about what they do all day: conduct business, raise children, vote for lawmakers, relate to neighbors, spend money. And you may be surprised at how emotional these thoughtful discussions become as people's hearts are pierced with new perspectives on their lives.

The questions typically progress along the following lines:

- What's being said?
- Is it true?
- So what?

That is, you'll begin by identifying exactly what the writer of the given selection is trying to say. Then you'll have a chance to react to it. Some people like to jump to expressing their opinions before taking the time to understand clearly what the author is saying. If this happens, it will be your job to slow participants down and ask them to look first at the text. An essential group skill is *listening*—listening both to the other members of the group and to the author of the selection being discussed. To speak one's own opinion without listening to others long enough to understand them is to shortchange oneself and the whole group.

Each session is designed to take about ninety minutes. During that time you will discuss three or four readings from *The Journey*, so you may have just twenty or thirty minutes for each one. Therefore, you won't have time to discuss all the questions listed in the book. It's not necessary to have an exhaustive discussion about any reading. Instead, you'll draw out the main points of each one so that group members can follow the inner logic that flows through the progression of readings. You won't have time to get bogged down in one reading because if you did, you would lose the thread of the big picture. Another benefit of keeping up the momentum is that in any given session, everyone is likely to find at least one of the readings especially meaningful to him or her personally. It is always better to cut off a good discussion than to drag it out until it dies.

This reader's guide will point out the questions for each reading that will be most helpful for group discussion. It will also trace the big picture from reading to reading so that you will have no trouble seeing where you're going. This guidance is meant to simplify your job. Nevertheless, you are still the group leader, so if you think your group will benefit most from questions other than those suggested here, then follow your intuition. Instead of the pointed questions that follow each reading, you may prefer to use open-ended questions, such as, "What is your perspective, feeling, or reaction to this reading?"

The reader's guide contains no suggestions for worship, such as prayer or the singing of hymns. This format makes the group open to everyone, regardless of faith convictions.

Guiding the Discussion

Most groups depend heavily on the leader in the beginning. The leader asks a question, and someone answers. The leader asks another question, and someone answers. People direct their responses to the leader. However, an effective leader nudges participants toward talking to each other. The leader plays referee and timekeeper so that the group stays on track.

One tool for nudging people to talk to each other is the follow-up question. For instance, one type of follow-up question invites others' input: "What do others of you think about Terry's view?" Other kinds of follow-up questions include:

- Rephrasing the question
- Probing gently for more information ("Can you say more about that?")
- Asking for clarification ("So are you saying that . . .?")
- Summarizing a portion of the discussion

You will probably want to summarize (or ask someone else to do so) at the end of your discussion of each reading. This will help people keep track of where each reading fits into the big picture.

Maintain eye contact with all participants, particularly those on your immediate left and right, so that everyone feels included in the discussion. It's a good idea to arrange the room in a circle before the meeting so that people will be able to see each other's faces.

Avoid answering your own questions. Allow silence, especially when people are looking at the readings to refresh their memories. If people seem not to understand your question, it's best to rephrase it rather than answer it.

Also, avoid commenting on each participant's response. Instead, ask a follow-up question to draw out others' comments.

Encourage participants to ask questions about one another's comments. Your ultimate goal is to foster a lively discussion among participants about the point under discussion. However, if you sense that the conversation is drifting off the main point of the reading, summarize the comments that have been made and move on to a new question that builds toward the focus of the reading.

Dealing with Talkative and Quiet People

In any small group, some people are naturally more talkative than others. While it's desirable for everyone to participate aloud, it's not essential for this group. One of the ground rules is that everyone is welcome to speak, but no one is obliged to speak. There are several reasons why a person might be quiet during the meeting, and you'll want to assess which reasons apply to each of your quiet people. Reasons for quietness include the following:

- A person may be overwhelmed by the material and not be following the discussion. This person needs you to listen to his or her concerns outside the group meeting.
- A person may be processing the discussion internally. Some people prefer to digest ideas and feelings inside and speak only when they have thought through what they want to say. By contrast, other people think out loud. They often don't know what they think until it comes out of their mouths. It's possible that both the talkative and the quiet people are getting what they need in your group. Don't assume that silence equals nonparticipation.
- A person may strongly disagree with what is being said but may be uncomfortable with overt conflict. There are ways of handling covert conflict that strengthen the group. See "Disagreement and Conflict" on the next page.

- A person may want to speak but may feel intimidated in a group. It's usually best to draw such people out in conversation outside the formal discussion, but not to call attention to them during the meeting.

This is not an exhaustive list of reasons for quietness. The important thing is to gauge each person individually and ask yourself, "What might this person need?"

With people whom you think talk too much, knowing why they're talking is less important than assessing their effect on the group. Are the quieter people getting something out of what the talker is saying? Or are they wishing they were somewhere else? If you think someone's talking is excessive, there are several subtle ways to discourage it. You can sit next to the person rather than facing him. You can avoid making eye contact or nodding, since these are signals that the speaker should continue. In extreme cases, you can take the person aside after the meeting and enlist his help in drawing out the quieter group members.

Above all, take care that you are not the group member who talks too much. Keep the group focused on the readings, not on you. Resist the temptation to fill silence with your observations. Silence can be productive if people are thinking.

Disagreement and Conflict

In a discussion group of this kind, disagreement is good. *Tough-minded discussion* occurs when one person's ideas, conclusions, or opinions are incompatible with another's, and the two seek a deeper understanding of truth or wisdom together. Views are aired openly, and everyone has a chance to evaluate the merits of each position. Someone might even change his or her mind.

Debate occurs when people's ideas, conclusions, or opinions are incompatible; each person argues for his or her position; and a winner is declared. Debate is not necessarily bad in a group either. People may feel strongly that they are right and someone else is wrong. A strenuous defense of one's position is fair play.

Some ground rules can make tough-minded discussion and debate constructive:

- Genuine disagreement is an achievement because it enables people to learn. We assume that a disagreement is valuable until proven otherwise.

- Deepening our understanding of truth or wisdom is more important in this group than winning an argument.
- Respect is important in this group. The merits of a position may be debated, but persons may not be attacked.
- If people feel attacked, they will say so respectfully, and the group will assess the situation together.

Many people fear all forms of conflict, including tough-minded discussion and debate. If you have group members who are uncomfortable with conflict in the group, you may want to have a discussion about constructive conflict. Explain that while quarreling is unproductive, disagreement is not. Emphasize that *concurrence-seeking* is less productive than open controversy. Concurrence-seeking happens when group members inhibit discussion in order to avoid disagreement. Concurrence-seeking can lead to *groupthink,* in which everyone feels obliged to think alike and people cease to think for themselves. Religious versions of political correctness are not uncommon.

A certain amount of concurrence-seeking is natural in a group of people who don't know each other well. However, the more you can draw covert conflict out into the open, the less likely people are to withdraw from the group because of unvoiced dissatisfaction. If you sense people simmering but not speaking, the best course may be to give a short speech about the value of healthy disagreement and to state some ground rules for tough-minded discussion.

The Roadmap

Because you'll cover a lot of ground in each group session, you'll find it helpful to keep in mind the book's "roadmap." The readings have been arranged as a journey leading logically from point to point, but they are not a self-contained logical proof. They require the group's involvement as participants, not spectators. Each reading contains many more interesting ideas than you have time to discuss, so you can avoid time-consuming side trips if you keep the roadmap or big picture in mind. Here is a detailed summary of the roadmap that you might use to orient the group as you begin each session:

The Journey is a process for arriving at a view of life that is both true and useful for responding to the experiences that life throws at you. Everybody has a view of life or "worldview." Some of us have adopted our worldview from our families or the surrounding culture without reflecting on whether our worldview is (a) adequate for understanding and dealing with life well or (b) true. *The Journey* offers us a chance to examine our worldviews and adjust them if we decide to do so.

Part 1 invites us to ask the big questions of life: What's really important? What am I to make of evil? Is there any meaning to the suffering I experience? Does anything exist outside my own mind or what I sense with my five senses? We begin with two readings that offer reasons for asking such questions. First, the Greek philosopher Plato tells a story that makes an unsettling point: our five senses may give us a severely distorted impression of reality as it actually is. Could Plato be right? Next, psychiatrist Viktor Frankl recounts an incident he experienced in a Nazi death camp; he shows how a person's life can literally depend on a sense of meaning and hope amid suffering. Then come two readings that explain why, despite our human need for a reliable sense of meaning, so few people invest energy toward asking the big questions. Scientist Blaise Pascal describes "diversion," the human drive to use any activity from work to entertainment that shields us from looking too closely at the inevitability of death. Second, *Faust* by the poet Goethe illustrates how we try to make bargains with life in order to fend off death and futility. Part 1 closes with four examples of experiences that shatter our attempts at diversion and bargaining and so force us to face the big questions. Scholar C. S. Lewis describes his experience of joy that transcends mere pleasure. Sociologist Peter Berger points to our hunger to believe that everything will be "all right" no matter what. Journalist G. K. Chesterton says gratitude for being alive was what first prodded him onto the journey toward faith. Poet W. H. Auden tells how confronting the realities of Nazism shook him out of his naïve optimism about human nature. The point of discussing these readings will be to help people overcome their reluctance to ask big questions and to help them put words to their questions. In order to come to deep convictions that can undergird a life, people need space to become open to the possibility of changing their minds about what they believe. Your goal in discussing part 1 will be to stir things up.

Part 2 offers a variety of answers to the questions raised in part 1. It focuses on one question in particular—the problem of why evil exists in the world and how humans should respond to it—in order to compare different worldviews. Your group will have a chance to evaluate how well each worldview throws light on this question. This is a time for asking, "What if this worldview is right about evil? What then?" In order to have a productive discussion, you'll need to grapple with the question not as mere idea-browsers, but as people who really do want an adequate way of viewing and responding to evil. Arnost

Lustig makes the case for taking the question of evil seriously. An excerpt from *The Gospel of Buddha* illustrates how the Eastern family of faiths deals with evil. Actress Shirley MacLaine speaks for the New Age view of evil. Philosopher Bertrand Russell explains how a secularist confronts evil, suffering, and death. Novelist Albert Camus makes a similar case for existential atheism. Then follow readings—two by C. S. Lewis, and one by Martin Luther King Jr.—that set out the Christian response to the problem of evil. Lastly, two readings highlight the seriousness of coming to grips with evil. Two nineteenth-century Germans (Heinrich Heine and Friedrich Nietzsche) foresaw what would happen in twentieth-century Europe when God "died," when Europeans abandoned the Christian stance toward evil in favor of paganism or atheism. As Nazism and other instances of genocide prove, Christian morality without Christian faith is a naïve fantasy.

While part 2 helps your group find a worldview that meets their needs, part 3 helps you decide whether that view is true. Faith that may be merely an illusion or a crutch is not the kind of answer for life that rational people want. Part 3 offers evidence—not absolute proof—of the truth of Christian faith. It also offers evidence that the alternatives do not match up with what we experience of the world. Three readings present the negative evidence. First, an excerpt from *Zen and the Art of Motorcycle Maintenance* by Robert Pirsig shows why Zen and other Eastern traditions fail to satisfy. The Japanese poet Issa offers further evidence against the Buddhist approach. And Charles Darwin's own letters show the inadequacy of scientific materialism as a philosophy for Darwin's life. After that, four readings present the positive evidence that the Christian faith makes sense. G. K. Chesterton shows that only Christian faith can explain both the optimistic truth about the world (the world is good) and the pessimistic truth (the world is going to hell in a handbasket). Philosopher Eleonore Stump thinks the God of the Bible is the best explanation for what she sees in the world of great wickedness and astonishing goodness. C. S. Lewis points to Jesus and lays out evidence that he was either a liar, a lunatic, a legend, or the Lord God. A story from the Gospel of Mark illustrates Lewis's argument.

Part 4 is meant to help your group members draw conclusions and commit themselves to a life of faith. The readings in this part display examples of what a genuine faith commitment looks like and show why mere intellectual belief is not enough. First come three perspectives on the step of commitment. Pascal presents faith as a wager, a smart bet that God exists and eternity matters now. Then the biblical account of St. Paul's conversion and C. S. Lewis's own experience show two instances of commitment to what is seen to be true.

Next, three readings illustrate the opposite, the choice to turn away from evidence one doesn't want to accept. Psychiatrist M. Scott Peck tells of a patient who chooses to reject God and live for herself. Art historian Kenneth Clark describes his own decision to reject an experience of grace because accepting it would require a change in his neatly ordered life. And novelist Aldous Huxley explains his atheism not as a rational choice based on evidence, but as the easy choice that left him free to indulge his desires. The contrast between the two options of part 4 is key: faith is not a decision to believe something because we need to believe it, in spite of the evidence; it is the decision to believe something because we have been convinced by the evidence, even if the journey of faith eventually takes us to painful places. Far from being a choice to believe an illusion for the sake of comfort, the step of faith often leads away from comfort but toward something more substantial: acts of integrity and great good. The final reading, from the letters of Helmut James von Moltke, reflects a man about to die for his faith.

The trajectory of the book then, is this:

- Become aware of what makes a seeker: that the big questions of life demand answers, and allow oneself to examine one's current answers.
- Confront the diversions that hinder a person from grappling with these questions and living by the answers that seem most true.
- Explore a varied but finite set of philosophies to seek answers to the crucial questions. For the sake of time, focus on the question of evil.
- Investigate whether the Christian, Buddhist, secularist, or other answers to life's questions are not just appealing to one's taste, but actually likely to be true.
- Understand what's involved in committing oneself to a particular view of life, and what's involved in ducking the commitment.
- Decide whether one is prepared to commit one's life to faith.

You may want to refer the group to this roadmap at the beginning of each session. This reader's guide will help you orient each session within the roadmap.

SESSION 1

Unless yours is an ongoing group, people will usually treat the first meeting as an opportunity to decide whether they want to participate. They will decide what they think about one another, the material, and the discussion format. Therefore, you'll want to do a few extra things in the first meeting that will help people feel comfortable with each other, have a sense of where the group is going, and become excited enough about the group to return.

Perhaps the best way to break the ice in a new group is to share a meal. Plan a simple enough meal that the focus will be on conversation. Schedule the meal so that people don't feel rushed as they eat, yet you still have ninety minutes for a full discussion session. You'll want the full ninety minutes in order to give people a realistic taste of what the group will be like. If sharing a full meal is impractical, consider planning a two-hour session in which the first half-hour is devoted to light refreshments and informal chatting.

Overview and Introductions   (25 minutes)

When the food is set aside and the group gathers formally, welcome everyone. Then take ten minutes to give people an overview of what to expect. Explain:

- *What the* Trinity Forum Study Series *is:* It makes the forum curricula available to study groups. It helps thoughtful people examine the foundational issues through which faith acts upon the public good of modern society. It is Christian in commitment but open to all who are interested in its vision. Issues are discussed in the context of faith and the sweep of Western civilization.
- *The theme of this particular study:* What answers to questions about life's meaning are convincing and satisfying enough to commit ourselves to?
- *The goals of this study:* See page 227.
- *The big picture of this study:* You may want to walk the group through "The Roadmap" section. See page 234.
- *The format of the group:* Your discussions will take about ninety minutes. In each session you will cover about thirty pages from the book. Ideally, everyone will have read the material ahead of time, but it is

possible to participate without having done so. As the leader, you'll select questions that you think are most helpful for the group to discuss. Your goal is an open give-and-take, and you will not be lecturing. Differing opinions are welcome.

Ground Rules

Here is a list of suggested ground rules for your group. You may want to add to this list the ones about disagreement on pages 233-234:

- *Leadership:* The leader is not an expert or an authority, merely a facilitator and fellow seeker. All in the group are teachers; all are students.
- *Confidentiality:* All discussion is free, frank, and *off-the-record.* Nothing will be repeated outside the group without permission.
- *Voluntary participation:* Everyone is free to speak; no one is required to take part. The only exception will be in the final session, when everyone will be asked to share two or three things he or she has found helpful or striking.
- *Non-denominational, non-partisan spirit:* Many people have strong beliefs and allegiances, both denominational and political. However, the desire here is to go deeper, so it will be important to transcend political advocacy and denominational differences. The book comes from the perspective of what C. S. Lewis called "mere Christianity" and reflects no particular denomination. Participants are welcome to express their own views and even to disagree with the readings.
- *Punctuality:* In order to get to all of the readings, the leader will keep the discussion moving. The formal meeting will begin and end on time.
- *Logistics:* Tell people anything they need to know about the location and schedule of the meetings. Explain that the group will finish promptly at the official ending time. That is the "soft" ending. However, if the host permits, you can also set a "hard" ending time thirty, sixty, or more minutes later. In that case, people are free to stay after the soft ending and talk informally until the hard ending time. (Setting a hard ending is a courtesy to the host if you are meeting in a home.)

Next, ask participants to go around and introduce themselves briefly. You'll go first to model the length and type of response you're looking for. That is, if your answer is one sentence, the others will usually give one sentence. If you take one minute, or three minutes, others will follow suit. The same is true for the content of your answer: if you say something brief and substantive, others will tend to do the same. Therefore, it will be a good idea to think ahead of time about how you can introduce yourself in a minute or less. In this way, you won't shortchange time for discussing the book. By way of introduction, ask each person to state his or her name and answer the following questions briefly:

- When you were a child, what was your family's stance on matters of faith?
- What is one thing that motivates you to get out of bed in the morning?

Introduction: The Journey   (10 minutes)

The introduction sets up the idea of life as a journey. It also addresses our modern condition of restless journeying without a clear idea of a destination. The readings by Plato and Frankl need the bulk of your attention in this session, but you might want to look briefly at the introduction. In this way you will draw attention to it, and anyone who has not had a chance to read it will be more motivated to do so.

Ask someone to read aloud the quotation from G. K. Chesterton at the end of the introduction: "Man has always lost his way. He has been a tramp ever since Eden; but he always knew, or thought he knew, what he was looking for. . . . For the first time in history he begins really to doubt the object of his wanderings on earth. He has always lost his way; but now he has lost his address." Then ask each participant to take one minute to respond to the following:

- Tell us something about your experience of wandering or journeying during the past ten years. You could talk about (a) the places you have lived during these years, (b) your business travel during this time, or (c) some part of your spiritual journey.

If everyone has responded and you still have time, ask participants to what extent they can identify with the image of life as a journey. If they see themselves as journeyers, do they feel they have a sense of where "home" is?

Plato   (30 minutes)

You'll spend the rest of this first group session looking at two readings that offer reasons for asking the big questions of life. The point of your discussion will be to help people overcome their reluctance to ask big questions and to help them put words to their questions. In order to come to deep convictions that can undergird a life, people need space to become open to the possibility of changing their minds about what they believe.

Before diving into Plato, summarize the introduction to part 1. Then take a minute to look at the Point to Ponder, "A World Within the World that Makes a World of Difference," to make sure everyone understands the term *worldview*. Your worldview is your philosophy of life, the framework of assumptions through which you interpret your experience of life. Everybody has a worldview. The following exercise might help your group see how a worldview works in practice:

Let's say you get a serious form of cancer. What assumptions about life will shape your interpretation of and response to this experience? Choose one or more of the following beliefs that you agree with. Add others if you choose.

- Heartless corporations are polluting the earth and causing cancer.
- Everything that happens is basically random.
- Everything happens for a reason.
- Disease and death prove that all life is meaningless and futile.
- A good God is in ultimate control of all that happens in the universe.
- What gives life meaning is to live bravely and die bravely.
- This life is all there is. After that, there's nothing.
- If I die, I will be reincarnated in another body.
- If I die, I will go to eternal joy.
- Death is the enemy to be fought by all means possible.
- My little life matters hardly at all in the vast scheme of the universe.

Now it may be clearer why worldviews make a world of difference. Carry this idea with you as you read the excerpt from Plato's *Republic*. In this reading, Plato tells a story that makes an unsettling point: our five senses may give us a severely distorted impression of reality as it actually is. Our worldviews may be way off base. Some members of your group may believe there's no such thing as "reality as it actually is." They may believe (this is a worldview assumption) that each person creates his own reality when he forms his own worldview. This is not the time to debate that assumption. Simply raise it as a possible belief, and ask participants to examine it as they go through the readings over the coming weeks. To begin with, what would Plato say in response to this belief?

The meaning of Plato's parable of the cave may not be obvious to readers who are not accustomed to sorting out this kind of closely reasoned allegory. Therefore, the introduction to the reading summarizes the salient points. Ask someone to read aloud from "The following reading . . ." to the end of the introduction (page 30). Ask the group to try to visualize the scene Plato is painting. Then have someone read the first seven paragraphs of the parable, from "And now . . ." through ". . . nothing but the shadows of the images." Discuss question 1. It might be helpful for you to compare the scene to a movie theater. The prisoners have spent their whole lives in the dark theater, seeing nothing but the images projected onto the movie screen, images of The World According to Hollywood. How accurate would be their understanding of the world outside the theater?

On page 32 read aloud the paragraph that begins, "And now look again . . ." and discuss question 2. Read "And if he is compelled . . ." and "Last of all he will . . .," then discuss question 3. "The light" in the parable is the sun, but it represents what Plato further on calls "the idea of good." "The idea of good" was Plato's term for a non-material Something that was beyond the reality we experience with our senses, was absolutely good, was the standard by which all goodness or evil on earth could be evaluated, and was even somehow the source of all goodness and beauty and reason on earth, just as the sun is the source of all daylight on earth.

Read aloud the paragraph that begins, "Imagine once more . . ." and discuss question 5.

Plato interprets his allegory (question 6) in the paragraph that begins, "This entire allegory . . ." on page 33. You may want to walk the group through this paragraph, because it is the key to making sense of Plato and is full of terms that carry unique meanings in Plato's vocabulary. "The idea of good" you've already addressed. What he calls "the intellectual world" is what we might call "the spiritual world"—that is, the world beyond the material world we sense with our senses and measure with our scientific instruments. He calls it "intellectual" because he thinks we can apprehend it if we train and use our minds properly, not through the kinds of religious rituals practiced in ancient Greece. When you think the group adequately understands this key paragraph, discuss question 7. What do participants think of the notion that there is a God out there, which is the source and standard of good, but which we can't know without effort?

See what you can do with question 10. Some atheists might say that Plato is simply wrong: there is no world outside that which we sense. Others might say there's a lot going on that is beyond our senses, but they might debate where there is an idea of good out there. A Hindu might understand the cave as the cycle of death and rebirth to which humans are doomed until they attain Nirvana. A Jew or Christian might say that the Creator God—an alive Being— is the idea of good, the source and standard of all beauty and goodness on earth. More important than comparing these various worldviews is dealing with the last part of question 10: what does your group think about the *possibility* that the way they see the world may not be the only way, or may even be disastrously wrong? The first step on a genuine journey is to admit the possibility that one might be wrong about something. If we cannot be wrong, we can never change our minds. While total open-mindedness—a refusal to commit to an opinion and live by it—is no virtue, neither is total close-mindedness.

Viktor Frankl   (30 minutes)

Some participants may be inclined to the safe, don't-rock-the-boat position that it doesn't matter whether Plato is right, that we can't know whether we live in a world of illusion, so we might as well go on as before and enjoy life as much as possible. This is an easy stance when life is easy. However, the next reading points out that at any moment life might cease to be easy, and it might suddenly be essential to know whether we have anything solid to hang onto. Using an incident he experienced in a Nazi death camp, Viktor Frankl shows how a person's life can literally depend on a sense of meaning and hope.

Summarize the background that explains who Frankl was and where this reading comes from. Have someone read the first paragraph of the selection on page 38. Discuss question 1. Then go on to question 2. What do you make of this idea that hope is not, "I'm confident that I'm going to get what I expect from life" but rather, "I know what life expects from me, and I know I have the resources to respond well"? Is that enough hope for you? Why was it the right kind of hope for people in the death camp?

Read the box on pages 38-39 and discuss question 3. For question 4, you might want to list the points Frankl makes in his talk. One could have hope because:

- There was still the possibility of recovering what one had lost in the war.
- There was the chance of getting assigned to exceptionally good working conditions, even in the camp.
- Nothing could take away one's good memories of the past.
- Each person knew that someone was watching with loving eyes, someone for whom one would like to be seen suffering proudly, even knowing how to die well.
- While sacrifice may seem pointless in a purely material world, there is a larger world in which every sacrifice has meaning.

Cover questions 7 and 9 with your remaining time. As you close your session, invite participants to bring to your next meeting any news items that show people either avoiding or facing the big questions of life. Also, ask them to read the selections by Pascal, Goethe, Lewis, Berger, Chesterton, and Auden for next time, along with the two essays labeled "Point to Ponder." In session 2 you will look at some habits that help us avoid the big questions and some experiences that can jolt us past those defenses.

SESSION 2

Session 2 continues your effort to stir up big questions about life in participants' minds. Answering these questions will come later; first people need to overcome their natural resistance to thinking about these issues at all.

But why should we resist dealing with the questions that are most central to our happiness and humanness? Your first two readings in this session explain why. Pascal describes "diversion," the human drive to use any activity from work to entertainment that shields us from looking too closely at the inevitability of death. Then *Faust* by the poet Goethe illustrates how we try to make bargains with life in order to fend off death and futility. Both diversion and bargaining are defenses against that which we fear the most: the inevitability of our own death.

Blaise Pascal   (15 minutes)

Take a minute to summarize "The Real Divide Is Between the Serious and the Indifferent" and then the introduction to Pascal. Note that diversion is "our drive toward an entertaining, distracting busyness that protects us from thinking too deeply about our human condition." One can be distracted equally well by busy work or busy entertainment. The goal of this discussion is to raise the possibility in participants' minds that *their* busyness may not be imposed on them from the outside (by bosses, family, and so on), but chosen by the fears in their own hearts.

Read aloud the first five paragraphs of the selection starting on page 46, and discuss questions 1 and 2. Read "Telling a man to rest . . ." and "Thus men . . ." and discuss questions 5 through 7.

Pascal's is just one of five readings you need to cover in this session, so you'll need to keep moving. The point here is to plant Pascal's idea about diversion in people's minds, not to exhaust the subject.

Goethe   (15 minutes)

Faust is challenging partly because it is poetry. Not everyone is practiced at extracting the meaning from two-hundred-year-old poetry. For this reason, and because you have a lot more to cover, you may want to help participants draw the meaning from this reading. Summarize the introduction on page 50. Ask someone to read the first ten lines or so of Faust's opening monologue. Then note the phrases that reveal what frustrates him: "The pain of life"; "Too old am I . . . Too young . . ." (he's middle aged); "Renunciation!" (life seems to be nothing but giving things up when one is middle aged); "None of my longings will come true" (life is hard, so he doesn't get what he wants, what he dreams of). He's alive with normal human desires, but beset by human limitations and the inevitability of death. Having outlined all this, ask the last two parts of question 1—about Faust's susceptibilities and his character.

Mephistopheles uses Faust's normal human desires (normal, but ungoverned) to ensnare him. Faust's problem is not that he wants pleasurable experiences; his problem is that he refuses to accept with humility life's "No." In Frankl's terms, his hope is in what he expects from life, not in what life expects from him. With this in mind, discuss questions 4 through 6. The box, "Sex Is Worth Dying For," points to one kind of human desire that can lead to a bad bargain. See if your group can think of other desires that can make us vulnerable, such as the desire for career success, youth, beauty, fame, power, or money.

C. S. Lewis   (20 minutes)

Part 1 closes with four examples of experiences that shatter our attempts at diversion and bargaining and so force us to face the big questions. In this reading, C. S. Lewis describes his experience of joy.

After summarizing who Lewis was, read the first paragraph of the selection on page 61. Discuss question 1.

Lewis believes that this piercing longing is not a longing for something past—some memory of a beautiful place, a thrilling piece of music we once heard, or a warm embrace. Instead, he thinks it's a longing for something we've never tasted in this world. He speaks of waking modern people from the spell of worldliness, the evil enchantment of believing that nothing exists beyond what we can sense scientifically. Our longing is for the "transtemporal." Make sure everyone in the group understands what he's saying, even if they don't agree.

Have someone read the box, "A Longing for the Longing." Discuss question 3. Read the next box, "Far, Far More than Happiness." Discuss question 4. Help the group understand Lewis's paradoxical words. Pleasure can be had in this world, while joy points to something beyond. Thus, many people settle for pleasure, but those who have acquired a taste for joy pursue it doggedly, even though they know their gratification will be delayed.

Use question 7 to give everyone a chance to voice a personal reaction. Some people greatly identify with this experience of longing; others have a temperament that tends to be oblivious to such experiences. That's why you'll be looking at three other kinds of experiences in the rest of the selections in part 1. Hopefully, everyone will find something to relate to.

Peter Berger   (5 minutes)

Because there are so many readings in the second half of part 1, you'll probably have to skip Peter Berger's. However, you may want to recommend it for those who have not read it. Berger points to the human instinct to believe and to reassure others that everything is "all right" as an indication that humans are wired for transcendence. If this world is all there is, then it's a lie to say that everything is all right. So much in life is far from all right, and that which we most fear—death—will come to us all. From this point of view, nothing is all right. Yet we persist. Why? Berger states the case well.

G. K. Chesterton   (20 minutes)

G. K. Chesterton's hint of things larger than himself is simple: gratitude. Summarize who he was, then read aloud the last couple of sentences of the first paragraph on page 70, "It was substantially this . . ." Discuss question 1. The question refers to "contemporary pessimism." You might pause to ask, "Where do you see pessimism in our culture?"

Read the next two paragraphs. Discuss questions 2 and 3.

It's easy to take Chesterton as simply an optimist. He sees the good in life. But he's not so simple. He doesn't close his eyes to life's difficulties and see only a great deal of good. Further down he speaks of "having a great deal of gratitude even for a very little good." What do you think about being grateful even if one has a difficult life, simply because one has any life at all? What do you think about being grateful for dandelions and the eyesight to see them, even if one has to struggle deeply with tight finances or poor health or difficult relationships?

Finally, Chesterton raises the question of whether one can be thankful for life if there is no one to thank. Read the last sentences of the selection from

"'What nonsense all this is . . .?'" Ask the group whether they think Chesterton is onto something here or not.

Finish this selection by discussing question 8.

W. H. Auden   (20 minutes)

Your final pointer to the big questions is much less cheerful. The poet Auden speaks of the moment when he came to grips with the human capacity for evil. Read the first paragraph of the selection on page 76 and discuss question 1. Read the next paragraph and discuss question 2. Read the paragraphs, "Auden began to remark . . ." and "'The whole trend of liberal thought . . .'" Discuss question 4. Spend a little time on questions 6 and 7.

Don't worry if you can't exhaust these last two questions. The problem of evil will come up again in part 2. In fact, Auden's experience appropriately sets up the question that you will set out to answer in part 2. You've begun to ask some big questions: Why do so many people have a longing for an undiscovered country that exists nowhere on earth? Why do we instinctively tell children and ourselves, "It's going to be all right"? Why is there so much to be grateful for if there's no one who deserves that gratitude? And why is there such evil in the world? These questions demand answers. In session 3 you'll look at several classic answers to the problem of evil and evaluate how convincing you find them. Ask the group to read Lustig, *The Gospel of Buddha*, Russell, and Camus for next time. And ask them to be aware over the next week of any of the pointers you've covered in this session: joy, or the longing for joy; the instinct for order; things that seem to deserve gratitude; or evil.

SESSION 3

Having come to grips with your questions, it's now time to look for answers. In the interest of time, this book focuses on just one of the big questions raised in part 1—the problem of why evil exists in the world and how humans should respond to it. This question provides a context for you to compare different worldviews. You'll be asking, "What does this worldview have to say about evil? Then, what if this worldview is right about evil? What then?"

Arnost Lustig   (15 minutes)

In order to have a productive discussion, you'll need to grapple with the question of evil not as mere idea-browsers but as people who desperately need an adequate way of viewing and responding to it. Arnost Lustig makes the case for taking the question of evil seriously. If "evil" feels like a distant abstraction to you, take a moment to sink down into the sights and smells of Auschwitz-Birchenau.

Read the fourth and fifth paragraphs on page 85, beginning with "Sometimes I wish . . ." Discuss questions 2 and 3. Read the rest of the selection. Allow a moment of silence. Ask, "What in this brief account helps you to take the problem of evil seriously?" Discuss questions 5 and 6 to the extent that you have time.

The Gospel of Buddha   (30 minutes)

This selection gives a concise account of what motivated Prince Siddhartha Gautama to set off on his pursuit of enlightenment. From the introduction to this selection, read aloud the definitions of *samsara* and *karma*. Then under the subhead "The Three Woes" on page 89, read the eleven short paragraphs beginning with, "There by the wayside . . ." Discuss questions 1 and 2.

It was indeed the problem of evil that motivated Siddhartha to seek enlightenment. However, you may want to note in your discussion that Siddhartha was dealing with a different face of evil than that of Auschwitz. Siddhartha was jolted out of his complacency simply by facing the inevitability of aging, disease, and death—all natural processes. These natural signs of life's futility motivated him to withdraw from the world to seek his own enlightenment. By contrast, there was nothing natural about the deaths at Auschwitz. That was evil deliberately planned and performed by humans. Is withdrawal a reasonable response to the evil of Auschwitz? What would a Buddhist say? What about a humanist? A Christian? A Jew? Should there be a difference in our response to impersonal evil (such as a disease caused by a microbe) as opposed to personal evil (something done deliberately by a person or other intelligent being)?

Read the paragraphs, "The prince hearing this greeting . . ." and "Then asked Kisa Gotami . . ." Discuss questions 3 and 4.

For question 5 read "In reply the vision . . ." For question 6 read "A thrill of joy . . ." For question 8 read the section called "Setting in Motion the Wheel of the Dharma."

Buddhism may be described as a "peace" worldview because the highest good is viewed to be Nirvana, a state of peace. Judaism is better classified as a "righteousness" worldview because while inner and outer peace are much esteemed in Judaism, a greater priority is placed on justice or righteousness. For the Jew, it is more important to work for justice in the world than to have peace or personal enlightenment for oneself. From the Buddhist point of view, the best thing you can do for the world is to withdraw to seek your own enlightenment. (On the other hand, some Buddhists interpret the right outlook, resolves, speech, and acts of the Noble Eightfold Path as including work for justice in this world. Most notable among these are those who have been exposed to Western ideas of human rights.) Which of these poles appeals to you more: a peace worldview or a righteousness worldview? Discuss question 10 to the extent that you have time.

Bertrand Russell   (20 minutes)

Because of limited time you may skip the New Age view of evil as represented by Shirley MacLaine. It's easy to laugh at MacLaine's ideas but hard not to be impressed by the nobility and intellect of Bertrand Russell, who makes the case for atheistic humanism. Summarize who Russell was. Read aloud the first paragraph of this selection on page 104 and discuss question 1. Ask the group to scan the rest of the selection for answers to question 3. Take a few minutes to discuss question 4. Then read "Not Such Good News After All" and discuss question 5.

Albert Camus   (30 minutes)

Both Russell and Camus were atheists, but they represent drastically different conclusions drawn from the assumption that there is no God and everything on earth happens by chance. Russell might recognize Camus's Dr. Rieux as the noble humanist battling bravely against the tragic inevitability of death, but Camus's existentialist version of the tale leaves quite a different taste in the reader's mouth.

Summarize who Camus was and what *The Plague* was basically about. Read the first two paragraphs of the selection starting on page 108 and discuss questions 1 and 2. What does the word "creation" mean if there is no Creator? Read the six paragraphs beginning with "Against whom?" Discuss questions 5 and 6. Further down, find the paragraph that begins, "*[Tarrou himself contracts . . .]*" Read the last half of that paragraph, beginning with, "And now Rieux had before him . . ." Read the final two paragraphs of the selection. Discuss question 7.

Ask the group to read the two Lewis selections, Martin Luther King Jr., Heine, and Nietzsche for next time, along with the Point to Ponder entitled, "The Image and the Mirror Image." Also, if they know of any additional information about Buddhist, humanist, or existentialist responses to evil and suffering, invite them to bring that information to share with the group.

SESSION 4

The first three readings in this session—two by C. S. Lewis and one by Martin Luther King Jr.—set out the Christian response to the problem of evil. The last two readings—Heine and Nietzsche—point toward the vacuum left in a formerly Christian society when the Christian view of evil is rejected. These positive and negative accounts are chosen to help you look closely at the Christian option. As you discuss these readings, you may find it helpful to refer back to the Buddhist, humanist, and existentialist worldviews for comparison.

C. S. Lewis   (45 minutes)

The first C. S. Lewis selection is from an essay about the Christian faith. The second is from a children's story that echoes the death and resurrection of Christ.

The quotation from Zaehner ("In, But Not Of") sets up the first Lewis selection. Lewis talks about the twin this-worldly and other-worldly aspects of the Christian faith, and Zaehner points to one of the cultural results of that twin quality. Technological advances happen in societies where life in this world matters, and so where improving life in this world matters. The other-worldly aspect of the Christian faith has given the West its belief in linear progress—the notion that history is going somewhere—as opposed to the Eastern view that life is cyclical and not directed toward a goal or culmination. Traditionally, Eastern societies have valued stability far more than progress. This distinction is harder to see these days, now that the East has developed a taste for technological progress and the West no longer links its value of progress with faith in an other-worldly culmination of life.

In the first Lewis selection beginning on page 114, read aloud the second and third paragraphs. Discuss question 3.

Take a moment to think of answers to question 4: Were the hospitals in your area originally run by Christian denominations? What about the elementary schools? The universities? The youth organizations? For example, few Americans stop to think about the fact that Harvard and Yale were founded by Puritans to educate clergy and other leaders, that their local hospital is called St. Jude's, that their children learn to swim at the YMCA (the Young Men's Christian Association), or that the local social services from poverty relief to drug treatment have their origins in overtly Christian efforts.

The biblical truths behind the two-edged character of the Christian faith are the Creation and the Fall. To see how these two truths organize the Christian worldview (question 5), ask the group to scan the paragraphs that begin, "Probably most of those . . ." and "This attitude will . . ." How does the idea of Creation lead a Christian to value this world? How does it lead a Christian to value the next world more? What about the idea of the Fall? (The Fall is the idea that evil entered the world through humans' choice to pursue becoming gods in their own right. Chapters 1 and 2 of the book of Genesis describe the Creation, and chapter 3 describes the Fall. A humanist interpretation of Genesis would say that rejecting a parental authority and choosing self-determination and self-knowledge are what makes us truly human. In this view, the "Fall" was a good thing. The classically Christian interpretation is that rejecting God's authority was the first step of alienation from our humanity, a step away from wisdom and true self-knowledge.)

Read the paragraph that begins, "And none of them . . ." Discuss questions 6 and 7. (The story of Jesus weeping at the tomb of Lazarus and then raising him from the dead is found in chapter 11 of the Gospel of John.)

In the interest of time, you'll need to move quickly through the second Lewis selection. Summarize what is going on in the story: Edmund betrayed his brother and sisters. This act of betrayal landed him in the clutches of the evil White Witch. The lion Aslan has rescued Edmund, but the Witch claims the legal right to kill the traitor. Even though his offense was against his family and friends, the Deep Magic of this land gives the Witch the right to the blood of all traitors. (For group members who aren't familiar with the Christian worldview, you might explain that Christians believe, similarly, that the Law of God laid down at the Creation gave Satan the right to the eternal souls of all humans who betrayed God or their fellow humans.) Aslan can't get around this Deep Magic because it is woven into the very creation of the land of Narnia, just as the law of gravity is woven into the land's physical laws. Narnia would be destroyed if the Law of this Deep Magic were ignored. Understanding this fact, the only way Aslan can save Edmund from the Witch's knife is to allow her to kill him instead. Pick up the story from the point where the Witch is about to stab the helpless Aslan, who is tied to the Stone Table where traitors are supposed to be executed. Have someone begin reading with the Witch's lines, "And now, who has won? . . .," and read through the end of the selection. Discuss questions 4 through 8.

For Christians, the meaning of this story is often obvious and the emotions positive. For people unfamiliar with the Christian worldview, it can seem bizarre. It's not obvious why God would require the death penalty for those who have rebelled against him. Few modern people think of themselves as having betrayed either God or their fellow humans and served the cause of someone as evil as the White Witch. Allow opportunity in your group for people to express honest bewilderment that Christians believe this. Don't try to argue people into believing that this Law is woven into the fabric of our world—that is a worldview assumption, and this group is designed to make space for people to assess the outlook of each worldview. Is it a capital crime to go about one's life putting Number One first? Is evil the result of human rebellion, and is it serious enough to warrant such a drastic response from God? Is the wrongdoing of your average group member utterly different from the wrongdoing of Auschwitz, or is there a continuum of evil in which even you have participated?

Martin Luther King Jr. (20 minutes)

The Buddha attempted to make sense of impersonal evil: aging, disease, death. Camus also portrayed evil as a disease. But Lewis presented evil as something like Auschwitz—personal, human, yet malevolent. Martin Luther King Jr. faced that same kind of institutionalized human evil as he sat in jail because of his opposition to racial injustice.

Summarize the occasion that prompted this letter. King is writing to white clergy. Read the second paragraph on page 126 ("I think I should indicate . . .") and discuss question 1. Further on, find the paragraph that begins, "Of course, there is nothing new . . ." Read aloud that paragraph and the one that begins, "But though I was initially . . ." Discuss question 4. King refers to the story of Shadrach, Meshach, and Abednego in the book of Daniel, chapter 3. He also refers to Jesus' words in Matthew 5, to the book of Amos, and to the end of Paul's letter to the Galatians.

Discuss question 7. Would King agree with Lewis that human evil is a serious problem requiring the most drastic response? Where do you see King's this-worldliness? His other-worldliness?

Heinrich Heine   (10 minutes)

The point of these last two readings in part 2 is that even those who despised the Christian faith could see that Europe faced a cataclysm when the culture as a whole turned away from thinking like Lewis or King. Russell believed God was dead, but morality would survive and flourish in Europe. Heine and Nietzsche did not. All three men wrote their selections before the two world wars and Stalinism ravaged Europe—whose predictions proved most accurate?

Session 5 will cover fewer readings than session 4. If you are running out of time, you could save Heine and Nietzsche for next time. However, it's not necessary to belabor them. Read aloud the brief Heine selection starting on page 134. Discuss questions 1 and 4. Discuss question 6 if you have time.

Friedrich Nietzsche   (15 minutes)

Summarize the introduction to Friedrich Nietzsche. Read in particular the last paragraph of the introduction. Note that for him the slogan "God is dead" meant "our culture has declared God to be dead." Some people today talk as though the death of God is liberating good news. Nietzsche believed it would unmake Western civilization. The goal of your discussion here is to understand why he believed that.

Read the first paragraph of this selection on page 137 and discuss question 1 briefly. The point here is to see what cataclysmic language Nietzsche uses to describe the change in Europe from faith in Christ to atheism.

Question 3 refers to the last two sentences of that first paragraph. Is it true that the worldviews that have replaced the Christian faith in the West—humanism, the New Age, Nazism, Stalinism, and materialism among others—more or less paint us humans as gods of our own world?

Take a few minutes for question 6. This is a chance to evaluate Russell's humanist point of view over against Nietzsche's view. What do the results of this comparison say about the Christian faith, if anything?

Sessions 5 and 6 will give you a chance to evaluate the truth or implausibility of the worldviews you have been discussing in sessions 3 and 4. Ask the group to read the Pirsig, Issa, and Darwin selections for next time, along with the Point to Ponder, "The Prelude to Confirmation Is Disconfirmation." This is a much shorter reading assignment and will give everyone a chance to assimilate the many ideas you have been dealing with. Session 5 will focus on Buddhism and atheism, while session 6 will address the Christian faith. Session 5 would be a good time for participants who know more about Buddhism, scientific materialism, humanism, or existentialism to bring that input to the group. The readings in session 5 present evidence against Buddhism and atheism; participants should feel free to bring evidence that represents a different point of view. Evidence for or against the Christian faith should wait for session 6.

SESSION 5

While part 2 helps your group find a worldview that meets their needs, part 3 helps you decide whether that view is true. Faith that may be merely an illusion or a crutch is not the kind of answer for life that rational people want. Part 3 offers evidence—not absolute proof—of the truth of Christian faith. It also offers evidence that the alternatives do not match up with what we experience of the world.

Here in session 5, three readings present evidence against Eastern philosophy and Western scientific materialism. Pirsig shows why Zen and other Eastern traditions fail to satisfy. The Japanese poet Issa offers further evidence against the Buddhist approach. And Charles Darwin's own letters show the inadequacy of scientific materialism as a philosophy for his life.

If participants have brought additional input about Buddhism or atheism, you'll need to get into the readings right away in order to have time for everything. If not, you will probably have time to spend a few minutes going over the introduction to part 3. Read aloud the first two paragraphs. What do you think of the statement, "If this question [about the truth of our worldview] is not answered . . . then the searcher may become a believer but will always be vulnerable to the doubt that faith is only a projection, . . . an illusion, or a crutch"? Ask participants whether, in the past, faith has been presented to them as something one believes without or despite evidence. If so, how has that affected their responses to faith?

Faith is often criticized for being irrational, a psychological crutch. On the other hand, Christian faith is simultaneously criticized (sometimes from the same people) for asserting that some worldviews are truer than others. This stance seems intolerant. Later, when you discuss the Point to Ponder, "Truth—The New Obscenity," you'll have a chance to talk about whether looking for evidence of a worldview's truth is a fool's errand or a necessary part of rational living.

Finally, underscore the fact that the evidence in part 3 is not ironclad proof. It is the kind of evidence that leads to convictions that "are more like a lover's reasons for accepting a marriage proposal than a student's reasons for accepting a mathematician's formula."

Robert Pirsig (30 minutes)

You begin with a reading that shows the inadequacy of Eastern philosophy (Buddhism or Hinduism) for understanding and responding to suffering on the level of nuclear disaster. The selection is short; read the whole of it aloud.

Take a moment to make sure everyone understands the Sanskrit doctrine of *Tat tvam asi* (question 1). Westerners often have difficulty grasping this idea, which is so contrary to the Western worldview. The Vietnamese Buddhist teacher Thich Nat Han explains this doctrine in a poem in which he says progressively, "I am the butterfly . . . I am the flower the butterfly sits on . . . I am the child who was raped . . . I am the rapist. . . ." The idea here is not recognition of one's capacity for evil (I *could be* that rapist, therefore my response to the rapist should include humility and compassion alongside a passion for justice). That would be a Christian view. Rather, the Eastern view is that it is meaningless to distinguish victim from perpetrator from witness to the crime. The evil of rape, then, vanishes into the mist of illusion. However, it should be noted that Thich Nat Han himself worked tirelessly for decades to help victims on both sides of the Vietnam War. He refused to identify one side or the other as the evil side, but gave aid to the wounded on both sides. *Tat tvam asi* can be a motivation toward evenhanded compassion, although it can be a barrier to the kind of justice that punishes criminals.

Next, be sure everyone grasps the concept of "Zen" or *dhyana* (question 2). The point of Zen is not to be more relaxed or better able to handle the stress of life. The point of Zen is to completely eliminate one's physical, mental, and emotional activity. The point is not to gain control over one's obsessive thoughts and raging emotions. The point is to stop having thoughts and emotions. Some of the techniques of meditation can be useful in stress management and even in Christian maturity. The Christian tradition includes spiritual practices aimed at learning to govern one's mind and emotions. But Zen, properly understood, has a deeper aim than mere self-governance.

Once participants digest those two concepts, you can probably move through questions 3 through 7 in the time allotted. Again, participants are free to provide evidence that puts Eastern philosophy in a better light. The intent here is not to stack a deck unfairly, nor to promote ethnic arrogance ("we in the West are better than those benighted souls in the East"). Still, the fact remains that Christian missionaries founded most of the hospitals in India. Indian philosophy provided no motivation for providing health care because disease was viewed as ultimately illusion. The few voices who struggle to improve education and housing for the poor in India continue to labor under the same philosophical burden. Those of us in the West who know nothing about India except Gandhi tend to romanticize that country, especially when Eastern philosophy and Western secularism are the only options on the table.

Issa   (30 minutes)

The Japanese poet Issa displays the tension between his Buddhist philosophy and his humanness. Read the entire introduction and both renderings of the poem, beginning on page 148. Discuss questions 1 through 3.

You might take a moment to compare the idea that "the world is dew" to C. S. Lewis's account of the two-edged nature of the Christian faith. In light of the ultimate reality of God's eternal realm and the finite limitations of the world, would a Christian say anything that sounds like "the world is dew"? On the other hand, in light of the fact that the world is God's creation, what would a Christian say about the idea that "the world is dew"? How would the lion Aslan have replied to Issa if asked about the reasons for the deaths of the man's wife and children?

Charles Darwin   (30 minutes)

The essence of naturalism (or materialism or empiricism) is that nothing exists other than what can be sensed with our five senses and/or scientific apparatus. Darwin's own letters are excerpted here to illustrate what happens to a person who attempts to live by naturalism as a philosophy of life.

On page 150 read the first paragraph of his letter to Mr. J. Fordyce down through the sentence that ends "not the least value as evidence" near the top of page 151. Discuss question 1. Read the portion of Darwin's letter to Mr. W. Graham, and discuss question 2. Read the letter to Sir J. D. Hooker and the passage from his autobiography. Discuss question 3. In your opinion, to what extent is Darwin's blindness to beauty and grandeur an argument against naturalism? What about his concern that a mind that has evolved purely through natural selection is not reliable for answering ultimate questions — is that an argument against naturalism in your eyes?

Save five or ten minutes for questions 6 and 7. The stories of part 3 have followed this logic: if a person has to deaden his or her humanity in order to live by a particular philosophy of life, then that philosophy is suspect. What do you think of that argument? The argument is not "Buddhism and naturalism are suspect because they don't work." Rather it is "Buddhism and naturalism are suspect because they don't make sense of important evidence: severe evil, the innate human response to suffering, natural beauty, and the innate human response to the arts."

For session 6, ask the group to read the Point to Ponder, "Truth—The New Obscenity," Stump, Lewis, and the Gospel of Mark.

SESSION 6

The readings in this session argue that the Christian view of God, humans, evil, and the world in general is true. Not just appealing, but objectively true. In previous sessions, participants may have raised doubts about whether any philosophy of life can claim that it is true and other philosophies are false. The Point to Ponder, "Truth—The New Obscenity," presents three reasons why a claim to objective truth is important:

- The Christian faith proclaims a God who entered the created world in all its gritty empirical reality, a God who—as a person—can be assessed as trustworthy or untrustworthy, speaking truth or false-hood.
- Unless we insist on objective truth, we are left with life philosophies built on unstable ground: personal preference, cultural bias, majority vote, feelings, wishful thinking, or pragmatism.
- Unless we insist on objective truth, we are vulnerable to religion that is only a helpful lie to ward off the terror of meaninglessness.

Take a few minutes to get the group's responses to this essay. Do partici-pants understand what "objective truth" is? What arguments might be used to claim that it's impossible to know whether Buddhism or naturalism or the Christian faith is true? What are the arguments in favor of believing it's pos-sible and important to know whether one's philosophy is objectively true?

In the interest of time, you'll be skipping G. K. Chesterton's selection. Chesterton argues that Christian faith alone enables a rational person to be both optimistic and pessimistic about the world. It alone of the world's philoso-phies makes sense of two aspects of his experience: (1) the world is good and beautiful; and (2) the world is a disastrous mess. The solution to the apparent contradiction of these two truths is solved by the Creation and the Fall. You encountered some of this argument before in part 1 from Chesterton and part 2 from Lewis. While some of Chesterton's references to history at the time of the Roman Empire may go over the heads of group members, you might rec-ommend his selection for their private reading.

Eleonore Stump   (30 minutes)

Eleonore Stump addresses one of the most common objections to the Christian idea of God: "If there is an omnipotent, omniscient, perfectly good God, how can it be that the world is full of evil?" State this question, and then (as Stump does in her second paragraph) make it concrete with some examples of severe evil as recorded in your current newspaper. Then, on page 165, read aloud the paragraph that begins, "This evil is a mirror for us" and the one that begins, "Some people believe that evil can be eliminated . . ." on page 166. Discuss question 1. (In the latter paragraph, Stump discusses global reformers and Good Samaritans. It might be helpful to summarize the two responses to evil in the preceding two paragraphs: the natural obliviousness of the hobbit and the labored obliviousness of Camus.)

Read the four paragraphs that begin "How does Hallie know . . .?" Discuss question 3. Stump argues that we must have a brain faculty that enables us to recognize evil intuitively.

Read the paragraph that begins, "It also seems clear . . ." Discuss the first part of question 4. Read the next paragraph ("What is perhaps less easy to see . . .") and discuss the second part of question 4. Read "Why tears, do you suppose? . . ." and discuss question 5. For question 6, read the three paragraphs beginning with, "Some people glimpse . . ."

Read the quotation from Philip Hallie that begins, "We are living in a time . . ." and the paragraph that follows ("So, in an odd sort of way . . ."). How can loathing evil give a person a taste for startling goodness? Discuss question 7.

Also ask, "How do you typically respond to extraordinary goodness? Do you tend to brush it off or pursue its source? Is your response to goodness similar to your typical response to evil? Do you tend to be a hobbit (naturally oblivious), a Camus (laboring to be oblivious of both great good and great evil all around us), a global reformer, or a Good Samaritan?"

C. S. Lewis   (30 minutes)

With this selection you get down to the evidence regarding the Christian faith specifically. The Christian faith stands or falls on the claims of who Jesus Christ was and what he did. From the first paragraph of this selection starting on page 175, read from "'How are we to solve the historical problem . . .'" to the end of the paragraph. Discuss question 1.

Read the next three paragraphs and discuss question 2. The selection from the Gospel of Mark that follows the Lewis selection illustrates Lewis's point here. It shows Jesus claiming the authority to forgive sins. You'll take a look at that story in a few minutes. Other biblical passages to which Lewis refers in this section are Matthew 9:14-15; 23:34; and John 8:58. The point to be clear about here is that if the biblical record is to be trusted, Jesus claimed Godlike status over and over.

For question 3, read the paragraph that begins, "Well, that is the other side."

Question 5 is important, for here Lewis deals with objections that participants may hear even from experts in the field of biblical studies. Read the paragraph that begins, "What are we to do . . .?" A number of widely read scholarly books claim to have proven that anytime the Gospels quote Jesus asserting the right to forgive sins or send prophets or do anything else Godlike, those passages were made up by followers decades after the Crucifixion. The argument tends to be, "A great moral teacher could not possibly have said such megalomaniac things, and we know that when stories are circulated orally over several decades they tend to be embellished, and we know that it was in the interests of Jesus' later followers to move their image of the Messiah in this grander direction, so it's logical to assume they made up these statements about Godlike authority." But even these scholars concede that the Gospel of Matthew was definitely written by a Jew for a Jewish audience—so strongly Jewish that instead of Jesus' familiar phrase "the kingdom of God," Matthew gives "the kingdom of heaven" because Jews avoided uttering any direct word for God. Lewis asks, would such a writer and such an audience make up words for Jesus that make him equal with God? The scholars tend not to address this objection. If any of your participants have heard the "legend" theory promoted, they need to be aware that the evidence for that theory is flawed.

The next paragraph, "Another point . . .," offers another piece of evidence for question 5. You might remind participants that Lewis was an acclaimed Oxford professor of medieval and Renaissance literature, so when he says, "I have read a great deal of legend," he means it. Your group may not know enough about ancient literature to evaluate Lewis's assertion that the Gospel of John is unusual, but help them grasp the reason why he says it's unusual. Today we are so accustomed to realistic fiction that it's hard for us to imagine a time when the techniques of realistic fiction had not been invented. But Lewis, who had read ancient Roman novels and knew what techniques they did and didn't use, was a scholar whose opinion needs to be taken seriously.

The "legend" theory is the one most commonly used today against the claims of the Gospels. "Liar" and "lunatic" are out of fashion, but you'll probably need to tackle "legend" directly.

For question 6, read "Then we come to the strangest story of all . . ." Help the group distinguish the idea of the Resurrection from ideas like reincarnation (which says everybody returns to this life in a new body) or life after death (which says people go on to a higher plane but no longer have bodies that can eat and walk around in this world) or ghost survival. The resurrection stories insist that Jesus had a physical body when he reappeared and that such reincarnation (literally a re-bodied soul) had never happened before.

Read the last two paragraphs of the selection and discuss question 7. The important thing now is not to push people to accept the gospel story but to help them understand that accepting the nice parts without the outrageous parts is not an option. The important thing is to help them grasp that the Jesus portrayed in the New Testament makes enormous claims that can be rejected but not softened.

The Gospel of Mark   (20 minutes)

With this reading you have a chance to look directly at one of the outrageous stories about Jesus that Lewis referred to. Read the story and discuss questions 1 through 3. Then ask, "If this account is not a mere legend, what does it say about Jesus as a person? What evidence does this story offer for or against the proposition that he was simply a great moral teacher?"

Much more evidence could be brought to bear on the question of whether the Gospels record genuine events rather than legends and whether Jesus was a liar, a lunatic, or the Lord. In session 7 you will consider the importance of pausing at some point in the journey to draw conclusions and decide whether or not to make a commitment to some philosophy of life. It might seem appealing to remain an explorer forever, never taking the risks or paying the prices of commitment. But the readings in session 7 will highlight the risks and costs of avoiding commitment. Still, sessions 7 and 8 will enable participants to understand what is involved in a real commitment and what is the downside of trying to avoid commitment. They will be equipped to make wise decisions at their own pace. Ask participants to read the Point to Ponder, "Step, Leap, or Wager?" as well as the selection by Pascal, the biblical account of the conversion of St. Paul, and the selection by Lewis.

SESSION 7

Part 4 is an ending and a beginning. Having gathered evidence, at some point we must draw conclusions and act on them. Otherwise, we were never really journeying, but merely playing. We may never have enough evidence for a mathematical proof, but at some point we have enough evidence for commitment.

The readings in session 7 offer three pictures of what a faith commitment looks like. The differences among the three are intended to suggest the diverse ways in which people come to faith. None of the three readings is normative—you must have an experience like this—but all illustrate aspects of what is called conversion.

Blaise Pascal   (30 minutes)

Take a minute to look at the Point to Ponder, "Step, Leap, or Wager?" Go over the important points:

- Faith is more than naked reason, but it is neither against reason nor without reason. We should have reason or evidence—though not proof—behind our faith.
- Faith means transferring our reliance from ourselves to God. It is not belief in a set of propositions but trust in a person.
- The choice to put our trust in God is one of the freest choices we will ever make.
- The choice involves real risk, but avoiding the choice is also risky.

Pascal's famous wager illustrates the last point. Gambling was a favored sport in the society to which he belonged, so he puts his description of the choice for or against faith in terms a gambler, investor, or entrepreneur would understand. Note that in the selection, the words in bold are Pascal's, while the commentary by philosopher Peter Kreeft is indented.

Read aloud the first two paragraphs of the selection on page 189 and discuss question 1.

Read the commentary after the bold sentences "Reason cannot decide this question" and "Infinite chaos separates us." Discuss question 2. Pascal argues that reason cannot prove the case one way or the other because our minds have only a limited capacity to reason, a limited scope for absorbing evidence, and the distorting, blinding effect of sin.

Read the section that begins, "Do not then condemn as wrong . . ." and the one that begins, "Yes, but you must wager." Discuss questions 4 and 5. Agnosticism is not an option because it places us by default in the position of those who are betting God does not exist. The agnostic ends up living like the atheist, as though there is no God who has a claim on his life. At death, then, the agnostic faces the same fate as the atheist. At death, the agnostic runs out of time to stall. "Wait" becomes "No."

Pascal argues that betting that God exists offers the best shot at both truth (living in reality, not being proved a fool) and happiness. We have everything to gain and little to lose. But eventually he acknowledges that the one who bets on God has *something* to lose. For a shot at infinite and eternal joy, we do have to risk not having our earthly "passion" satisfied. Read from the bold heading "Yes, but my hands are tied . . ." to the end of the selection. Discuss question 8. See if you can draw out the particular "passions" that are the most alluring for your group members. Is it the pleasure of entertainment that keeps them from betting everything on God? A passion for power in the workplace that seems too valuable to risk? Sexual pleasure? Possessions? The safety of a comfortable life? The good opinion of people who may view us with contempt if they hear we have bet our lives on God?

Save a minute for question 10. Some people find the idea of risk stimulating; others are put off by the coldness of a wager. Sometimes those who don't relate to a wager are more drawn to a romance—the step of faith is like accepting or rejecting a marriage proposal. What keeps us from trusting the lover and saying yes? Do we have enough evidence to take the risk? Or is the issue not evidence but rather the fear of trusting someone and sacrificing our independence?

The Apostle Paul   (30 minutes)

Set up who Saul/Paul was from the introduction to the selection. Then have someone read the whole selection beginning on page 197. You will probably have time for all the questions. Saul's is the classic conversion story—no long journey, but a bolt from the blue that produces instant turnaround. Saul had been brooding on the subject of Jesus for some time, but when the moment of encounter came, it was dramatic. Unlike Saul, some people can point to no moment in time when they switched from unbeliever to believer. Others, like

C. S. Lewis in the next reading, recall several turning points in a long process. But while few of us are literally knocked off our horses, most of us face moments of decision along the path.

C. S. Lewis   (30 minutes)

Read the first paragraph of the selection on page 200 and discuss question 1. Read the paragraph that begins, "Really, a young Atheist . . ." Discuss question 2. Lewis has a vivid way of describing how God goes into action when a person gives God even the slightest opening. Read the next paragraph and discuss question 3. Notice that Lewis had hoped to be an idle explorer but was now cornered into taking the journey seriously.

Read "People who are naturally religious . . ." and "Remember, I had always wanted . . ." Discuss question 4. Notice that when Lewis uses the phrase "leap in the dark," he's not talking about a leap to believe something his reason said was silly. He means a leap—led by reason and more than reason—to trust someone with a completely blank check. He was reporting for duty with no idea what the orders might be.

Read "As soon as I became a Theist . . ." and "But though I liked clergymen . . ." What do you think of his reaction to church? What was the significance of "flying one's flag?"

Summarize the parts of the story you've skipped: kneeling one night to acknowledge the Ultimate, no promise of joy or a future life, the decrease in his self-examination, wrestling with the story of Jesus in the Gospels, and finally believing that Jesus was the Son of God. How does Lewis's progressive conversion add to your picture of how conversion happens?

If you have time, close by reading the last paragraph of the selection. Does it surprise you that those stabs of joy became less important?

Ask the group to read the rest of the book for your final session. Also ask them to consider where they are on the journey, what choices they have made, if any. Assure them that they will not be obliged to state their convictions or commitments to the whole group. (However, if anyone does make any decisions, telling one or two people is usually helpful.) There must be no pressure tactics! Session 8 addresses a serious subject: not eternal damnation, but the earthly tragedy of people who avoid a moment of decision when it comes.

SESSION 8

There is a point at which the honesty of our seeking is revealed. Either we conform our desires to truth, which leads to repentance, or we conform the truth to our desires, which leads to rationalization. The first three readings of this session illustrate the second possibility.

You'll need to keep the discussion moving. The readings are short—let the group get the point and move on. Save time for each person to have at least two minutes for closing thoughts.

M. Scott Peck   (15 minutes)

A psychiatric client named Charlene teaches M. Scott Peck about rejecting truth. Read the whole selection. Charlene presents her problem as a feeling that life has no meaning. She knows the meaning of life according to Christians: the meaning of life is to glorify God. How does she *feel* (emotionally) about that answer? What beliefs and desires lie behind that feeling? Look at the next to last paragraph. Note the "flat, low monotone" that gives way to "a quavering voice" and then "a roar." What are her deepest emotions and beliefs about the idea of glorifying God? Discuss questions 3 through 5.

Kenneth Clark   (15 minutes)

Charlene preferred the misery of meaninglessness to the terror of surrendering to a God she hated and feared. Unlike C. S. Lewis, she refused to bow the knee to a God who demanded everything and made no guarantees. She chose to keep her armor on.

The eminent art historian Kenneth Clark describes his own rejection of God with less pathos than Peck uses to describe Charlene's. Make sure everyone knows who Clark was. Then read the whole selection on page 212. Discuss questions 1 through 4.

Aldous Huxley   (15 minutes)

In this reading, novelist Aldous Huxley admits that his rejection of the Christian faith was not based on evidence but on passion. Confronted with a choice between truth and desire, he chose desire.

On page 214 read the paragraph that begins, "Most ignorance is vincible . . ." and the first few sentences of the paragraph after that. (The word "vin–cible" means "capable of being overcome.") Discuss question 2. Read the last paragraph of the selection and discuss question 4. Take a few minutes for question 5.

Helmuth von Moltke   (15 minutes)

In the Point to Ponder, "Journeying to Arrive," read aloud the last paragraph: "To those who say . . ." Helmuth von Moltke was a man who finished well because he had made the wager, chosen his path, and stuck to it to the end. Summarize the introduction to von Moltke. Read the first paragraph beginning on page 220 and discuss question 1. Read "The decisive phrase of the trial . . ." and discuss question 2. If you have time, discuss questions 4, 6, and 7.

Closing Thoughts   (30 minutes)

To close your session, let each person respond to this question: "What key thoughts, ideas, and comments struck you personally during our study? What stands out to you?" Think carefully ahead of time whom you will ask to answer this question first, since that person's answer will set the tone for the other responses. Choose someone who you think is reflective and has been taking the readings to heart.

Thank everyone for participating. Some light refreshments and informal time to talk would be a fitting way to end the meeting.

AUTHORS

Os Guinness is a Senior Fellow at The Trinity Forum in McLean, Virginia. Born in China and educated in England, he earned his D.Phil from Oxford University. He is the author or editor of numerous books, including *The Call, The American Hour, Invitation to the Classics,* and *Long Journey Home.*

Karen Lee-Thorp (author of the reader's guide) is the senior editor of Bible studies and small group resources at NavPress and the author of more than fifty study guides. Karen has spent almost two decades exploring how people grow spiritually. A graduate of Yale University, she speaks at women's groups and writes from her home in Brea, California.

For a catalog of The Trinity Forum's publications, including others in this series, please write: The Trinity Forum, 7902 Westpark Drive, Suite A, McLean, VA 22102. The catalog is also online at The Trinity Forum's website, www.ttf.org.

OTHER BOOKS IN THE TRINITY FORUM STUDY SERIES.

Entrepreneurs of Life

Through the writings of men and women who fought slavery, reinvented healthcare, or composed great music, you'll find models to follow as you discover and answer your own call.

Entrepreneurs of Life (Os Guinness) $16

The Great Experiment

Discover the critical role faith played in the formation of America and why it's essential to freedom in society today.

The Great Experiment (Os Guinness) $16

Doing Well and Doing Good

What does the way we make and dispose of money say about us as a nation? Discover the connection between a society's character and its view of money, giving, and caring.

Doing Well and Doing Good (Os Guinness) $16

Steering Through Chaos

There is a huge difference between knowing about good and becoming a good person. This thoughtful, probing study examines the seven deadly vices and contrasts them with the beatitudes from Jesus' Sermon on the Mount.

Steering Through Chaos (Os Guinness) $16

When No One Sees

True character is demonstrated by what you do when no one else is around. This compelling book illustrates how character is built and tested, and offers practical help for bringing about radical change in your own character.

When No One Sees (Os Guinness) $16

Get your copies today at your local bookstore, visit our website at www.navpress.com, or call (800) 366-7788. Ask for offer **#6179** or a FREE catalog of NavPress products.

NAVPRESS
BRINGING TRUTH TO LIFE
www.navpress.com

Prices subject to change.